A Functional Approach to Java
Augmenting Object-Oriented Code with Functional Principles

Ben Weidig

Beijing · Boston · Farnham · Sebastopol · Tokyo

A Functional Approach to Java

by Ben Weidig

Copyright © 2023 Benjamin Weidig. All rights reserved.

Published by O'Reilly Media, Inc., 1005 Gravenstein Highway North, Sebastopol, CA 95472.

O'Reilly books may be purchased for educational, business, or sales promotional use. Online editions are also available for most titles (*http://oreilly.com*). For more information, contact our corporate/institutional sales department: 800-998-9938 or *corporate@oreilly.com*.

Acquisitions Editor: Brian Guerin
Development Editor: Rita Fernando
Production Editor: Ashley Stussy
Copyeditor: Liz Wheeler
Proofreader: Piper Editorial Consulting, LLC

Indexer: WordCo Indexing Services, Inc.
Interior Designer: David Futato
Cover Designer: Karen Montgomery
Illustrator: Kate Dullea

May 2023:   First Edition

Revision History for the First Edition
2023-05-09:   First Release

See *http://oreilly.com/catalog/errata.csp?isbn=9781098109929* for release details.

978-1-098-10992-9

[LSI]

Table of Contents

Part II.   A Functional Approach

Preface

A mind that is stretched by a new experience can never go back to its old dimensions.
—Oliver Wendell Holmes, Jr.

Developing software is quite a complex endeavor. As Java developers, we usually try to tame this complexity with object-oriented programming (OOP) as a metaphor to represent the things we are developing, such as data structures, and use a primarily imperative-focused coding style to handle our program's state. Although OOP is a well-known and battle-tested approach to developing sensible software, not every problem is a good match for it. We might introduce a certain amount of unnecessary complexity by forcing OOP principles on every problem instead of using more appropriate tools and paradigms also available to us. The functional programming (FP) paradigm offers an alternative approach to solving problems.

Functional programming isn't a new idea. In fact, it's even older than object-oriented programming! It first appeared in the early years of computing, in the 1950s, in the *Lisp*[1] programming language and has been used quite commonly in academia and niche fields. In recent years, however, there has been an increasing interest in functional paradigms.

Many new functional languages have emerged, and non-functional languages are including functional features to various degrees. The ideas and concepts behind FP are now adopted in almost every mainstream multiparadigm and general-purpose language, allowing us to use some form of functional programming regardless of the context and chosen language. Nothing stops us from taking the best parts of FP and

---

[1] Originally specified in 1958, *Lisp* is the second-oldest high-level programming language still in common use. It also builds the foundation of a variety of programming languages, like *Emacs Lisp* (*https://oreil.ly/5piWN*), or the functional JVM language *Clojure* (*https://clojure.org*).

augmenting our existing way of programming and software development tools—and that's what this book is about!

In this book, you'll learn the fundamentals of functional programming and how to apply this knowledge to your daily work using Java.

New Hardware Needs a New Way of Thinking

Hardware is evolving in a new direction. For quite some time, single-core performance improvements haven't been as significant as with each previous processor generation. *Moore's law*[2] seems to slow down, but such a slowdown doesn't mean that hardware isn't improving anymore. But instead of primarily focussing on single-core performance and even higher GHz numbers, the manufacturers favor more and more cores.[3] So, for modern workloads to reap all the benefits of new hardware that favors more cores rather than faster ones, we need to adopt techniques that can use more cores to their advantage without compromising productivity or introducing additional complexity.

Scaling your software horizontally through parallelism isn't an easy task in OOP. Not every problem is a good fit for parallelism. More painters might paint a room faster, but you can't speed up pregnancy by involving more people. If the problem consists of serial or interdependent tasks, concurrency is preferable to parallelism. But parallelism really shines if a problem breaks down into smaller, non-related subproblems. That's where functional programming comes in. The stateless and immutable nature of idiomatic FP provides all the tools necessary to build small, reliable, reusable, and higher-quality tasks that elegantly fit into parallel and concurrent environments.

Adopting a functional mindset adds another set of tools to your toolbelt that will allow you to tackle your daily development problems in a new way and scale your code more easily and safely than before.

Next, let's look at why Java can be a good choice for functional programming.

Java Can Be Functional, Too

Many programming languages out there are great for functional programming. *Haskell (https://oreil.ly/xd-ZC)* is a favorite if you prefer a *pure* functional language

---

2 *Moore's law* was coined in 1965 by the cofounder of Intel, Gordon Moore, as the observation of transistor counts doubling every two years and, therefore, the performance per core available to us. Chris Edwards, "Moore's Law: What Comes Next?" *Communications of the ACM*, Vol. 64, No. 2 (Feb. 2021): 12-14 (*https://oreil.ly/U6ee2*).

3 N. C. Thompson and Svenja Spanuth, "The Decline of Computers as a General-Purpose Technology," *Communications of the ACM*, Vol. 64, No. 3 (Mar. 2021): 64-72 (*https://oreil.ly/YR8lp*).

with almost no support for an imperative coding style. *Elixir (https://oreil.ly/097Ve)* is another exciting option that leverages the *Erlang Virtual Machine.*[4] However, you don't have to leave the vast JVM ecosystem behind to find FP-capable languages. *Scala (https://oreil.ly/fOCAH)* shines in combining OOP and FP paradigms into a concise, high-level language. Another popular choice, *Clojure (https://oreil.ly/q0Hw5),* was designed from the ground up as a functional language with a dynamic type system at heart.

In a perfect world, you'd have the luxury of choosing the perfect functional language for your next project. In reality, you might not have a choice at all about what language to use, and you'll have to play the cards you're dealt.

As a Java developer, you'd use Java, which was historically seen as not ideal for functional programming. Before we continue, though, I need to stress that you can implement most functional principles in Java, regardless of deeply integrated language-level support[5]. Still, the resulting code won't be as concise and easy to reason with as it would in other languages that allow a functional approach in the first place. This caveat scares many developers away from even trying to apply functional principles to Java, despite the fact that it might have provided a more productive approach or better overall solution.

In the past, many people thought of Java as a slow-moving behemoth, a "too big to become extinct" enterprise language, like a more modern version of COBOL or Fortran. And in my opinion that's partially true, or at least it was in the past. The pace didn't pick up until Java 9 and the shortened release timeframes[6]. It took Java five years to go from version 6 to 7 (2006-2011). And even though there were significant new features, like `try-with-resources`, none of them were "groundbreaking." The few and slow changes in the past led to projects and developers not adopting the "latest and greatest" Java Development Kit (JDK) and missing out on many language improvements. Three years later, in 2014, the next version, Java 8, was released. This time, it introduced one of the most significant changes to Java's future: *lambda expressions.*

---

4 *Erlang (https://oreil.ly/aKQbP)* is a functional and concurrency-oriented programming language that is known for building low-latency, distributed, and fault-tolerant systems.

5 Dean Wampler shows in his book *Functional Programming for Java Developers (https://oreil.ly/MgVEW)* (O'Reilly) in detail how to implement and facilitate the missing functional programming features in Java all by yourself. He describes many techniques that weren't easily feasible before version 8. But now, many of the shortcomings and gaps in the JDK are closed up, and it provides many of the tools necessary to incorporate FP concisely and more straightforwardly.

6 Oracle introduced a faster release schedule *(https://oreil.ly/yLj1p)* for Java with the release of versions beyond 9 with a fixed release cadence of six months. To meet such a tight schedule, not every release is considered "long-term-support," in favor of releasing features faster than before.

A better foundation for functional programming had finally arrived in arguably the most prominent object-oriented programming language of the world, changing the language and its idioms significantly:

```
Runnable runnable = () -> System.out.println("hello, functional world!");
```

The addition of lambda expressions was monumental in making it possible to finally use functional programming in Java as an integrated language and runtime feature. Not only that, but a whole new world of ideas and concepts was made available to Java developers. Many of the JDK's new features, like Streams, the Optional type, or CompletableFuture, are only possible in such a concise and straightforward way thanks to language-level lambda expressions and Java's other functional additions.

These new idioms and new ways of doing things with FP in Java may seem strange and might not come naturally, especially if you're primarily accustomed to OOP. Throughout this book, I'll show you how to develop a mindset that'll help you apply FP principles to your code and how to make it better without needing to go "fully functional."

Why I Wrote This Book

After using another multipurpose language with excellent functional programming support—*Swift* (*https://oreil.ly/hqIYc*)—and seeing the benefits firsthand, I gradually introduced more and more functional principles in my Java-based projects, too. Thanks to lambda expressions and all the other features introduced in Java 8 and later, all the tools necessary were readily available. But after using these tools more frequently and discussing them with my colleagues, I realized something: *How* to use lambdas, Streams, and all the other functional goodies provided by Java is easy to grasp. But without a deeper understanding of *why* and *when* you should use them— and when not to—you won't unlock their full potential, and it will just be "new wine in old wineskins."

So I decided to write this book to highlight the different concepts that make a language *functional*, and how you can incorporate them into your Java code, either with the tools provided by the JDK or by creating them yourself. A functional approach to your Java code will most likely challenge the status quo and go against *best practices* you were using before. But by embracing a more functional way of doing things, like *immutability* and *pure functions*, you will be able to write more concise, more reasonable, and future-proof code that is less prone to bugs.

Who Should Read This Book

This book is for you if you are curious about functional programming and want to know what all the fuss is about and apply it to your Java code. You might already be using some functional Java types but desire a more profound knowledge of why and how to apply them more effectively.

There is no need to be an expert on OOP, but the book is not a beginner's guide to Java or OOP. You should already be familiar with the Java standard library. No prior knowledge of functional programming is required. Every concept is introduced with an explanation and examples.

The book covers Java 17 as the latest Long-Term-Support (LTS) version available at publication. Knowing that many developers need to support projects with earlier versions, the general baseline will be the previous LTS, Java 11. But even if you're stuck on Java 8, many of the discussed topics are relevant. However, some chapters will rely on newer features, like *Records*, which were introduced in Java 14.

This book might not be for you if you are looking for a compartmentalized, recipe-style book presenting "ready-to-implement" solutions. Its main intention is to introduce functional concepts and idioms and teach you how to incorporate them into your Java code.

What You Will Learn

By the end of this book, you will have a fundamental knowledge of functional programming and its underlying concepts and how to apply this knowledge to your daily work. Every Java functional type will be at your disposal, and you will be able to build anything missing from the JDK by yourself, if necessary.

You will learn about the concepts and importance of the following aspects of functional programming:

Composition
   Build modular and easy composable blocks.

Expressiveness
   Write more concise code that clearly expresses its intent.

Safer code
   Create safer data structures without side effects that don't need to deal with race conditions or locks, which are hard to use without introducing bugs.

Modularity
   Break down larger projects into more easily manageable modules.

Maintainability
   Use smaller functional blocks with less interconnection to make changes and refactoring safer without breaking other parts of your code.

Data manipulation
> Build efficient data manipulation pipelines with less complexity.

Performance
> Immutability and predictability allow you to scale horizontally with parallelism without much thought about it.

Even without going fully functional, your code will benefit from the concepts and idioms presented in this book. And not only your Java code. You will tackle development challenges with a functional mindset, improving your programming regardless of the used language or paradigm.

What about Android?

It's hard to talk about Java without bringing up Android as well. Even though you can write Android applications in Java, the underlying API and runtime aren't the same. So what does this mean for adopting a functional approach to Java for Android apps? To better understand that, we first need to look at what makes Java for Android different from "normal" Java.

Android doesn't run Java bytecode directly on a minimalistic JVM optimized for smaller devices, like Java Platform Micro Edition (*https://oreil.ly/H0slD*). Instead, the bytecode gets recompiled. The *Dex-compiler* creates Dalvik bytecode, which is then run on a specialized runtime: the *Android Runtime* (ART) and previously on the *Dalvik virtual machine*.[7]

Recompiling Java bytecode to Dalvik bytecode allows the devices to run highly optimized code, getting the most out of their hardware constraints. For you as a developer, however, that means that even though your code looks and feels like Java on the surface—most of the public API is identical—there isn't a feature parity between the JDK and Android SDK you can rely on. For example, the cornerstones of this book—lambda expressions and Streams—were among the missing features in Android for a long time.

The Android Gradle plugin started supporting some of the missing functional features (lambda expressions, method references, default and static interface methods) with version 3.0.0 by using so-called *desugaring*: the compiler uses bytecode transformations to replicate a feature behind the scenes without supporting the new syntax or providing an implementation in the runtime itself.

---

7 The Android Open Source Project provides a good overview (*https://oreil.ly/_iVa4*) of the features and the reasoning behind Android's runtime.

The next major version, 4.0.0, added even more functional features: Streams, Optionals, and the `java.util.function` package. That allows you to benefit from the functional paradigms and tools discussed in this book, even as an Android developer.

 Even though most of the JDK's functional features are available on Android, too, they are not verbatim copies[8] and might have different performance characteristics and edge cases. The available features are listed in the official documentation on the Java 8+ support (*https://oreil.ly/1XTsQ*).

A Functional Approach to Android

In 2019, Kotlin (*https://oreil.ly/HxrtK*) took the mantle of preferred language for Android developers from Java. It's a multiplatform language that mainly targets the JVM but also compiles to JavaScript and multiple native platforms.[9] It aims to be a "modern and more concise" Java, fixing many of Java's debatable shortcomings and cruft accumulated over the years due to backward compatibility, without forgoing all the frameworks and libraries available to Java. And it's 100% interoperable: you can easily mix Java and Kotlin in the same project.

One obvious advantage of Kotlin over Java is that many functional concepts and idioms are integral to the language itself. Still, as a different language, Kotlin has its own idioms and best practices that differ from Java's. The generated bytecode might differ, too, like that used to generate lambdas.[10] The most significant advantage of Kotlin is its attempt to create a more concise and predictable language compared to Java. And just like you can be more functional in Java without going fully functional, you can use Kotlin-only features without going *full Kotlin* in your Android projects, too. By mixing Java and Kotlin, you can pick the best features from both languages.

Keep in mind that this book's primary focus is the Java language and the JDK. Still, most of the ideas behind what you will learn are transferrable to Android, even if you use Kotlin. However, there won't be any special considerations for Android or Kotlin throughout the book.

Navigating This Book

This book consists of two different parts:

---

8 Jake Wharton, a well-known Android developer, provides a detailed insight (*https://oreil.ly/l6yJU*) on how Android desugars modern Java code.

9 See the official Kotlin documentation for an overview of supported platforms (*https://oreil.ly/W4-FG*).

10 Each lambda compiles to an anonymous class extending `kotlin.jvm.internal.FunctionImpl`, as explained in the function type specs (*https://oreil.ly/C2qnh*).

- Part I, *Functional Basics*, introduces the history and core concepts of functional programming, how Java implements these concepts, and what types are already available to us as developers.

- Part II, *A Functional Approach*, is a topic-based deep dive through the more generalized programming concepts and how to augment them with functional principles and the newly available tools. Certain features, like Records and Streams, are highlighted with extended examples and use cases.

Reading the chapters in their respective order will let you get the most out of them because they usually build on each other. But feel free to skim for the bits that might interest you and jump around. Any necessary connections are cross-referenced to fill in any blanks if needed.

Conventions Used in This Book

The following typographical conventions are used in this book:

Italic
: Indicates new terms, URLs, email addresses, filenames, and file extensions.

`Constant width`
: Used for program listings, as well as within paragraphs, to refer to program elements such as variable or function names, databases, data types, environment variables, statements, and keywords.

`Constant width bold`
: Shows commands or other text that should be typed literally by the user.

`Constant width italic`
: Shows text that should be replaced with user-supplied values or by values determined by context.

This element signifies a tip or suggestion.

This element signifies a general note.

This element indicates a warning or caution.

Using Code Examples

The source code for the book is available on GitHub: *https://github.com/benweidig/a-functional-approach-to-java*. Besides compilable Java code, there are also *JShell* scripts available to run the code more easily.

If you have a technical question or a problem using the code examples, please send an email to *support@oreilly.com*.

This book is here to help you get your job done. In general, if example code is offered with this book, you may use it in your programs and documentation. You do not need to contact us for permission unless you're reproducing a significant portion of the code. For example, writing a program that uses several chunks of code from this book does not require permission. Selling or distributing examples from O'Reilly books does require permission. Answering a question by citing this book and quoting example code does not require permission. Incorporating a significant amount of example code from this book into your product's documentation does require permission.

We appreciate, but generally do not require, attribution. An attribution usually includes the title, author, publisher, and ISBN. For example: "*A Functional Approach to Java* by Ben Weidig (O'Reilly). Copyright 2023 Benjamin Weidig, 978-1-098-10992-9."

If you feel your use of code examples falls outside fair use or the permission given above, feel free to contact us at *permissions@oreilly.com*.

O'Reilly Online Learning

 For more than 40 years, *O'Reilly Media* has provided technology and business training, knowledge, and insight to help companies succeed.

Our unique network of experts and innovators share their knowledge and expertise through books, articles, and our online learning platform. O'Reilly's online learning platform gives you on-demand access to live training courses, in-depth learning paths, interactive coding environments, and a vast collection of text and video from O'Reilly and 200+ other publishers. For more information, visit *https://oreilly.com*.

Please address comments and questions concerning this book to the publisher:

O'Reilly Media, Inc.
1005 Gravenstein Highway North
Sebastopol, CA 95472
800-889-8969 (in the United States or Canada)
707-829-7019 (international or local)
707-829-0104 (fax)
support@oreilly.com
https://www.oreilly.com/about/contact.html

We have a web page for this book, where we list errata, examples, and any additional information. You can access this page at *https://oreil.ly/functional-approach-to-java-1e*.

For news and information about our books and courses, visit *https://oreilly.com*.

Find us on LinkedIn: *https://linkedin.com/company/oreilly-media*

Follow us on Twitter: *https://twitter.com/oreillymedia*

Watch us on YouTube: *https://www.youtube.com/oreillymedia*

Acknowledgments

This book is for Alexander Neumer, the best mentor I could've wished for in my early career. Without him, I wouldn't be the developer I am today.

I want especially to thank Zan McQuade for her encouragement and for proposing to aggregate my ramblings about functional Java into a book in the first place.

The technical reviewers deserve special thanks, too: Dean Wampler, Venkat Subramaniam, Thiago H. de Paula Figueiredo, and A N M Bazlur Rahman. Their support, suggestions, and sometimes harsh critique throughout the different stages of the book made it better than I ever could have by myself.

I would also like to thank Felix Gonschorek and Benjamin Quenzer, the two friends and colleagues that "suffered" with me from the beginning and provided invaluable feedback up to the end.

Last but not least, I want to thank my Acquisitions Editor Brian Guerin and everyone at O'Reilly. My Editor Rita Fernando, who always found a way to polish a few rough edges and get the best out of what I wrote. Ashley Stussy, the Production Editor, and her team, who made all my layout requests possible. Nick and Theresa from the O'Reilly Tools Team, who patiently helped me through any Asciidoc issues that arose. And all the other ones involved behind the scenes. Thank you!

PART I

Functional Basics

Functional programming isn't more complicated than object-oriented programming with its primarily imperative coding style. It's just a different way of approaching the same problems. Every problem that you can solve imperatively can also be solved functionally.

Mathematics builds the foundation for functional programming, making it harder to approach than an object-oriented mindset. But just like learning a new foreign language, the similarities and shared roots become more visible over time until it *just clicks*.

You can implement almost any of the upcoming concepts without Java lambda expression. Compared to other languages, though, the result won't be as elegant and concise. The functional tools available in Java allow your implementations of these concepts and functional idioms to be less verbose and more concise and efficient.

CHAPTER 1

An Introduction to Functional Programming

To better understand how to incorporate a more functional programming style in Java, you first need to understand what it means for a language to be functional and what its foundational concepts are.

This chapter will explore the roots of functional programming needed to incorporate a more functional programming style into your workflow.

What Makes a Language Functional?

Programming Paradigms, like object-oriented, functional, or procedural, are synthetic overall concepts that classify languages and provide ways to structure your programs in a specific style and use different approaches to solving problems. Like most paradigms, functional programming doesn't have a single agreed-upon definition, and many turf wars are fought about what defines a language as *actually* functional. Instead of giving my own definition, I will go over different aspects of what makes a language functional.

A language is considered functional when there's a way to express computations by creating and combining abstract functions. This concept is rooted in the formal mathematical system *lambda calculus*, invented by the logician Alonzo Church in the 1930s.[1] It's a system to express computations with abstract functions and how to apply variables to them. The name "lambda calculus" came from the Greek letter "lambda" chosen for its symbol: λ.

---

[1] Alonzo Church, "An Unsolvable Problem of Elementary Number Theory," *American Journal of Mathematics*, Vol. 58 (1936): 345-363 (*https://oreil.ly/a8qUg*).

Lambda Calculus

Three pillars build the foundation for the general concept of lambda calculus:

Abstraction
> An anonymous function—a *lambda*—that accepts a single input.

Application
> An *abstraction* is applied to a value to create a result. From a developer's perspective, it's a function or method call.

β-Reduction
> The substitution of the abstraction's variable with the applied argument.

A mathematical function declaration looks like this: $f = \lambda x \,.\, E$

Such a declaration consists of multiple parts:

x
> The *variable*, or argument, representing a value

E
> The *expression*, or *term*, containing the logic

$\lambda x \,.\, E$
> The *abstraction*, an anonymous function accepting a single input x

f
> The resulting function that can apply an argument to its abstraction

These parts are very similar to how Java lambdas, the core of its new functional programming style, are implemented. For example, the abstraction of a function that calculates a quadratic value—$\lambda x \,.\, x * x$—is almost identical to the Java version if you include the types:

```
Function<Integer, Integer> quadratic =
    value -> value * value;
```

The code should be self-explanatory in context, but the lambda syntax will be explained in detail in Chapter 2.

As an object-oriented developer, you are used to *imperative* programming: by defining a series of statements, you are telling the computer *what* to do to accomplish a particular task with a sequence of *statements*.

For a programming language to be considered functional, a *declarative* style to express the logic of computations without describing their actual control flow needs to be achievable. In such a declarative programming style, you describe the outcome and *how* your program should work with *expressions*, not *what* it should do with *statements*.

In Java, an *expression* is a sequence of operators, operands, and method invocations that define a computation and evaluate to a single value:

```
x * x
2 * Math.PI * radius
value == null ? true : false
```

Statements, on the other hand, are actions taken by your code to form a complete unit of execution, including method invocations without a return value. Any time you assign or change the value of a variable, call a void method, or use control-flow constructs like if-else, you're using statements. Usually, they're intermixed with expressions:

```
int totalTreasure = 0; ❶

int newTreasuresFound = findTreasure(6); ❷

totalTreasure = totalTreasure + newTreasuresFound; ❸

if (totalTreasure > 10) { ❹
  System.out.println("You have a lot of treasure!"); ❺
} else {
  System.out.println("You should look for more treasure!"); ❺
}
```

❶ Assigns an initial value to a variable, introducing state into the program.

❷ The function call findTreasure(6) is a functional expression, but the assignment of newTreasuresFound is a statement.

❸ The reassignment of totalTreasure is a statement using the result of the expression on the right-hand side.

❹ The control-flow statement if-else conveys what action should be taken based on the result of the (totalTreasure > 10) expression.

❺ Printing to System.out is a statement because there's no result returned from the call.

The primary distinction between expressions and statements is whether or not a value is returned. In a general-purpose, multiparadigm language like Java, the lines between them are often up for debate and can quickly blur.

Functional Programming Concepts

Since functional programming is based primarily on abstract functions, its many concepts that form the paradigm can focus on "what to solve" in a declarative style, in contrast to the imperative "how to solve" approach.

We will go through the most common and significant aspects that functional programming uses at its foundation. These aren't exclusive to the functional paradigm, though. Many of the ideas behind them apply to other programming paradigms as well.

Pure Functions and Referential Transparency

Functional programming categorizes functions into two categories: *pure* and *impure*.

Pure functions have two elemental guarantees:

The same input will always create the same output
  The return value of a *pure* function must solely depend on its input arguments.

They are self-contained without any kind of side effect
  The code cannot affect the global state, like changing argument values or using any I/O.

These two guarantees allow pure functions to be safe to use in any environment, even in a parallel fashion. The following code shows a method being a pure function that accepts an argument without affecting anything outside of its context:

```java
public String toLowercase(String str) {
  return str;
}
```

Functions violating either of the two guarantees are considered *impure*. The following code is an example of an *impure function*, as it uses the current time for its logic:

```java
public String buildGreeting(String name) {
  var now = LocalTime.now();
  if (now.getHour() < 12) {
    return "Good morning " + name;
  } else {
    return "Hello " + name;
  }
}
```

The signifiers "pure" and "impure" are rather unfortunate names because of the connotation they might invoke. Impure functions aren't inferior to pure functions in general. They are just used in different ways depending on the coding style and paradigm you want to adhere to.

Another aspect of side-effect-free expressions or pure functions is their deterministic nature, which makes them *referentially transparent*. That means you can replace them with their respective evaluated result for any further invocations without changing the behavior of your program.

Function:

$$f(x) = x * x$$

Replacing Evaluated Expressions:

$$result = f(5) + f(5)$$
$$= 25 + f(5)$$
$$= 25 + 25$$

All these variants are equal and won't change your program. Purity and referential transparency go hand in hand and give you a powerful tool because it's easier to understand and reason with your code.

Immutability

Object-oriented code is usually based around a mutable program state. Objects can and will usually change after their creation, using *setters*. But mutating data structures can create unexpected side effects. Mutability isn't restricted to data structures and OOP, though. A local variable in a method might be mutable, too, and can lead to problems in its context as much as a changing field of an object.

With *immutability*, data structures can no longer change after their initialization. By never changing, they are always consistent, side-effect-free, predictable, and easier to reason with. Like pure functions, their usage is safe in concurrent and parallel environments without the usual issues of unsynchronized access or out-of-scope state changes.

If data structures never change after initialization, a program would not be very useful. That's why you need to create a new and updated version containing the mutated state instead of changing the data structure directly.

Creating new data structures for every change can be a chore and quite inefficient due to copying the data every time. Many programming languages employ "structure sharing" to provide efficient copy mechanisms to minimize the inefficiencies of requiring new data structures for every change. This way, different instances of data structures share immutable data between them. Chapter 4 will explain in more detail why the advantages of having side-effect-free data structures outweigh the extra work that might be necessary.

Recursion

Recursion is a problem-solving technique that solves a problem by partially solving problems of the same form and combining the partial results to finally solve the original problem. In layperson's terms, recursive functions call themselves, but with a slight change in their input arguments, until they reach an end condition and return an actual value. Chapter 12 will go into the finer details of recursion.

A simple example is calculating a factorial, the product of all positive integers less than or equal to the input parameter. Instead of calculating the value with an intermediate state, the function calls itself with a decremented input variable, as illustrated in Figure 1-1.

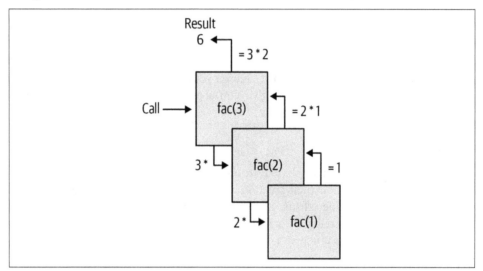

Figure 1-1. Calculating a factorial with recursion

Pure functional programming often prefers using recursion instead of loops or iterators. Some of them, like Haskell, go a step further and don't have loops like for or while at all.

The repeated function calls can be inefficient and even dangerous due to the risk of the stack overflowing. That's why many functional languages utilize optimizations like "unrolling" recursion into loops or *tail-call optimization* to reduce the required stack frames. Java doesn't support any of these optimization techniques, which I'll talk more about in Chapter 12.

First-Class and Higher-Order Functions

Many of the previously discussed concepts don't have to be available as deeply integrated language features to support a more functional programming style in your code. The concepts of first-class and higher-order functions, however, are absolute must-haves.

For functions to be so-called "first-class citizens," they must observe all the properties inherent to other entities of the language. They need to be assignable to variables and be used as arguments and return values in other functions and expressions.

Higher-order functions use this *first-class* citizenship to accept functions as arguments or to return a function as their result, or both. This is an essential property for the next concept, *functional composition*.

Functional Composition

Pure functions can be combined to create more complex expressions. In mathematical terms, this means that the two functions $f(x)$ and $g(y)$ can be combined to a function $h(x) = g(f(x))$, as seen in Figure 1-2.

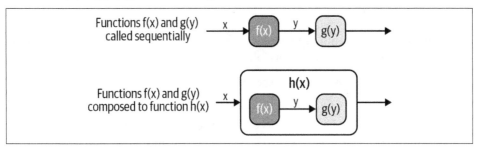

Figure 1-2. Composing functions

This way, functions can be as small and on point as possible, and therefore easier to reuse. To create a more complex and complete task, such functions can be quickly composed as needed.

Currying

Function *currying* means converting a function from taking multiple arguments into a sequence of functions that each takes only a single argument.

The currying technique borrows its name from the mathematician and logician Haskell Brooks Curry (1900-1982). He's not only the namesake of the functional technique called *currying*, he also has three different programming languages named after him: Haskell (*https://oreil.ly/xd-ZC*), Brook (*https://oreil.ly/RGwNw*), and Curry (*https://oreil.ly/EFbC4*).

Imagine a function that accepts three arguments. It can be curried as follows:

Initial function:

$$x = f(a, b, c)$$

Curried functions:

$$h = g(a)$$
$$i = h(b)$$
$$x = i(c)$$

Sequence of curried functions:

$$x = g(a)(b)(c)$$

Some functional programming languages reflect the general concept of *currying* in their type definitions, like Haskell, as follows:

```
add :: Integer -> Integer -> Integer ❶
add x y = x + y ❷
```

❶ The function add is declared to accept an Integer and returns another function accepting another Integer, which itself returns an Integer.

❷ The actual definition reflects the declaration: two input parameters and the result of the body as return value.

At first glance, the concept can feel weird and foreign to an OO or imperative developer, like many principles based on mathematics. Still, it perfectly conveys how a function with more than one argument is representable as a function of functions, and that's an essential realization to support the next concept.

Partial Function Application

Partial function application is the process of creating a new function by providing only a subset of the required arguments to an existing one. It's often conflated with currying, but a call to a partially applied function returns a result and not another function of a currying chain.

The currying example from the previous section can be partially applied to create a more specific function:

```
add :: Integer -> Integer -> Integer ❶
add x y =  x + y

add3 = add 3 ❷

add3 5 ❸
```

❶ The add function is declared as before, accepting two arguments.

❷ Calling the function add with only a value for the first argument x returns as
    a partially applied function of type Integer → Integer, which is bound to the
    name add3.

❸ The call add3 5 is equivalent to add 3 5.

With partial application, you can create new, less verbose functions on the fly or
specialized functions from a more generic pool to match your code's current context
and requirements.

Lazy Evaluation

Lazy evaluation is an evaluation strategy that delays the evaluation of an expression
until its result is literally needed by separating the concerns of how you create an
expression from whether or when you actually use it. It's also another concept not
rooted in or restricted to functional programming, but it's a must-have for using
other functional concepts and techniques.

Many nonfunctional languages, including Java, are primarily *strict*—or *eagerly*—evaluated, meaning an expression evaluates immediately. Those languages still have a few
lazy constructs, like control-flow statements such as if-else statements or loops, or
logical short-circuit operators. Immediately evaluating both branches of an if-else
construct or all possible loop iterations wouldn't make much sense, would it? So
instead, only the branches and iterations absolutely required are evaluated during
runtime.

Laziness enables certain constructs that aren't possible otherwise, like infinite data
structures or more efficient implementations of some algorithms. It also works very
well with *referential transparency*. If there is no difference between an expression and
its result, you can delay the evaluation without consequences to the result. Delayed
evaluation might still impact the program's performance because you might not know
the precise time of evaluation.

In Chapter 11 I will discuss how to achieve a lazy approach in Java with the tools at
your disposal, and how to create your own.

Advantages of Functional Programming

After going through the most common and essential concepts of functional programming, you can see how they are reflected in the advantages that a more functional approach provides:

Simplicity
> Without mutable state and side effects, your functions tend to be smaller, doing "just what they are supposed to do."

Consistency
> Immutable data structures are reliable and consistent. No more worries about unexpected or unintended program state.

(Mathematical) correctness
> Simpler code with consistent data structures will automatically lead to "more correct" code with a smaller bug surface. The "purer" your code, the easier it will be to reason with, leading to simpler debugging and testing.

Safer concurrency
> Concurrency is one of the most challenging tasks to do right in "classical" Java. Functional concepts allow you to eliminate many headaches and gain safer parallel processing (almost) for free.

Modularity
> Small and independent functions lead to simpler reusability and modularity. Combined with functional composition and partial application, you have powerful tools to build more complex tasks out of these smaller parts easily.

Testability
> Many of the functional concepts, like pure functions, referential transparency, immutability, and the separation of concerns make testing and verification easier.

Disadvantages of Functional Programming

While functional programming has many advantages, it's also essential to know its possible pitfalls.

Learning curve
> The advanced mathematical terminology and concepts that functional programming is based on can be quite intimidating. To augment your Java code, though, you definitely don't need to know that "a monad is just a monoid in the category

of endofunctors.[2]" Nevertheless, you're confronted with new and often unfamiliar terms and concepts.

Higher level of abstraction

Where OOP uses objects to model its abstraction, FP uses a higher level of abstraction to represent its data structures, making them quite elegant but often harder to recognize.

Dealing with state

Handling state isn't an easy task, regardless of the chosen paradigm. Even though FP's immutable approach eliminates a lot of possible bug surfaces, it also makes it harder to mutate data structures if they actually need to change, especially if you're accustomed to having setters in your OO code.

Performance implications

Functional programming is easier and safer to use in concurrent environments. This doesn't mean, however, that it's inherently faster compared to other paradigms, especially in a single-threaded context. Despite their many benefits, many functional techniques, like immutability or recursion, can suffer from the required overhead. That's why many FP languages utilize a plethora of optimizations to mitigate, like specialized data structures that minimize copying, or compiler optimizations for techniques like recursion[3].

Optimal problem context

Not all problem contexts are a good fit for a functional approach. Domains like high-performance computing, I/O heavy problems, or low-level systems and embedded controllers, where you need fine-grained control over things like data locality and explicit memory management, don't mix well with functional programming.

As programmers, we must find the balance between the advantages and disadvantages of any paradigm and programming approach. That's why this book shows you how to pick the best parts of Java's functional evolution and utilize them to augment your object-oriented Java code.

---

2 James Iry used this phrase in his humorous blog post "A Brief, Incomplete, and Mostly Wrong History of Programming Languages" (*https://oreil.ly/FUnJM*) to illustrate Haskell's complexity. It's also a good example of how you don't need to know all the underlying mathematical details of a programming technique to reap its benefits. But if you really want to know what it means, see Saunders Mac Lane's book, *Categories for the Working Mathematician* (Springer, 1998), where the phrase was used initially.

3 The *Java Magazine* article "Curly Braces #6: Recursion and tail-call optimization" (*https://oreil.ly/UivsD*) provides a great overview about the importance of tail-call optimization in recursive code.

Takeaways

- Functional programming is built on the mathematical principle of lambda calculus.
- A declarative coding style based on expressions instead of statements is essential for functional programming.
- Many programming concepts feel inherently functional, but they are not an absolute requirement to make a language or your code "functional." Even non-functional code benefits from their underlying ideas and overall mindset.
- Purity, consistency, and simplicity are essential properties to apply to your code to get the most out of a functional approach.
- Trade-offs might be necessary between the functional concepts and their real-world application. Their advantages usually outweigh the disadvantages, though, or can at least be mitigated in some form.

CHAPTER 2

Functional Java

Unsurprisingly, *lambda expressions* are the key to having a functional approach in Java.

In this chapter, you will learn how to use lambdas in Java, why they are so important, how to use them efficiently, and how they work internally.

What Are Java Lambdas?

A lambda expression is a single line or block of Java code that has zero or more parameters and might return a value. From a simplified point of view, a lambda is like an *anonymous method* that doesn't belong to any object:

```
() -> System.out.println("Hello, lambda!")
```

Let's look at the details of the syntax and how lambdas are implemented in Java.

Lambda Syntax

The Java syntax for lambdas is quite similar to the mathematical notation you saw in Chapter 1 for lambda calculus:

```
(<parameters>) -> { <body> }
```

The syntax consists of three distinct parts:

Parameters
> A comma-separated list of parameters, just like a method argument list. Unlike method arguments, though, you can omit the argument types if the compiler can infer them. Mixing implicitly and explicitly typed parameters is not allowed. You don't need parentheses for a single parameter, but they are required if none or more than one parameter is present.

Arrow

> The -> (arrow) separates the parameters from the lambda body. It's the equivalent to λ in lambda calculus.

Body

> Either a single expression or a code block. Single-line expressions don't require curly braces, and their evaluated result returns implicitly without a `return` statement. A typical Java code block is used if the body is represented by more than a single expression. It must be wrapped in curly braces and explicitly use a `return` statement if a value is supposed to be returned.

That is all the syntax definition there is for lambdas in Java. With its multiple ways of declaring a lambda, you can write the same lambda with different levels of verbosity, as seen in Example 2-1.

Example 2-1. Different ways of writing the same lambda

```
(String input) -> { ❶
  return input != null;
}

input -> { ❷
  return input != null;
}

(String input) -> input != null ❸

input -> input != null ❹
```

❶ The most verbose variant: an explicitly typed parameter in parentheses and a body block.

❷ The first mixed variant: type inference for parameters allows removing the explicit type, and a single parameter doesn't need parentheses. That shortens the lambda declaration slightly without removing information due to the surrounding context.

❸ The second mixed variant: an explicitly typed parameter in parentheses but a single expression body instead of a block; no curly braces or `return` statement needed.

❹ The most concise variant, as the body is reducible to a single expression.

Which variant to choose depends highly on the context and personal preference. Usually, the compiler can infer the types, but that doesn't mean a human reader is as good at understanding the shortest code possible as a compiler is.

Even though you should always strive for clean and more concise code, that doesn't mean it has to be as minimal as possible. A certain amount of verbosity might help any reader—you included—to understand the reasoning behind the code better and make the mental model of your code easier to grasp.

Functional Interfaces

So far, we've looked only at the general concept of lambdas in isolation. However, they still have to exist inside Java and its concepts and language rules as well.

Java is known for its backward compatibility. That's why even though the lambda syntax is a breaking change to the Java syntax itself, it's still based on ordinary interfaces to be backward compatible and feel quite familiar to any Java developer.

To achieve their first-class citizenship, lambdas in Java require a representation comparable to the existing types, like objects and primitives, as discussed in "First-Class and Higher-Order Functions" on page 8. Therefore, lambdas are represented by a specialized subtype of interfaces, so-called *functional interfaces*.

Interfaces in Java

Interface declarations consist of a name with optional generic bounds, inherited interfaces, and its body. Such a body is allowed to contain the following content:

Method signatures
> Body-less—`abstract`—method signatures that must be implemented by any class conforming to the interface. Only these method signatures count towards the *single abstract method* constraint of *functional interfaces*.

Default methods
> Methods signatures can have a "default" implementation, signified by the `default` keyword and a body block. Any class implementing the interface *can* override it but *isn't required* to do so.

Static methods
> Like the class-based counterparts, they're associated with the type itself and must provide an implementation. However, unlike `default` methods, they aren't inherited and can't be overridden.

Constant values
> Values that are automatically `public`, `static`, and `final`.

There isn't any explicit syntax or language keyword for functional interfaces. They look and feel like any other interface, can extend or be extended by other interfaces, and classes can implement them. If they are just like "normal" interfaces, what makes them a "functional" interface then? It's their enforced requirement that they may only define a *single abstract method* (SAM).

As the name signifies, the SAM count only applies to `abstract` methods. There's no limit to any additional, non-`abstract` methods. Neither `default` nor `static` methods are abstract, hence not relevant for the SAM count. That's why they are often used to complement the capabilities of the lambda type.

 Most functional interfaces of the JDK give you additional `default` and `static` methods related to the type. Checking out the interface declarations of any functional interface might reveal many hidden gems of functionality.

Consider Example 2-2, which shows a simplified version[1] of the functional interface `java.util.function.Predicate<T>`. A `Predicate` is a functional interface for testing conditions, which will be explained in more detail in "The Big Four Functional Interface Categories" on page 39. Besides having a single abstract method, `boolean test(T t)`, it provides five additional methods (three `default`, two `static`).

Example 2-2. Simplified `java.util.function.Predicate<T>`

```
package java.util.function;

@FunctionalInterface ❶
public interface Predicate<T> {

  boolean test(T t); ❷

  default Predicate<T> and(Predicate<? super T> other) { ❸
    // ...
  }

  default Predicate<T> negate() { ❸
    // ...
  }

  default Predicate<T> or(Predicate<? super T> other) { ❸
    // ...
```

---

1 The simplified version of `java.util.function.Predicate` is based on the source code for the latest Git tag of the LTS version at the time of writing: 17+35. You can check out the official repository (*https://oreil.ly/Amx25*) to see the full source code.

```
  }

  static <T> Predicate<T> isEqual(Object targetRef) { ❹
    // ...
  }

  static <T> Predicate<T> not(Predicate<? super T> target) { ❹
    // ...
  }
}
```

❶ The type uses the `@FunctionalInterface` annotation, which isn't explicitly required.

❷ The type's single abstract method.

❸ Several `default` methods provide support for functional composition.

❹ Convenience `static` methods are used to simplify creation or to wrap existing lambdas.

Any interface with a single abstract method is automatically a functional interface. Therefore, any of their implementations is representable by a lambda, too.

Java 8 added the marker annotation `@FunctionalInterface` to enforce the SAM requirement at the compiler level. It isn't mandatory, but it tells the compiler and possibly other annotation-based tooling that an interface should be a functional interface and, therefore, that the single abstract method requirement must be enforced. If you add another `abstract` method, the Java compiler will refuse to compile your code. That's why adding the annotation to any functional interface makes a lot of sense, even if you don't explicitly need it. It clarifies the reasoning behind your code and the intention of such an interface and fortifies your code against unintentional changes that might break it in the future.

The optional nature of the `@FunctionalInterface` annotation also enables the backward compatibility of existing interfaces. As long as an interface fulfills the SAM requirements, it's representable as a lambda. I'll talk about the functional interfaces of the JDK later in this chapter.

Lambdas and Outside Variables

"Pure Functions and Referential Transparency" on page 6 introduced the concept of *pure*—self-contained and side-effect-free—functions that won't affect any outside state and only rely on their arguments. Even though lambdas follow the same gist, they also allow a certain degree of impurity to be more flexible. They can "capture" constants and variables from their creation scope in which the lambda is defined, which makes such variables available to them even if the original scope no longer exists, as shown in Example 2-3.

Example 2-3. Lambda variable capture

```
void capture() {
  var theAnswer = 42; ❶

  Runnable printAnswer =
    () -> System.out.println("the answer is " + theAnswer); ❷

  run(printAnswer); ❸
}

void run(Runnable r) {
  r.run();
}

capture();
// OUTPUT:
// the answer is 42
```

❶ The variable `theAnswer` is declared in the scope of the `capture` method.

❷ The lambda `printAnswer` captures the variable in its body.

❸ The lambda can be run in another method and scope but still has access to `theAnswer`.

The big difference between *capture* and *non-capture* lambdas is the optimization strategies of the JVM. The JVM optimizes lambdas with different strategies based on their actual usage pattern. If no variables get captured, a lambda might end up being a simple `static` method behind the scenes, beating out the performance of alternative approaches like anonymous classes. The implications of capturing variables on performance are not as clear-cut, though.

There are multiple ways the JVM might translate your code if it captures variables, leading to additional object allocation, affecting performance and garbage collector times. That doesn't mean that capturing variables is inherently a bad design choice. The main goal of a more functional approach should be improved productivity, more straightforward reasoning, and more concise code. Still, you should avoid unnecessary capturing, especially if you require the least amount of allocations or the best performance possible.

Another reason to avoid capturing variables is their necessity of being *effectively* `final`.

Effectively final

The JVM has to make special considerations to use captured variables safely and achieve the best performance possible. That's why there's an essential requirement: only *effectively* final variables are allowed to be captured.

In simple terms, any captured variable must be an immutable reference that isn't allowed to change after its initialization. They must be final, either by explicitly using the final keyword or by never changing after their initialization, making them effectively final.

Be aware that this requirement is actually for the *reference* to a variable and not the underlying data structure itself. A reference to a List<String> might be final, and therefore usable in a lambda, but you can still add new items, as seen in Example 2-4. Only reassigning the variable is prohibited.

Example 2-4. Change data behind a final variable

```
final List<String> wordList = new ArrayList<>(); ❶

// COMPILES FINE
Runnable addItemInLambda = () -> wordList.add("adding is fine"); ❷

// WON'T COMPILE
wordList = List.of("assigning", "another", "List", "is", "not"); ❸
```

❶ The variable wordList is explicitly final, making the reference immutable.

❷ Capturing and using the variable in a lambda works without problems. However, the keyword final does not affect the List<String> itself, allowing you to add additional items.

❸ Reassigning the variable is prohibited due to the final keyword and won't compile.

The simplest way to test whether a variable is effectively final is by making it explicitly final. If your code still compiles with the additional final keyword, it will compile without it. So why not make every variable final? Because the compiler ensures that "out-of-body" references are effectively final, the keyword won't help with actual immutability anyway. Making every variable final would only create more visual noise in your code without much benefit. Adding a modifier like final should always be a conscious decision with intent.

If you run any of the shown effectively final-related examples in jshell, they might not behave as expected. That's because jshell has special semantics regarding top-level expressions and declarations, which affect final or effectively final values at top-level[2]. Even though you can reassign any reference, making them non-effectively final, you can still use them in lambdas, as long as you're not in the top-level scope.

Re-finalizing a reference

Sometimes a reference might not be effectively final, but you still need it to be available in a lambda. If refactoring your code isn't an option, there's a simple trick to *re-finalize* them. Remember, the requirement is just for the reference and not the underlying data structure itself.

You can create a new effectively final reference to the non-effectively final variable by simply referencing the original one and not changing it further, as shown in Example 2-5.

Example 2-5. Re-finalize a reference

```
var nonEffectivelyFinal = 1_000L; ❶

nonEffectivelyFinal = 9_000L; ❷

var finalAgain = nonEffectivelyFinal; ❸

Predicate<Long> isOver9000 = input -> input > finalAgain;
```

❶ At this point, nonEffectivelyFinal is still effectively final.

❷ Changing the variable after its initialization makes it unusable in lambda.

❸ By creating a new variable and not changing it after its initialization, you "re-finalized" the reference to the underlying data structure.

Keep in mind that re-finalizing a reference is just a band-aid, and needing a band-aid means you scraped your knees first. So the best approach is trying not to need it at all. Refactoring or redesigning your code should always be the preferred option instead of bending the code to your will with tricks like re-finalizing a reference.

---

2 The official documentation (*https://oreil.ly/dvmJp*) sheds some light on the special semantics and requirements for top-level expressions and declarations.

Such safeguards for using variables in lambdas like the effectively final requirement might feel like an additional burden at first. However, instead of capturing "out-of-body" variables, your lambdas should strive to be self-sufficient and require all necessary data as arguments. That automatically leads to more reasonable code, increased reusability, and allows for easier refactoring and testing.

What about Anonymous Classes?

After learning about lambdas and functional interfaces, you're most likely reminded of their similarities to *anonymous inner classes*: the combined declaration and instantiation of types. An interface or extended class can be implemented "on the fly" without needing a separate Java class, so what differs between a lambda expression and an anonymous class if they both have to implement a concrete interface?

On the surface, a functional interface implemented by an anonymous class looks quite similar to its lambda representation, except for the additional boilerplate, as seen in Example 2-6.

Example 2-6. Anonymous class versus lambda expression

```
// FUNCTIONAL INTERFACE (implicit)
interface HelloWorld {
  String sayHello(String name);
}

// AS ANONYMOUS CLASS
var helloWorld = new HelloWorld() {
  @Override
  public String sayHello(String name) {
    return "hello, " + name + "!";
  }
};

// AS LAMBDA
HelloWorld helloWorldLambda = name -> "hello, " + name + "!";
```

Does this mean that lambda expressions are just *syntactic sugar* for implementing a functional interface as an anonymous class?

Syntactic Sugar

Syntactic sugar describes features that are additions to a language to make your life as a developer "sweeter," so certain constructs can be expressed more concisely or clearly, or in an alternative manner.

Peter J. Landin coined the term in 1964[3], describing how the keyword where replaced λ in an ALGOL-like language.

Java's import statement, for example, allows you to use types without their fully qualified names. Another example is type inference with var for references or the <> (diamond) operator for generic types. Both features simplify your code for "human consumption." The compiler will "desugar" the code and deal directly with its "bitterness."

Lambda expressions might look like syntactic sugar, but they're so much more in reality. The *real* difference—besides verbosity—lies in the generated bytecode, as seen in Example 2-7, and how the runtime handles it.

Example 2-7. Bytecode differences between anonymous classes and lambdas

```
// ANONYMOUS CLASS
0: new #7 // class HelloWorldAnonymous$1 ❶
3: dup
4: invokespecial #9 // Method HelloWorldAnonymous$1."<init>":()V ❷
7: astore_1
8: return

// LAMBDA
0: invokedynamic #7, 0 // InvokeDynamic #0:sayHello:()LHelloWorld; ❸
5: astore_1
6: return
```

❶ A new object of the anonymous inner class HelloWorldAnonymous$1 is created in the surrounding class HelloWorldAnonymous.

❷ The constructor of the anonymous class is called. Object creation is a two-step process in the JVM.

❸ The invokedynamic opcode hides the whole logic behind creating the lambda.

---

3 Peter J. Landin, "The Mechanical Evaluation of Expressions," *The Computer Journal*, Vol. 6, Issue 4 (1964): 308-320 (*https://oreil.ly/Ee6kW*).

Both variants have the `astore_1` call in common, which stores a reference into a local variable, and the `return` call, so both won't be part of analyzing the bytecode.

The anonymous class version creates a new object of the anonymous type `HelloWorldAnonymous$1`, resulting in three opcodes:

`new`
> Create a new uninitialized instance of a type.

`dup`
> Put the value on top of the stack by duplicating it.

`invokespecial`
> Call the constructor method of the newly created object to finalize its initialization.

The lambda version, on the other hand, doesn't need to create an instance that needs to be put on the stack. Instead, it delegates the whole task of creating the lambda to the JVM with a single opcode: `invokedynamic`.

The invokedynamic Instruction

Java 7 introduced the new JVM opcode `invokedynamic`[4] to allow more flexible method invocation to support dynamic languages like Groovy (*https://oreil.ly/Db9Q4*) or JRuby (*https://oreil.ly/gW1Uh*). The opcode is a more versatile invocation variant because its actual target, like a method call or lambda body, is unknown on class-loading. Instead of linking such a target at compile time, the JVM instead links a dynamic call site with the actual target method.

The runtime then uses a "bootstrap method"[5] on the first `invokedynamic` call to determine what method should actually be called.

You can think of it as a recipe for lambda creation that utilizes reflection directly in the JVM. This way, the JVM can optimize the creation task by using different strategies, like dynamic proxies, anonymous inner classes, or `java.lang.invoke.Method Handle`.

Another big difference between lambdas and anonymous inner classes is their respective scope. An inner class creates its own scope, hiding its local variables from the

---

4 The *Java Magazine* has an article (*https://oreil.ly/KrkQo*) by Java Champion Ben Evans that explains method invocation with `invokedynamic` in more detail.

5 The class `java.lang.invoke.LambdaMetafactory` (*https://oreil.ly/3E-fO*) is responsible for creating "bootstrap methods."

enclosing one. That's why the keyword `this` references the instance of the inner class itself, not the surrounding scope. Lambdas, on the other hand, live fully in their surrounding scope. Variables can't be redeclared with the same name, and `this` refers to the instance the lambda was created in, if not `static`.

As you can see, lambda expressions are *not* syntactic sugar at all.

Lambdas in Action

As you saw in the previous section, lambdas are an extraordinary addition to Java to improve its functional programming abilities that are much more than just syntactic sugar for previously available approaches. Their first-class citizenship allows them to be statically typed, concise, and anonymous functions that are just like any other variable. Although the arrow syntax might be new, the overall use pattern should feel familiar to any programmer. In this section, we'll jump right into actually using lambdas and seeing them in action.

Creating Lambdas

To create a lambda expression, you need to represent a singular functional interface. The actual type might not be evident because a receiving method argument dictates the required type, or the compiler will infer it if possible.

Let's take a look at `Predicate<T>` again to better illustrate that point.

Creating a new instance requires the type to be defined on the left-hand side:

```
Predicate<String> isNull = value -> value == null;
```

Even if you use explicit types for the arguments, the functional interface type is still required:

```
// WON'T COMPILE
var isNull = (String value) -> value == null;
```

The method signature of `Predicate<String>` SAM might be inferable:

```
boolean test(String input)
```

Still, the Java compiler requires a concrete type for the reference, not just a method signature. This requirement stems from Java's propensity for backward compatibility, as I previously mentioned. By using the preexisting statically-typed system, lambdas fit perfectly into Java, granting lambdas the same compile-time safety as any other type or approach before them.

However, obeying the type system makes Java lambdas less dynamic than their counterparts in other languages. Just because two lambdas share the same SAM signature doesn't mean they are interchangeable.

Take the following functional interface, for example:

```
interface LikePredicate<T> {
  boolean test(T value);
}
```

Even though its SAM is identical to `Predicate<T>`, the types can't be used interchangeably, as shown in the following code:

```
LikePredicate<String> isNull = value -> value == null; ❶

Predicate<String> wontCompile = isNull; ❷
// Error:
// incompatible types: LikePredicate<java.lang.String> cannot be converted
// to java.util.function.Predicate<java.lang.String>
```

❶ The lambda is created as before.

❷ Trying to assign it to a functional interface with an identical SAM won't compile.

Due to this incompatibility, you should try to rely on the available interfaces in the `java.util.function` package that will be discussed in Chapter 3 to maximize interoperability. You're still going to encounter pre-Java 8 interfaces like `java.util.concurrent.Callable<V>` that are identical to a Java 8+ one, in this case, `java.util.function.Supplier<T>`, though. If that happens, there's a neat shortcut for switching a lambda to another identical type. You'll learn about this in "Bridging Functional Interfaces" on page 46.

Ad hoc created lambdas as method arguments and return types don't suffer from any type incompatibility, as demonstrated by the following:

```
List<String> filter1(List<String> values, Predicate<String> predicate) {
  // ...
}

List<String> filter2(List<String> values, LikePredicate<String> predicate) {
  // ...
}

var values = Arrays.asList("a", null, "c");

var result1 = filter1(values, value -> value != null);

var result2 = filter2(values, value -> value != null);
```

The compiler infers the type of ad hoc lambdas directly from the method signature, so you can concentrate on *what* you want to achieve with the lambda. The same is true for return types:

```
Predicate<Integer> isGreaterThan(int value) {
  return compareValue -> compareValue > value;
}
```

Now that you know how to create lambdas, you then need to call them.

Calling Lambdas

Lambdas are effectively concrete implementations of their respective functional interfaces. Other, more functionally inclined, languages usually treat lambdas more dynamically. That's why Java's usage patterns can differ from such languages.

In JavaScript, for example, you can call a lambda and pass an argument directly, as shown in the following code:

```
let helloWorldJs = name => "hello, " + name + "!"

let resultJs = helloWorldJs("Ben")
```

In Java, however, lambdas behave like any other instances of an interface, so you need to explicitly call its SAM, as demonstrated as follows:

```
Function<String, String> helloWorld = name -> "hello, " + name + "!";

var result = helloWorld.apply("Ben");
```

Calling the *single abstract method* might not be as concise as in other languages, but the benefit is Java's continued backward compatibility.

Method References

Besides lambdas, Java 8 introduced another new feature with a language syntax change as a new way to create lambda expressions: *method references*. It's shorthand syntactic sugar, using the new :: (double-colon) operator to reference an existing method in place of creating a lambda expression from an existing method and therefore streamlining your functional code.

Example 2-8 shows how a Stream pipeline's readability is improved by converting the lambdas to method references. Don't worry about the details! You will learn about Streams in Chapter 6; just think of it as a fluent call with lambda accepting methods.

Example 2-8. Method references and Streams

```
List<Customer> customers = ...;

// LAMBDAS
customers.stream()
        .filter(customer -> customer.isActive())
        .map(customer -> customer.getName())
        .map(name -> name.toUpperCase())
```

```
            .peek(name -> System.out.println(name))
            .toArray(count -> new String[count]);

// METHOD REFERENCES
customers.stream()
        .filter(Customer::isActive)
        .map(Customer::getName)
        .map(String::toUpperCase)
        .peek(System.out::println)
        .toArray(String[]::new);
```

Replacing lambdas with method references removes a lot of "noise" without compromising the readability or understandability of your code. There is no need for the input arguments to have actual names or types, or to call the reference method explicitly. Also, modern IDEs usually provide automatic refactoring to convert lambdas to method references, if applicable.

There are four types of method references you can use, depending on the lambda expression you want to replace and what kind of method you need to reference:

- static method references
- Bound non-static method references
- Unbound non-static method references
- Constructor references

Let's take a look at the different kinds and how and when to use them.

Static method references

A *static method reference* refers to a static method of a specific type, like the toHexString method available on Integer:

```
// EXCERPT FROM java.lang.Integer
public class Integer extends Number {

  public static String toHexString(int i) {
    // ..
  }
}

// LAMBDA
Function<Integer, String> asLambda = i -> Integer.toHexString(i);

// STATIC METHOD REFERENCE
Function<Integer, String> asRef = Integer::toHexString;
```

The general syntax for static method references is ClassName::staticMethodName.

Bound non-static method references

If you want to refer to a non-`static` method of an already existing object, you need a *bound non-static method reference*. The lambda arguments are passed as the method arguments to the reference method of that specific object:

```
var now = LocalDate.now();

// LAMBDA BASED ON EXISTING OBJECT
Predicate<LocalDate> isAfterNowAsLambda = date -> $.isAfter(now);

// BOUND NON-STATIC METHOD REFERENCE
Predicate<LocalDate> isAfterNowAsRef = now::isAfter;
```

You don't even need an intermediate variable; you can combine the return value of another method call or field access directly with the :: (double-colon) operator:

```
// BIND RETURN VALUE
Predicate<LocalDate> isAfterNowAsRef = LocalDate.now()::isAfter;

// BIND STATIC FIELD
Function<Object, String> castToStr = String.class::cast;
```

You can also reference methods from the current instance with `this::` or the `super` implementation with `super::`, as follows:

```
public class SuperClass {

  public String doWork(String input) {
    return "super: " + input;
  }
}

public class SubClass extends SuperClass {

  @Override
  public String doWork(String input){
    return "this: " + input;
  }

  public void superAndThis(String input) {
    Function<String, String> thisWorker = this::doWork;
    var thisResult = thisWorker.apply(input);
    System.out.println(thisResult);

    Function<String, String> superWorker = SubClass.super::doWork;
    var superResult = superWorker.apply(input);
    System.out.println(superResult);
  }
}

new SubClass().superAndThis("hello, World!");
```

```
// OUTPUT:
// this: hello, World!
// super: hello, World!
```

Bound method references are a great way to use already existing methods on variables, the current instance, or super. It also allows you to refactor nontrivial or more complex lambdas to methods and use method references instead. Especially fluent pipelines, like Streams in Chapter 6 or Optionals in Chapter 9, profit immensely from the improved readability of short method references.

The general syntax for bound non-static method references is used in the following pattern:

```
objectName::instanceMethodName
```

Unbound non-static method references

Unbound non-static method references are, as their name suggests, not bound to a specific object. Instead, they refer to an instance method of a type:

```
// EXCERPT FROM java.lang.String
public class String implements ... {

  public String toLowerCase() {
    // ...
  }
}

// LAMBDA
Function<String, String> toLowerCaseLambda = str -> str.toLowerCase();

// UNBOUND NON-STATIC METHOD REFERENCE
Function<String, String> toLowerCaseRef = String::toLowerCase;
```

The general syntax for unbound non-static method references is used in the following pattern:

```
ClassName::instanceMethodName
```

This type of method reference can be confused with a static method reference. For *unbound non-static method references*, however, the ClassName signifies the instance type in which the referenced instance method is defined. It's also the first argument of the lambda expression. This way, the reference method is called on the incoming instance and not on an explicitly referenced instance of that type.

Constructor references

The last type of method reference refers to a type's constructor. A constructor method reference looks like this:

```
// LAMBDA
Function<String, Locale> newLocaleLambda = language -> new Locale(language);

// CONSTRUCTOR REFERENCE
Function<String, Locale> newLocaleRef = Locale::new;
```

At first glance, constructor method references look like static or unbound non-static method references. The referenced method isn't an actual method but a reference to a constructor via the new keyword.

The general syntax for constructor method references is `ClassName::new`.

Functional Programming Concepts in Java

Chapter 1 tackled the core concepts that make a programming language functional from a mostly theoretical viewpoint. So let's take another look at them from a Java developer's point of view.

Pure Functions and Referential Transparency

The concept of pure functions is based on two guarantees that aren't necessarily bound to functional programming:

- Function logic is self-contained without any kind of side effect.
- The same input will always create the same output. Therefore, repeated calls can be replaced by the initial result, making the call referentially transparent.

These two principles make sense even in your imperative code. Making your code self-contained makes it predictable and more straightforward. From a Java perspective, how can you achieve these beneficial properties?

First, check for uncertainty. Is there non-predictive logic that doesn't depend on the input arguments? Prime examples are random number generators or the current date. Using such data in a function removes a function's predictability, making it *impure*.

Next, look for side effects and mutable state:

- Does your function affect any state outside of the function itself, like an instance or global variable?
- Does it change the inner data of its arguments, like adding new elements to a Collection or changing an object property?
- Does it do any other impure work, like I/O?

However, side effects aren't restricted to mutable state. For example, a simple `System.out.println` call is a side effect, even if it might look harmless. Any kind of I/O, like accessing the file system, or making network requests is a side effect. The reasoning is simple: repeated calls with the same arguments can't be replaced with the result of the first evaluation. A good indicator for an *impure* method is a void return type. If a method doesn't return anything, all it does are side effects, or it does nothing at all.

Pure functions are inherently referentially transparent. Hence, you can replace any subsequent calls using the same arguments with the previously calculated result. This interchangeability allows for an optimization technique called *memoization*. Originating from the Latin word "memorandum"—to be remembered—this technique describes "remembering" previously evaluated expressions. It trades memory space for saving computational time.

Space-Time Trade-Off

Algorithms depend on two significant factors: *space* (memory) and *time* (computational or response time). Both might be available in vast quantities these days, but they are still finite.

The *space-time trade-off* states that you can decrease one of the factors by increasing the other. If you want to save time, you need more memory for storing results. Or you can save permanently needed memory by constantly recalculating them.

You're most likely already using the general idea behind referential transparency in your code in the form of *caching*. From dedicated cache libraries, like Ehcache[6] to simple HashMap-based lookup tables, it's all about "remembering" a value against a set of input arguments.

The Java compiler doesn't support automatic memoization of lambda expressions or methods calls. Some frameworks provide annotations, like @Cacheable in Spring[7] or @Cached in Apache Tapestry[8], and generate the required code automatically behind the scenes.

Creating your own lambda expression caching isn't too hard either, thanks to some of the newer additions to Java 8+. So let's do that right now.

Building your own memoization by creating an "on-demand" lookup table requires the answer to two questions:

---

6 Ehcache (*https://oreil.ly/5E0BT*) is a widely used Java caching library.

7 The official documentation of @Cacheable (*https://oreil.ly/30P7w*) explains the inner workings, including key mechanics.

8 The Tapestry annotation (*https://oreil.ly/taX6J*) doesn't support key-based caching but can be bound to a field instead.

- How do you identify the function and its input arguments uniquely?

- How can you store the evaluated result?

If your function or method call has only a single argument with a constant hashCode or other deterministic value, you can create a simple Map-based lookup table. For multi-argument calls, you must first define how to create a lookup key.

Java 8 introduced multiple functional additions to the Map type. One of these additions, the computeIfAbsent method, is a great aid to easily implement memoization, as shown in Example 2-9.

Example 2-9. Memoization with Map#computeIfAbsent

```
Map<String, Object> cache = new HashMap<>(); ❶

<T> T memoize(String identifier, Supplier<T> fn) { ❷
  return (T) cache.computeIfAbsent(identifier, key -> fn.get());
}

Integer expensiveCall(String arg0, int arg1) { ❸
    // ...
}

Integer memoizedCall(String arg0, int arg1) { ❹
  var compoundKey = String.format("expensiveCall:%s-%d", arg0, arg1);
  return memoize(compoundKey, () -> expensiveCall(arg0, arg1));
}

var calculated = memoizedCall("hello, world!", 42); ❺

var cached = memoizedCall("hello, world!", 42); ❻
```

❶ The results are cached in a simple HashMap<String, Object> so it can cache any kind of call based on an identifier. Depending on your requirements, there might be special considerations, like caching results per request in a web application or requiring a "time-to-live" concept. This example is supposed to show the simplest form of a lookup table.

❷ The memoize method accepts an identifier and a Supplier<T> in case the cache doesn't have a result yet.

❸ The expensiveCall is the method that gets memoized.

❹ For convenience, a specialized memoized call method exists, so you don't have to build an identifier manually each time you call memoize. It has the same arguments as the calculation method and delegates the actual memoization process.

❺ The convenience method allows you to replace the method name of the call to use the memoized version instead of the original one.

❻ The second call returns the cached result immediately without any additional evaluation.

This implementation is quite simplistic and is not a one-size-fits-all solution. Still, it confers the general concept of storing a call result via an intermediate method doing the actual memoization.

The functional additions to Map don't stop there. It provides the tools to create associations "on the fly," and more tools giving you more fine-grained control whether a value is already present or not. You will learn more about it in Chapter 11.

Immutability

The classical approach to Java with OOP is based on mutable program state, most prominently represented by JavaBeans and POJOs, also discussed in Chapter 4. There's no clear definition of how program state should be handled in OOP, and immutability is no prerequisite or unique feature of FP. Still, mutable state is a thorn in the side of many functional programming concepts because they expect immutable data structures to ensure data integrity and safe overall use.

POJOs are "plain old Java objects" that aren't bound by special restrictions, other than those imposed by the Java language. JavaBeans are a special type of POJOs. You will learn more about them in "Mutability and Data Structures in OOP" on page 59.

Java's support for immutability is quite limited compared to other languages. That's why it has to enforce constructs like effectively final as discussed in "Lambdas and Outside Variables" on page 19. To support "full" immutability, you need to design your data structures from the ground up as immutable, which can be cumbersome and error-prone. Third-party libraries are an often chosen approach to minimize the required boilerplate code and rely on battle-tested implementations. Finally, with Java 14+, immutable data classes—Records—were introduced to bridge the gap, which I will discuss in Chapter 5.

Immutability is a complex subject that you'll learn more about, as well as its importance and how to utilize it properly—either with built-in tools or with a do-it-yourself approach—in Chapter 4.

First-Class Citizenship

With Java lambdas being concrete implementations of functional interfaces, they gain first-class citizenship and are usable as variables, arguments, and return values, as seen in Example 2-10.

Example 2-10. First-class Java lambdas

```
// VARIABLE ASSIGNMENT

UnaryOperator<Integer> quadraticFn = x -> x * x;  ❶
quadraticFn.apply(5);  ❷
// => 25

// METHOD ARGUMENT

public Integer apply(Integer input, UnaryOperator<Integer> operation) {
  return operation.apply(input);  ❸
}

// RETURN VALUE

public UnaryOperator<Integer> multiplyWith(Integer multiplier) {
  return x -> multiplier * x;  ❹
}

UnaryOperator<Integer> multiplyWithFive = multiplyWith(5);
multiplyWithFive.apply(6);
// => 30
```

❶ Assigning a Java lambda to the variable `quadraticFn`.

❷ It can be used like any other "normal" Java variable, calling the `apply` method of its interface.

❸ Lambdas are usable, like any other type, for arguments.

❹ Returning a lambda is like returning any other Java variable.

Accepting lambdas as arguments and returning lambdas is essential for the next concept, functional composition.

Functional Composition

The idea of creating complex systems by composing smaller components is a cornerstone of programming, regardless of the chosen paradigm to follow. In OOP, objects can be composed of smaller ones, building a more complex API. In FP, two functions are combined to build a new function, which then can be combined further.

Functional composition is arguably one of the essential aspects of a functional programming mindset. It allows you to build complex systems by composing smaller, reusable functions into a larger chain, fulfilling a more complex task, as illustrated in Figure 2-1.

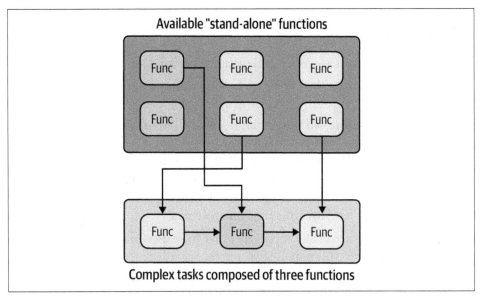

Figure 2-1. Composing complex tasks from multiple functions

Java's functional composition capabilities depend highly on the involved concrete types. In "Functional Composition" on page 47, I will discuss how to combine the different functional interfaces provided by the JDK.

Lazy Evaluation

Even though Java, at least in principle, is a non-lazy—strict or eager—language, it supports multiple lazy constructs:

- Logical short-circuit operators
- `if-else` and `:?` (ternary) operator
- `for` and `while` loops

Logical short-circuit operators are a simple example of laziness:

```
var result1 = simple() && complex();

var result2 = simple() || complex();
```

The evaluation of the `complex` method depends on the outcome of the `simple` class and the logical operator used in the overall expression. That's why the JVM can discard expressions that don't need evaluation, as will be explained in more detail in Chapter 11.

Takeaways

- Functional interfaces are concrete types and representations of Java lambdas.
- Java's lambda syntax is close to the underlying mathematical notation of lambda calculus.
- Lambdas can be expressed with multiple levels of verbosity, depending on the surrounding context and your requirements. Shorter isn't always as expressive as it should be, especially if others are reading your code.
- Lambda expressions are not syntactic sugar thanks to the JVM using the opcode `invokedynamic`. This allows for multiple optimization techniques to get better performance as alternatives like anonymous classes.
- Outside variables need to be effectively `final` to be used in lambdas, but this makes only the references immutable, not the underlying data structure.
- Method references are a concise alternative for matching method signatures and lambda definitions. They even provide a simple way to use "identical but incompatible" functional interface types.

CHAPTER 3

Functional Interfaces of the JDK

Many functional programming languages use only a singular and dynamic concept of "functions" to describe their lambdas, regardless of their arguments, return type, or actual use case. Java, on the other hand, is a strictly typed language requiring tangible types for everything, including lambdas. That's why the JDK provides you with over 40 readily available functional interfaces in its `java.util.function` package to kick-start your functional toolset.

This chapter will show you the most important functional interfaces, explain why there are so many variations, and show how you can extend your own code to be more functional.

The Big Four Functional Interface Categories

The 40+ functional interfaces in `java.util.function` fall into four main categories, with each category representing an essential functional use case:

- *Functions* accept arguments and return a result.
- *Consumers* only accept arguments but do not return a result.
- *Suppliers* do not accept arguments and only return a result.
- *Predicates* accept arguments to test against an expression and return a `boolean` primitive as their result.

These four categories cover many use cases, and their names relate to functional interface types and their variants.

Let's take a look at the four main categories of functional interfaces.

Functions

Functions, with their corresponding `java.util.function.Function<T, R>` interface, are one of the most central functional interfaces. They represent a "classical" function with a single input and output, as seen in Figure 3-1.

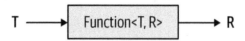

Figure 3-1. java.util.function<T, R>

The single abstract method of `Function<T, R>` is called `apply` and accepts an argument of a type T and produces a result of type R:

```
@FunctionalInterface
public interface Function<T, R> {
  R apply(T t);
}
```

The following code shows how to `null` check and convert a `String` to its length as an `Integer`:

```
Function<String, Integer> stringLength = str -> str != null ? str.length() : 0;

Integer result = stringLength.apply("Hello, Function!");
```

The input type T and output type R can be identical. However, in "Function Arity" on page 42 I discuss specialized functional interface variants with identical types.

Consumers

As the name suggests, a Consumer only consumes an input parameter but doesn't return anything, as shown in Figure 3-2. The central Consumer functional interface is `java.util.function.Consumer<T>`.

Figure 3-2. java.util.function.Consumer<T>

The single abstract method of `Consumer<T>` is called `accept` and requires an argument of a type T:

```
@FunctionalInterface
public interface Consumer<T> {
  void accept(T t);
}
```

The following code consumes a String to print it:

```
Consumer<String> println = str -> System.out.println(str);

println.accept("Hello, Consumer!");
```

Even though the sole consumption of a value in an expression might not fit into "pure" functional concepts, it's an essential component for employing a more functional coding style in Java, bridging many gaps between non-functional code and higher-order functions.

The Consumer<T> interface is similar to the Java 5+ Callable<V> found in the java.util.concurrent package, except the latter throws a checked Exception. The concept of checked and unchecked Exceptions and their implications for functional code in Java will be explored in detail in Chapter 10.

Suppliers

Suppliers are the antithesis of Consumers. Based around the central functional interface java.util.function.Supplier<T>, the different Supplier variants don't accept any input parameters but return a single value of type T, as shown in Figure 3-3.

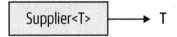

Figure 3-3. java.util.function.Supplier<T>

The single abstract method of Supplier<T> is called get:

```
@FunctionalInterface
public interface Supplier<T> {
   T get();
}
```

The following Supplier<Double> provides a new random value on calling get():

```
Supplier<Double> random = () -> Math.random();

Double result = random.get();
```

Suppliers are often used for deferred execution, like when an expensive task gets wrapped by them to call get only when needed, as I will discuss in Chapter 11.

Predicates

Predicates are functions that accept a single argument to be tested against its logic and return either true or false. The syntax for the main functional interface java.util.function.Predicate<T> is illustrated in Figure 3-4.

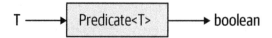

Figure 3-4. java.util.function.Predicate<T>

The single abstract method is called test and accepts an argument of a type T and returns a boolean primitive:

```
@FunctionalInterface
public interface Predicate<T> {
  boolean test(T t);
}
```

It's the go-to functional interface for decision-making, like filter methods of the functional pattern *map/filter/reduce* you will learn more about in Chapter 6.

The following code tests an Integer to be over 9000:

```
Predicate<Integer> over9000 = i -> i > 9_000;

Integer result = over9000.test(1_234);
```

Why So Many Functional Interface Variants?

Although the big four categories and their main functional interface representations already cover many use cases, there are also variations and more specialized variants you can use. All these different types are necessary to fit lambdas into Java without a trade-off in backward compatibility. Due to this, though, using lambdas in Java is a little bit more complicated than in other languages. Still, integrating such a feature without breaking the vast ecosystem is worth it, in my opinion.

There are ways to bridge between different functional interfaces, and each variant has its own optimal problem context to be used in. Handling so many different types might seem intimidating at first, but it will become almost second nature to know which type to use for what scenario after using a more functional approach for a while.

Function Arity

The concept of *arity* describes the number of operands that a function accepts. For example, an arity of one means that a lambda accepts a single argument:

```
Function<String, String> greeterFn = name -> "Hello " + name;
```

As the number of arguments in Java methods, like a SAM, is fixed[1], there must be an explicit functional interface representing every required arity. To support arities higher than one, the JDK includes specialized variants of the main functional interface categories that accept arguments, as listed in Table 3-1.

Table 3-1. Arity-based functional interfaces

Arity of one	Arity of two
Function<T, R>	BiFunction<T, U, R>
Consumer<T>	BiConsumer<T, U>
Predicate<T>	BiPredicate<T, U>

Only functions interfaces with an arity of up to two are supported out of the box. Looking at the functional APIs and use cases in Java, arities of one or two cover the most common tasks. That's most likely why the Java language designers decided to stop there and didn't add any higher arities.

Adding higher arities is simple though, like in the following code:

```
@FunctionalInterface
public interface TriFunction<T, U, V, R> {
  R accept(T t, U u, V v);
}
```

However, I wouldn't recommend this unless it's an absolute necessity. As you will see throughout this chapter and the book, the included functional interface gives you a lot of additional functionality through `static` and `default` methods. That's why relying on them ensures the best compatibility and well understood usage patterns.

The concept of *functional operators* simplifies the two most commonly used arities by giving you functional interfaces with identical generic types. For example, if you require a function to accept two `String` arguments to create another `String` value, the type definition of `BiFunction<String, String, String>` would be quite repetitive. Instead, you can use a `BinaryOperator<String>` which is defined as:

```
@FunctionalInteface
interface BinaryOperator<T> extends BiFunction<T, T, T> {
  // ...
}
```

Implementing a common `super` interface allows you to write more concise code with more meaningful types.

---

1 Varargs method arguments, like `String-`, appear to have a dynamic arity, as the method accepts a non-fixed number of arguments. However, behind the scenes, the arguments are converted to an array, making the actual arity one.

The available operator functional interfaces are listed in Table 3-2.

Table 3-2. Operator functional interfaces

Arity	Operator	Super Interface
1	UnaryOperator<T>	Function<T, T>
2	BinaryOperator<T>	BiFunction<T, T, T>

Be aware, though, that operator types and their super interface aren't interchangeable. That's especially important when designing APIs.

Imagine a method signature requires a `UnaryOperator<String>` as an argument; it won't be compatible with `Function<String, String>`. However, the other way around works, as shown in Example 3-1.

Example 3-1. Java arity compatibility

```
UnaryOperator<String> unaryOp = String::toUpperCase;
Function<String, String> func = String::toUpperCase;

void acceptsUnary(UnaryOperator<String> unaryOp) { ... };
void acceptsFunction(Function<String, String> func) { ... };

acceptsUnary(unaryOp); // OK
acceptsUnary(func); // COMPILE-ERROR

acceptsFunction(func); // OK
acceptsFunction(unaryOp); // OK
```

This example highlights that you should choose the most common denominator for method arguments, in this case, `Function<String, String>`, as it gives you the most compatibility. Even though it increases the verbosity of your method signatures, it's an acceptable trade-off, in my opinion, because it maximizes usability and doesn't restrict an argument to a specialized functional interface. When creating a lambda, on the other hand, the specialized type allows for more concise code without losing any expressiveness.

Primitive Types

Most of the functional interfaces you've encountered so far had a generic type definition, but that's not always the case. Primitive types can't be used as generic types (yet). That's why there are specialized functional interfaces for primitives.

You *could* use any generic functional interface for the object wrapper type and let autoboxing take care of the rest. However, autoboxing isn't free, so it can have a performance impact.

Autoboxing and unboxing is the automatic conversion between primitive value types and their object-based counterparts so they can be used indiscriminately. For example, autoboxing an `int` to an `Integer`. The other way around is called unboxing.

That's why many of the functional interfaces provided by the JDK deal with primitive types to avoid autoboxing. Such primitive functional interfaces, like the arity specializations, aren't available for all primitives, though. They are mostly concentrated around the numeric primitives `int`, `long`, and `double`.

Table 3-3 lists only the available functional interfaces for `int`; there are equivalent interfaces for `long` and `double` as well.

Table 3-3. Functional interfaces for the integer primitive

Functional Interface	Boxed Alternative
Functions	
IntFunction<R>	Function<Integer, R>
IntUnaryOperator	UnaryOperator<Integer>
IntBinaryOperator	BinaryOperator<Integer>
ToIntFunction<T>	Function<T, Integer>
ToIntBiFunction<T, U>	BiFunction<T, U, Integer>
IntToDoubleFunction	Function<Integer, Double>
IntToLongFunction	Function<Integer, Long>
Consumers	
IntConsumer	Consumer<Integer>
ObjIntConsumer<T>	BiConsumer<T, Integer>
Suppliers	
IntSupplier	Supplier<Integer>
Predicates	
IntPredicate	Predicate<Integer>

The `boolean` primitive has only a single specialized variant: `BooleanSupplier`.

Functional interfaces for primitives aren't the only special consideration in the new functional parts of Java to accommodate primitives. As you will learn later in this book, Streams and Optionals provide specialized types, too, to reduce the unnecessary overhead incurred by autoboxing.

Project Valhalla and Specialized Generics

The OpenJDK Project Valhalla (*https://oreil.ly/KzoGD*) is an experimental JDK project to develop multiple changes to the Java language itself. One change they're working on that is quite relevant to simplifying lambdas is "specialized generics."

As it stands, generic type arguments are constrained to types that extend `java.lang.Object`, meaning that they are not compatible with primitives. Your only option is to use autoboxed types like `java.lang.Integer`, etc., which has performance implications and other caveats compared to using primitives directly.

The project started in 2014, and in March 2020, the team behind it previewed five distinct prototypes to tackle the associated aspects of the problems. At the time of writing, there isn't an official release date.

Bridging Functional Interfaces

Functional interfaces are, well, interfaces, and lambda expressions are concrete implementations of these interfaces. Type inference makes it easy to forget that you can't use them interchangeably or simply cast between unrelated interfaces. Even if their method signatures are identical, an Exception is thrown, as seen previously in "Creating Lambdas" on page 26:

```
interface LikePredicate<T> {
  boolean test(T value);
}

LikePredicate<String> isNull = str -> str == null;

Predicate<String> wontCompile = isNull;
// Error:
// incompatible types: LikePredicate<java.lang.String> cannot be
// converted to java.util.function.Predicate<java.lang.String>

Predicate<String> wontCompileEither = (Predicate<String>) isNull;
// Exception java.lang.ClassCastException: class LikePredicate
// cannot be cast to class java.util.function.Predicate
```

From a lambda-based point of view, both SAMs are identical. They both accept a `String` argument and return a `boolean` result. For Java's type system, though, they have no connection whatsoever, making a cast between them impossible. Still, the gap between "lambda-compatible but type-incompatible" functional interfaces can be bridged by a feature discussed in "Method References" on page 28.

By using a method reference instead of trying to cast between the "identical but incompatible" functional interfaces, you can refer to the SAM instead to make your code compile:

```
Predicate<String> thisIsFine = isNull::test;
```

Using a method reference creates a new dynamic call site to be invoked by the bytecode opcode invokedynamic instead of trying to implicitly or explicitly cast the functional interface itself.

Like re-finalizing variables that you've learned about in "Re-finalizing a reference" on page 22, bridging functional interfaces with method references is another band-aid to deal with code that can't be refactored or redesigned another way. Still, it's an easy-to-use and sometimes necessary tool to have in your functional kit, especially if you're transitioning from a legacy codebase to a more functional approach, or you are working with third-party code that provides its own functional interfaces.

Functional Composition

Functional composition is an essential part of the functional approach to combine small functional units into a bigger, more complex task, and Java's got you covered. However, it's done in a typical Java fashion to ensure backward compatibility. Instead of introducing a new keyword or changing any language semantics, Java uses "glue" methods that are directly implemented on the functional interfaces themselves as default methods. With their help, you easily can compose the big four categories of functional interfaces. Such glue methods build the bridge between two functional interfaces by returning a new one with the combined functionality.

In the case of Function<T, R>, two default methods are available:

- <V> Function<V, R> compose(Function<? super V, ? extends T> before)
- <V> Function<T, V> andThen(Function<? super R, ? extends V> after)

The difference between these two methods is the direction of the composition, as indicated by the argument names and the returned Function and its generic types. The first one, compose, creates a composed function that applies the before argument to its input and the result to this. The second one, andThen, is the antagonist to compose, as it evaluates this and then applies after to the previous result.

Which direction of functional composition to choose, compose or andThen, depends on the context and personal preference. The call fn1.compose(fn2) leads to an equivalent call like fn1(fn2(input)). To achieve the same flow with the andThen method, the compositional order must be reversed to a fn2.andThen(fn1(input)) call, as illustrated in Figure 3-5.

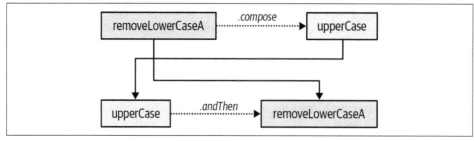

Figure 3-5. Function<T, R> composition order

Personally, I prefer the andThen method because the resulting prose-like fluent method call-chain mirrors the logical flow of functions that's easier to grasp for other readers not well versed in functional programming naming conventions.

Think of manipulating a String by removing occurrences of any lowercase "a" and uppercasing the result. The overall tasks consist of two Function<String, String>, each doing a singular thing. Composing them can be done either way without a difference in the final result, if you use the appropriate glue method, as seen in Example 3-2.

Example 3-2. Functional composition direction

```
Function<String, String> removeLowerCaseA = str -> str.replace("a", "");
Function<String, String> upperCase = String::toUpperCase;


var input = "abcd";

removeLowerCaseA.andThen(upperCase)
                .apply(input);
// => "BCD"

upperCase.compose(removeLowerCaseA)
        .apply(input);
// => "BCD"
```

Be aware that not every functional interface provides such "glue methods" to easily support composition, even if it would be sensible to do so. The following list summarizes how the different main interfaces of the big four categories support composition out of the box:

Function<T, R>

    Function<T, R> and its specialized arities, like UnaryOperator<T>, support composition in both directions. The -Bi variants only support andThen.

`Predicate<T>`

Predicates support various methods to compose a new Predicate with common operations associated with them: `and`, `or`, `negate`.

`Consumer<T>`

Only `andThen` is supported, which will compose two Consumers to accept a value in sequence.

Specialized primitive functional interfaces

The support for functional composition among the specialized functional interfaces for primitives is not on par with their generic brethren. Even among themselves, the support differs between the primitive types.

But don't fret! Writing your own functional composition helper is easy, as I will discuss in the next section.

Extending Functional Support

Most functional interfaces give you more than just their single abstract method defining the lambda signature. Usually, they provide additional `default` methods to support concepts like functional composition, or `static` helpers to simplify common use cases of that type.

Even though you can't change the types of the JDK, you can still make your own types more functional instead. Three approaches you can choose are also used by the JDK:

- Add `default` methods to an interface to make existing types more functional.
- Implement a functional interface explicitly.
- Create `static` helpers to provide common functional operations.

Adding Default Methods

Adding new functionality to an interface always requires you to implement new methods on all implementations. When dealing with a small project, it might be fine just to update any implementation, but in bigger and shared projects it's often not as easy. In library code it's even worse; you might break the code of anyone using your library. That's where `default` methods come in to save the day.

Instead of solely changing the contract of a type's interface and letting anyone implementing it deal with the fallout—adding the new method on any type that implements the interface—you can use `default` methods to supply a "common-sense" implementation. This provides a general variant of the intended logic to all other types down the line, so you don't have to throw an `UnsupportedOperationException`.

This way, your code is backward-compatible because only the interface itself has changed, but any type that implements the interface still has a chance to create its own more fitting implementation if necessary. That's exactly how the JDK added Stream support to any type implementing the interface `java.util.Collection<E>`.

The following code shows the actual `default` methods that give any `Collection`-based type Stream capabilities out of the box at no additional (implementation) cost:

```
public interface Collection<E> extends Iterable<E> {

  default Stream<E> stream() {
    return StreamSupport.stream(spliterator(), false);
  }

  default Stream<E> parallelStream() {
    return StreamSupport.stream(spliterator(), true);
  }

  // ...
}
```

The two `default` methods create new `Stream<E>` instances by calling the static helper `StreamSupport.stream` and the `default` method `spliterator`. The `spliterator` method is initially defined in `java.util.Iterable<E>` but is overridden as necessary, as shown in Example 3-3.

Example 3-3. default method hierarchy

```
public interface Iterable<T> { ❶

  default Spliterator<T> spliterator() {
    return Spliterators.spliteratorUnknownSize(iterator(), 0); ❶
  }

  // ...
}

public interface Collection<E> extends Iterable<E> {

  @Override
  default Spliterator<E> spliterator() {
    return Spliterators.spliterator(this, 0); ❷
  }

  // ...
}

public class ArrayList<E> extends AbstractList<E> implements List<E>, ... {

  @Override
```

```
public Spliterator<E> spliterator() {
    return new ArrayListSpliterator(0, -1, 0); ❸
}

// ...
}
```

❶ The original definition of the `spliterator` method with a commonsense implementation based on all the available information for the type.

❷ The `Collection` interface can use more information to create a more specific `Spliterator<E>` that is available to all of its implementations.

❸ The concrete implementation `ArrayList<E>`, which implements `Collection<E>` via `List<E>`, provides an even more specialized `Spliterator<E>`.

A hierarchy of `default` methods gives you the power to add new functionality to an interface without breaking any implementations and still providing a commonsense variant of the new method. Even if a type never implements a more specific variant for itself, it can fall back to the logic provided by the `default` method.

Implementing Functional Interfaces Explicitly

Functional interfaces can be implemented implicitly via lambda or method references, but they are also useful when implemented explicitly by one of your types so they are usable in higher-order functions. Some of your types might already implement one of the retroactively functional interfaces like `java.util.Comparator<T>` or `java.lang.Runnable`.

Implementing a functional interface directly creates a bridge between previously "non-functional" types and their easy usage in functional code. A good example is the object-oriented *command design pattern*[2].

 The command pattern encapsulates an action, or "command," and all data required to execute it in an object. This approach decouples the creation of commands from consuming them.

---

2 The command pattern is one of many object-oriented design patterns described by the *Gang of Four*. E. Gamma, R. Helm, R. Johnson, and J. Vlissides, *Design Patterns: Elements of Reusable Object-Oriented Software* (Boston, MA: Addison-Wesley Professional, 1994).

Usually, a command already has a dedicated interface. Imagine a text editor with its common commands like opening a file or saving it. A shared command interface between these commands could be as simple as:

```
public interface TextEditorCommand {
  String execute();
}
```

The concrete command classes would accept the required arguments, but the executed command would simply return the updated editor content. If you look closely, you see that the interface matches a Supplier<String>.

As I discussed in "Bridging Functional Interfaces" on page 46, the mere logical equivalency between functional interfaces isn't enough to create compatibility. However, by extending TextEditorCommand with Supplier<String>, you bridge the gap with a default method, as follows:

```
public interface TextEditorCommand extends Supplier<T> {

  String execute();

  default String get() {
    return execute();
  }
}
```

Interfaces allow multiple inheritance, so adding a functional interface shouldn't be an issue. The functional interface's SAM is a simple default method calling the actual method doing the work. This way, not a single command needs to be changed, but all of them gain compatibility with any higher-order function accepting a Supplier<String> without requiring a method reference as a bridge.

 Look out for method signature collisions if existing interfaces implement a functional interface, so you don't accidentally override an existing one.

Implementing one or more functional interfaces is a great way to give your types a functional starting point, including all the additional default methods available on the functional interfaces.

Creating Static Helpers

Functional interfaces usually extend their versatility by having default methods and static helpers for common tasks. If you don't have control over the type, though, like a functional interface provided by the JDK itself, you can create a helper type that accumulates static methods.

In "Functional Composition" on page 47, I discussed functional composition with the help of the available `default` methods on the big four interfaces. Even though the most common use cases are covered, certain different functional interfaces aren't covered. You can create them yourself, however.

Let's take a look at how `Function<T, R>` implements[3] its `compose` method in Example 3-4, so we can develop a compositor helper type to accept other types, too.

Example 3-4. Simplified Function<T, R> interface

```
@FunctionalInterface
public interface Function<T, R> {

    default <V> Function<V, R> compose(Function<V, T> before) { ❶
        Objects.requireNonNull(before); ❷

        return (V v) -> { ❸
          T result = before.apply(v); ❹
          return apply(result); ❺
        };
    }

    // ...
}
```

❶ The composed function isn't bound to the original type T and introduces V in its method signature.

❷ A `null`-check helper to throw a `NullPointerException` on composition and not only on the first use of the returned lambda.

❸ The returned lambda accepts a value of the newly introduced type V.

❹ The `before` function is evaluated first.

❺ The `result` is then applied to the original `Function<T, R>`.

To create your own compositional methods, you first have to think about what exactly you want to achieve. The involved functional interfaces and their compositional order dictate the overall type chain that the method signature has to reflect, as listed in Table 3-4.

---

3 The shown `Function<T, R>` interface is a simplified variant of the source code (*https://oreil.ly/QfW6N*) present in the JDK to increase readability.

Table 3-4. Functional composition type chains for `Function<T, R>`

Method Signature	Type chain
`Function<V, R> compose(Function<V, T>`	$V \rightarrow T \rightarrow R$
`Function<T, V> andThen(Function<R, V>)`	$T \rightarrow R \rightarrow V$

Let's develop a compositor for `Function<T, R>` and `Supplier`/`Consumer`.

Only two combinations are possible because `Supplier` won't accept arguments, so it can't evaluate the result of the `Function<T, R>`. The opposite reason is true for `Supplier`. Because you can't extend the `Function<T, R>` interface directly, an indirect compositor in the form of a `static` helper is needed. That leads to the following method signatures in which the compositional order is reflected by the argument order:

- `Supplier<R> compose(Supplier<T> before, Function<T, R> fn)`
- `Consumer<T> compose(Function<T, R> fn, Consumer<R> after)`

Example 3-5 shows a simple compositor implementation that won't differ much from the JDK's implementation of equivalent methods.

Example 3-5. Functional compositor

```
public final class Compositor {

  public static <T, R> Supplier<R> compose(Supplier<T> before,
                                            Function<T, R> fn) {
    Objects.requireNonNull(before);
    Objects.requireNonNull(fn);

    return () -> {
      T result = before.get();
      return fn.apply(result);
    };
  }

  public static <T, R> Consumer<T> compose(Function<T, R> fn,
                                           Consumer<R> after) {
    Objects.requireNonNull(fn);
    Objects.requireNonNull(after);

    return (T t) -> {
      R result = fn.apply(t);
      after.accept(result);
    };
  }

  private Compositor() {
```

```
    // suppress default constructor
  }
}
```

Composing the previous `String` operation from Example 3-2 with an additional `Consumer<String>` for printing the result is now easy, as shown in Example 3-6.

Example 3-6. Using the functional compositor

```
// SINGULAR STRING FUNCTIONS
Function<String, String> removeLowerCaseA = str -> str.replace("a", "");
Function<String, String> upperCase = String::toUpperCase;

// COMPOSED STRING FUNCTIONS
Function<String, String> stringOperations =
  removeLowerCaseA.andThen(upperCase);

// COMPOSED STRING FUNCTIONS AND CONSUMER
Consumer<String> task = Compositor.compose(stringOperations,
                                    System.out::println);

// RUNNING TASK
task.accept("abcd");
// => BCD
```

A simple compositor passing values between functional interfaces is an obvious use case for functional composition. Still, it's useful for other use cases, too, like introducing a certain degree of logic and decision-making. For example, you could safeguard a `Consumer` with a `Predicate` as shown in Example 3-7.

Example 3-7. Improved functional compositor

```
public final class Compositor {

  public static Consumer<T> acceptIf(Predicate<T> predicate,
                                Consumer<T> consumer) {
    Objects.requireNonNull(predicate);
    Objects.requireNonNull(consumer);

    return (T t) -> {
      if (!predicate.test(t)) {
        return;
      }
      consumer.accept(t);
    }
  }

  // ...
}
```

You can fill the gaps left by the JDK by adding new `static` helpers to your types as needed. From personal experience, I would suggest adding helpers only as required instead of trying to fill the gaps proactively. Implement only what you currently need because it can be quite hard to foresee what you will need in the future. Any additional line of code that's not used right now will need maintenance over time, and it might need changes or refactoring anyway if you want to use it and the actual requirements become clear.

Takeaways

- The JDK provides 40+ functional interfaces because Java's type system requires tangible interfaces for different use cases. The available functional interfaces fall into four categories: Functions, Consumers, Suppliers, and Predicates.

- More specialized functional interface variants exist for arities up to two. Method signatures, however, should use their equivalent `super` interface instead to maximize compatibility.

- Primitives are supported either by using autoboxing or a respective functional interface variant for `int`, `long`, `double`, and `boolean`.

- Functional interfaces behave like any other interface and require a common ancestor to be used interchangeably. However, bridging the gap between "identical but incompatible" functional interfaces is possible by using a method reference of a SAM.

- Adding functional support to your own types is easy. Use `default` methods on your interfaces to cover functional use cases without requiring you to change any implementations.

- Common or missing functional tasks can be accumulated in a helper type with `static` methods.

PART II

A Functional Approach

Even though Java is a multiparadigm language, it clearly incentivizes an object-oriented and imperative coding style. However, many functional idioms, concepts, and techniques are still available to you, even without deeply integrated language support.

The JDK has a multitude of tools available to solve common problems with a functional approach and benefit from FP's advantages even without going fully functional.

CHAPTER 4

Immutability

Dealing with data structures—constructs dedicated to storing and organizing data values—is a core task of almost any program. In OOP, this usually means dealing with a *mutable* program state, often encapsulated in objects. For a functional approach, however, *immutability* is the preferred way to handle data and is a prerequisite for many of its concepts.

In functional programming languages like Haskell or even multiparadigm but more functionally inclined ones like Scala, immutability is treated as a prevalent feature. In those languages, immutability is a necessity and often strictly enforced, not just an afterthought to their design. Like most other principles introduced in this book, immutability isn't restricted to functional programming and provides many benefits, regardless of your chosen paradigm.

In this chapter, you will learn about immutable types already available in the JDK and how to make your data structures immutable to avoid side effects, either with the tools provided by the JDK or with the help of third-party libraries.

 The term "data structure" used in this chapter represents any construct that stores and organizes data, like Collections, or custom types.

Mutability and Data Structures in OOP

As an object-oriented inclined language, typical Java code encapsulates an object's state in a mutable form. Its state is usually mutable by using "setter" methods. This approach makes the program state *ephemeral*, meaning any change to an existing data structure updates its current state in-place, which also affects anyone else who references it, and the previous state is lost.

Let's take a look at the most common forms used to handle mutable state in OOP Java code as discussed in Chapter 2: *JavaBeans* and *plain old Java objects (POJO)*. A lot of confusion exists about those two data structures and their distinct properties. In a sense, they are both ordinary Java objects supposed to create reusability between components by encapsulating all relevant states. They have similar goals, although their design philosophies and rules differ.

POJOs don't have any restrictions regarding their design. They are supposed to "just" encapsulate the business logic state, and you can even design them to be immutable. How you implement them is up to you and what matches your environment best. They usually provide "getters" and "setters" for their fields to be more flexible in an object-oriented context with a mutable state.

JavaBeans, on the other hand, are a special kind of POJO that allows easier introspection and reusability, which requires them to follow certain rules. These rules are necessary because JavaBeans were initially designed to be a standardized shareable machine-readable state between components, like a UI widget in your IDE[1]. The differences between POJOs and JavaBeans are listed in Table 4-1.

Table 4-1. POJOs versus JavaBeans

	POJO	JavaBean
General Restrictions	Imposed by Java language rules	Imposed by JavaBean API specification
Serialization	Optional	Must implement `java.io.Serializable`
Field Visibility	No restrictions	`private` only
Field Access	No restrictions	Accessible only via getters and setters
Constructors	No restrictions	No-arg constructor must exist

Many of the available data structures in the JDK, like the *Collections framework*,[2] are mostly built around the concept of mutable state and in-place changes. Take `List<E>` for an example. Its mutating methods, like `add(E value)` or `remove(E value)`, only return a `boolean` to indicate that a change occurred, and they change the Collection in place, so the previous state is lost. You might not need to think much about it in a local context, but as soon as a data structure leaves your direct sphere of influence,

---

1 JavaBeans are specified in the official JavaBeans API Specification 1.01 (*https://oreil.ly/jLlK3*), which is over a hundred pages long. For the scope of this book, however, you don't need to know all of it, but you should be familiar with the mentioned differences to other data structures.

2 Since Java 1.2, the Java Collections framework provides a multitude of common reusable data structures, like `List<E>`, `Set<E>`, etc. The Oracle Java documentation (*https://oreil.ly/nQjAL*) has an overview of the available types included in the framework.

it's no longer guaranteed to remain in its current state as long as you hold a reference to it.

Mutable state breeds complexity and uncertainty. You must include all possible state changes in your mental model at any time to understand and reason with your code. This isn't restricted to a single component, though. Sharing mutable state increases the complexity to cover the lifetime of any components having access to such shared state. Concurrent programming especially suffers under the complexities of shared state, where many problems originate in mutability and require intricate and often misused solutions like access synchronization and atomic references.

Ensuring the correctness of your code and shared state becomes a Sisyphean task of endless unit tests and state validation. And the required additional work multiplies as soon as mutable state interacts with more mutable components, resulting in even more verification of their behavior.

That's where immutability provides another approach to handling data structures and restoring reasonability.

Immutability (Not Only) in FP

The core idea of immutability is simple: data structures can no longer change after their creation. Many functional programming languages support it by design at their core. The concept isn't bound to functional programming per se, and it has many advantages in any paradigm.

 Immutability provides elegant solutions to many problems, even outside of programming languages. For example, the distributed version control system Git[3] essentially uses a tree of pointers to immutable blobs and diffs to provide a robust representation of historical changes.

Immutable data structures are persistent views of their data without a direct option to change it. To "mutate" such a data structure, you must create a new copy with the intended changes. Not being able to mutate data "in place" can feel weird in Java at first. Compared to the usually mutable nature of object-oriented code, why should you take the extra steps necessary to simply change a value? Such creation of new instances by copying data incurs a particular overhead that accumulates quickly for naive implementations of immutability.

---

3 Git is a free and open source distributed version control system. Its website (*https://oreil.ly/-67zg*) provides ample documentation about its inner workings.

Despite the overhead and initial weirdness of not being able to change data in place, the benefits of immutability can make it worthwhile even without a more functional approach to Java:

Predictability

Data structures won't change without you noticing because they simply can't. As long as you reference a data structure, you know it is the same as at the time of its creation. Even if you share that reference or use it in a concurrent fashion, no one can change your copy of it.

Validity

After initialization, a data structure is complete. It needs to be verified only once and stays valid (or invalid) indefinitely. If you need to build a data structure in multiple steps, the *builder pattern*, shown later in "Step-by-step creation" on page 93, decouples the building and initialization of a data structure.

No hidden side effects

Dealing with side effects is a really tough problem in programming—besides naming and cache invalidation[4]. A byproduct of immutable data structures is the elimination of side effects; they're always as-is. Even if moved around a lot through different parts of your code or using them in a third-party library out of your control, they won't change their values or surprise you with an unintended side effect.

Thread safety

Without side effects, immutable data structures can move freely between thread boundaries. No thread can change them, so reasoning about your program becomes more straightforward due to no more unexpected changes or race conditions.

Cacheability and optimization

Because they are as-is right after creation, you can cache immutable data structures with ease of mind. Optimization techniques, like memoization, are possible only with immutable data structures, as discussed in Chapter 2.

Change tracking

If every change results in a whole new data structure, you can track their history by storing the previous references. You no longer need to intricately track single property changes to support an *undo* feature. Restoring a previous state is as simple as using a prior reference to the data structure.

---

4 Phil Karton, an accomplished software engineer who for many years was a principal developer at Xerox PARC, Digital, Silicon Graphics, and Netscape, said, "There are only two hard things in Computer Science: cache invalidation and naming things." It became a mainstream joke in the software community over the years and is often amended by adding "one-off errors" without changing the count of two.

Remember, all these benefits are independent of the chosen programming paradigm. Even if you decide that a functional approach might not be the right solution for your codebase, your data handling can still benefit immensely from immutability.

The State of Java Immutability

Java's initial design didn't include immutability as a deeply integrated language feature or provide a variety of immutable data structures. Certain aspects of the language and its types were always immutable, but it was nowhere close to the level of support offered in other more functional languages. This all changed when Java 14 was released and introduced *Records*, a built-in language-level immutable data structure.

Even if you might not know it yet, you're already using immutable types in all your Java programs. The reasons behind their immutability might differ, like runtime optimizations or ensuring their correct usage, but regardless of their intentions, they'll make your code safer and less error-prone.

Let's take a look at all the different immutable parts available in the JDK today.

java.lang.String

One of the first types every Java developer learns about is the `String` type. Strings are everywhere! That's why it needs to be a highly optimized and safe type. One of these optimizations is that it's immutable.

`String` is not a primitive value-based type, like `int` or `char`. Still, it supports the + (plus) operator to concatenate a `String` with another value:

```
String first = "hello, ";
String second = "world!";

String result = first + second;
// => "hello, world!"
```

Like any other expression, concatenating strings creates a result and, in this case, a new `String` object. That's why Java developers are taught early not to overuse manual `String` concatenation. Each time you concatenate strings by using the + (plus) operator, a new `String` instance is created on the heap, occupying memory, as depicted in Figure 4-1. These newly created instances can add up quickly, especially if concatenation is done in a loop statement like `for` or `while`.

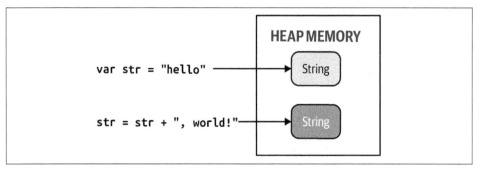

Figure 4-1. String memory allocation

Even though the JVM will garbage-collect instances that are no longer needed, the memory overhead of endless `String` creation can be a real burden on the runtime. That's why the JVM uses multiple optimization techniques behind the scenes to reduce `String` creation, like replacing concatenations with a `java.lang.String Builder`, or even using the opcode `invokedynamic` to support multiple optimization strategies.[5]

Because `String` is such a fundamental type, it is sensible to make it immutable for multiple reasons. Having such a base type being thread-safe by design solves issues associated with concurrency, like synchronization, before they even exist. Concurrency is hard enough without worrying about a `String` to change without notice. Immutability removes the risk of race conditions, side effects, or a simple unintended change.

`String` literals also get special treatment from the JVM. Thanks to *string pooling*, identical literals are stored only once and reused to save precious heap space. If a `String` could change, it would change for everyone using a reference to it in the pool. It's possible to allocate a new `String` by explicitly calling one of its constructors instead of creating a literal to circumvent pooling. The other way around is possible, too, by calling the `intern` method on any instance, which returns a `String` with the same content from the string pool.

String equality

The specialized handling of `String` instances and literals is why you should *never* use the equality operator `==` (double-equal) to compare Strings. That's why you should always use either the `equals` or `equalsIgnoreCase` method to test for equality.

---

5 The JDK Enhancement Proposal (JEP) 280, "Indify String Concatenation" (*https://oreil.ly/Xx2v5*), describes the reasoning behind using `invokedynamic` in more detail.

However, the `String` type isn't "completely" immutable, at least from a technical point of view. It calculates its `hashCode` lazily due to performance considerations because it needs to read the whole `String` to do so. Still, it's a pure function: the same `String` will always result in the same `hashCode`.

Using lazy evaluation to hide expensive just-in-time calculations to achieve logical immutability requires extra care during the design and implementation of a type to ensure it remains thread-safe and predictable.

All these properties make `String` something between a primitive and an object type, at least from a usability standpoint. Performance optimization possibilities and safety might have been the main reasons for its immutability, but the implicit advantages of immutability are still a welcome addition to such a fundamental type.

Immutable Collections

Another fundamental and ubiquitous group of types that benefit significantly from immutability is Collections, like `Set`, `List`, `Map`, etc.

Although Java's Collection framework wasn't designed with immutability as a core principle, it still has a way of providing a certain degree of immutability with three options:

- Unmodifiable Collections
- Immutable Collection factory methods (Java 9+)
- Immutable copies (Java 10+)

All options aren't `public` types you can instantiate directly using the `new` keyword. Instead, the relevant types have `static` convenience methods to create the necessary instances. Also, they're only *shallowly* immutable, meaning that you cannot add or remove any elements, but the elements themselves aren't guaranteed to be immutable. Anyone holding a reference to an element can change it without the knowledge of the Collection it currently resides in.

Shallow immutability

Shallowly immutable data structures provide immutability only at their topmost level. This means that the reference to the data structure itself can't be changed. The referenced data structure, however—in the case of a Collection, its elements—can still be mutated.

To have a fully immutable Collection, you need to have only fully immutable elements, too. Nevertheless, the three options still provide you with helpful tools to use against unintended modification.

Unmodifiable Collections

The first option, *unmodifiable Collections*, is created from an existing Collection by calling one of the following generic static methods of java.util.Collections:

- Collection<T> unmodifiableCollection(Collection<? extends T> c)
- Set<T> unmodifiableSet(Set<? extends T> s)
- List<T> unmodifiableList(List<? extends T> list)
- Map<K, V> unmodifiableMap(Map<? extends K, ? extends V> m)
- SortedSet<T> unmodifiableSortedSet(SortedSet<T> s)
- SortedMap<K, V> unmodifiableSortedMap(SortedMap<K, ? extends V> m)
- NavigableSet<T> unmodifiableNavigableSet(NavigableSet<T> s)
- NavigableMap<K, V> unmodifiableNavigableMap(NavigableMap<K, V> m)

Each method returns the same type as was provided for the method's single argument. The difference between the original and the returned instance is that any attempt to modify the returned instance will throw an UnsupportedOperationException tion, as demonstrated in the following code:

```
List<String> modifiable = new ArrayList<>();
modifiable.add("blue");
modifiable.add("red");

List<String> unmodifiable = Collections.unmodifiableList(modifiable);
unmodifiable.clear();
// throws UnsupportedOperationException
```

The obvious downside of an "unmodifiable view" is that it's only an abstraction over an existing Collection. The following code shows how the underlying Collection is still modifiable and affects the unmodifiable view:

```
List<String> original = new ArrayList<>();
original.add("blue");
original.add("red");

List<String> unmodifiable = Collections.unmodifiableList(original);

original.add("green");

System.out.println(unmodifiable.size());
// OUTPUT:
// 3
```

The reason for still being modifiable via the original reference is how the data structure is stored in memory, as illustrated in Figure 4-2. The unmodified version is only a view of the original list, so any changes directly to the original circumvent the intended unmodifiable nature of the view.

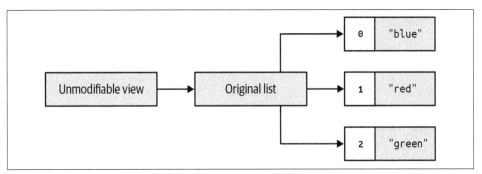

Figure 4-2. Memory layout of unmodifiable Collections

The common use for unmodifiable views is to freeze Collections for unwanted modification before using them as a return value.

Immutable Collection factory methods

The second option—*immutable Collection factory methods*—has been available since Java 9 and isn't based on preexisting Collections. Instead, the elements must be provided directly to the `static` convenience methods available on the following Collection types:

- `List<E> of(E e1, …)`
- `Set<E> of(E e1, …)`
- `Map<K, V> of(K k1, V v1, …)`

Each factory method exists with zero or more elements and uses an optimized internal Collection type based on the number of elements used.

Immutable copies

The third option, *immutable copies*, is available in Java 10+ and provides a deeper level of immutability by calling the `static` method copyOf on the following three types:

- `Set<E> copyOf(Collection<? extends E> coll)`
- `List<F> copyOf(Collection<? extends E> coll)`
- `Map<K, V> copyOf(Map<? extends K, ? extends V> map)`

Instead of being a mere view, copyOf creates a new container, holding its own references to the elements:

```
// SETUP ORIGINAL LIST
List<String> original = new ArrayList<>();
original.add("blue");
original.add("red");

// CREATE COPY
List<String> copiedList = List.copyOf(original);

// ADD NEW ITEM TO ORIGINAL LIST
original.add("green");

// CHECK CONTENT
System.out.println(original);
// [blue, red, green]
System.out.println(copiedList);
// [blue, red]
```

The copied Collection prevents any addition or removal of elements through the original list, but the actual elements are still shared, as illustrated in Figure 4-3, and open to changes.

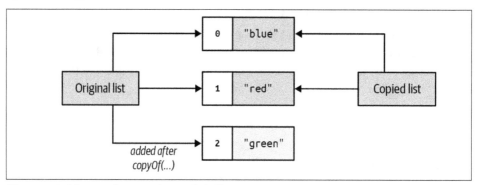

Figure 4-3. Memory layout of copied Collections

Which option of immutable Collections you choose depends on your context and intentions. If a Collection can't be created in a single call, like in a for-loop, an unmodifiable view or immutable copy is a sensible approach. Use a mutable Collection locally and "freeze" it by returning an unmodifiable view or copy it when the data leaves your current scope. Immutable Collection factory methods don't support an intermediary Collection that might get modified but requires you to know all the elements beforehand.

Primitives and Primitive Wrappers

So far, you've learned mostly about immutable object types, but not everything in Java is an object. Java's *primitive* types—byte, char, short, int, long, float, double, boolean—are handled differently from object types. They are simple values that are initialized by either a literal or an expression. Representing only a single value, they are practically immutable.

Besides the primitive types themselves, Java provides corresponding object wrapper types, like Byte or Integer. They encapsulate their respective primitives in a concrete object type to make them usable in scenarios where primitives aren't allowed (yet), like generics. Otherwise, autoboxing—the automatic conversion between the object wrapper types and their corresponding primitive type—could lead to inconsistent behavior.

Immutable Math

Most simple calculations in Java rely on primitives types like int or long for whole numbers, and float or double for floating-point calculations. The package java.math, however, has two immutable alternatives for safer and more precise integer and decimal calculations, which are both immutable: java.math.BigInteger and java.math.BigDecimal.

In this context, "integer" means a number without a fractional component and not Java's int or Integer type. The word integer comes from Latin and is used in mathematics as a colloquial term to represent whole numbers in the range from $-\infty$ to $+\infty$, including zero.

Just like with String, why should you burden your code with the overhead of immutability? Because they allow side-effect-free calculations in a greater range with higher precision.

The pitfall of using immutable math objects, though, is the possibility of simply forgetting to use the actual result of a calculation. Even though method names like add or subtract suggest modification, at least in an OO context, the java.math types return a new object with the result, as follows:

```
var theAnswer = new BigDecimal(42);

var result = theAnswer.add(BigDecimal.ONE);

// RESULT OF THE CALCULATION
System.out.println(result);
// OUTPUT:
// 43
```

```
// UNCHANGED ORIGINAL VALUE
System.out.println(theAnswer);
// OUTPUT:
// 42
```

The immutable math types are still objects with the usual overhead and use more memory to achieve their precision. Nevertheless, if calculation speed is not your limiting factor, you should always prefer the BigDecimal type for floating-point arithmetic due to its arbitrary precision.[6]

The BigInteger type is the integer equivalent to BigDecimal, also with built-in immutability. Another advantage is the extended range of at least[7] from $-2^{2,147,483,647}$ up to $2^{2,147,483,647}$ (both exclusive), compared to the range of int from -2^{31} to 2^{31}.

Java Time API (JSR-310)

Java 8 introduced the Java Time API (JSR-310 (*https://oreil.ly/NKu-y*)), which was designed with immutability as a core tenet. Before its release, you only had three[8] types in the package java.util at your disposal for all your date- and time-related needs: Date, Calendar, and TimeZone. Performing calculations was a chore and error-prone. That's why Joda Time library (*https://oreil.ly/PYr6_*) became the de facto standard for date and time classes before Java 8 and subsequently became the conceptual foundation for JSR-310.

 Like with immutable math, any calculation with methods such as plus or minus won't affect the object they're called on. Instead, you have to use the return value.

Rather than the previous three types in java.util, there now are multiple date- and time-related types with different precisions, with and without timezones, available in the java.time package. They are all immutable, giving them all the related advantages like no side effects and safe use in concurrent environments.

---

6 Arbitrary-precision arithmetic—also known as bignum arithmetic, multiple-precision arithmetic, or sometimes infinite-precision arithmetic—performs calculations on numbers whose digits of precision are limited only by the available memory, not a fixed number.

7 The actual range of BigInteger depends on the actual implementation of the used JDK, as stated in an implementation note in the official documentation (*https://oreil.ly/0x5wo*).

8 Technically there's a fourth type, java.sql.Date, which is a thin wrapper to improve JDBC support.

Enums

Java enums are special types consisting of constants. And constants are, well, *constant*, and therefore immutable. Besides the constant values, an enum can contain additional fields which aren't implicitly constant.

Usually, `final` primitives or Strings are used for these fields, but no one stops you from using a mutable object type or a setter for a primitive. It will most likely lead to problems, and I strongly advise against it. Also, it's considered a *code smell*.[9]

The final Keyword

Since Java's inception, the `final` keyword provides a certain form of immutability depending on its context, but it's not a magic keyword to make any data structure immutable. So what exactly does it mean for a reference, method, or class to be `final`?

The `final` keyword is similar to the `const` keyword of the programming language C. It has several implications if applied to classes, methods, fields, or references:

- `final` classes cannot be subclassed.
- `final` methods cannot be overridden.
- `final` fields must be assigned exactly once—either by the constructors or on declaration—and can never be reassigned.
- `final` variable references behave like a field by being assignable *exactly* once—at declaration. The keyword affects only the reference itself, not the referenced variable content.

The `final` keyword grants a particular form of immutability for fields and variables. However, their immutability might not be what you expect because the reference itself becomes immutable but not the underlying data structure. That means you can't reassign the reference but can still change the data structure, as shown in Example 4-1.

---

9 A *code smell* is a known code characteristic that might indicate a deeper problem. It's not a bug or error per se, but it might cause trouble in the long run. These smells are subjective and vary by programming language, developer, and paradigms. Sonar (*https://oreil.ly/ldteU*), the well-known company that develops open source software for continuous code quality and security, lists mutable enums as rule RSPEC-3066 (*https://oreil.ly/VGsgP*).

Example 4-1. Collections and final references

```
final List<String> fruits = new ArrayList<>(); ❶

System.out.println(fruits.isEmpty());
// OUTPUT:
// true

fruits.add("Apple"); ❷

System.out.println(fruits.isEmpty());
// OUTPUT:
// false

fruits = List.of("Mango", "Melon"); ❸
// => WON'T COMPILE
```

❶ The final keyword affects only the reference fruits, not the actually referenced ArrayList.

❷ The ArrayList itself doesn't have any concept of immutability, so you can freely add new items to it, even if its reference is final.

❸ Reassigning a final reference is prohibited.

As discussed in "Effectively final" on page 21, having effectively final references is a necessity for lambda expressions. Making every reference in your code final is an option; however, I wouldn't recommend it. The compiler detects automatically if a reference behaves like a final reference even without adding an explicit keyword. Most problems created by the lack of immutability come from the underlying data structure itself and not reassigned references anyway. To ensure a data structure won't change unexpectedly as long as it's in active use, you must choose an immutable data structure from the get-go. The newest addition to Java to achieve this goal is *Records*.

Records

In 2020, Java 14 introduced a new type of class with its own keyword to complement or even replace POJOs and JavaBeans in certain instances: *Records*.

Records are "plain data" aggregates with less ceremony than POJOs or Java Beans. Their feature set is reduced to an absolute minimum to serve that purpose, making them as concise as they are:

```
    public record Address(String name,
                          String street,
                          String state,
                          String zipCode,
                          Country country) {
      // NO BODY
    }
```

Records are shallowly immutable data carriers primarily consisting of their state's declaration. Without any additional code, the Address record provides automatically generated getters for the named components, equality comparison, toString and hashCode methods, and more.

Chapter 5 will do a deep dive into Records on how to create and use them in different scenarios.

How to Achieve Immutability

Now that you know about the immutable parts the JVM provides, it's time to look at how to combine them to achieve immutability for your program state.

The easiest way to make a type immutable is by not giving it a chance to change in the first place. Without any setters, a data structure with final fields won't change after creation because it can't. For real-world code, though, the solution might not be as simple as that.

Immutability requires a new way of thinking about data creation because shared data structures are seldom created in one fell swoop. Instead of mutating a single data structure over time, you should work with immutable constructs along the way, if possible, and compose a "final" and immutable data structure in the end. Figure 4-4 depicts the general idea of different data components contributing to a "final" immutable Record. Even if the individual components aren't immutable, you should always strive to wrap them in an immutable shell, Record or otherwise.

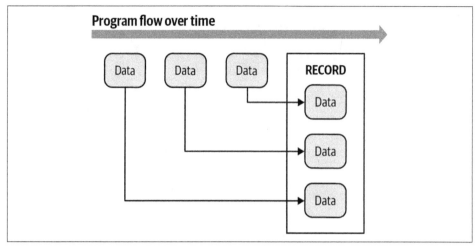

Figure 4-4. Records as data aggregators

Keeping track of the required components and their validation might be challenging in more complicated data structures. In Chapter 5, I'll discuss tools and techniques that improve data structure creation and reduce the required cognitive complexity.

Common Practices

Like the functional approach in general, immutability doesn't have to be an all-or-nothing approach. Due to their advantages, having only immutable data structures sounds intriguing, and your key goal should be to use them and immutable references as your default approach. Converting existing mutable data structures to immutable ones, though, is often a pretty complex task requiring a lot of refactoring or conceptual redesign. Instead, you could introduce immutability gradually by following common practices like those listed below and treating your data as if it were already immutable:

Immutability by default
Any new data structure, like data transfer objects, value objects, or any kind of state, should be designed as immutable. If the JDK or another framework or library you're using provides an immutable alternative, you should consider it over a mutable type. Dealing with immutability right from the start with a new type will influence and shape any code that will use it.

Always expect immutability
Assume all data structures are immutable unless you created them or it's stated explicitly otherwise, especially when dealing with Collection-like types. If you need to change one, it's safer to create a new one based on the existing one.

Modifying existing types

Even if a preexisting type isn't immutable, new additions should be, if possible. There might be reasons for making it mutable, but unnecessary mutability increases the bug surface, and all the advantages of immutability vanish instantly.

Break immutability if necessary

If it doesn't fit, don't force it, especially in legacy codebases. The main goal of immutability is providing safer, more reasonable data structures, which requires their environment to support them accordingly.

Treat foreign data structures as immutable

Always treat any data structure not under your scope's control as immutable. For example, Collection-like types received as method arguments should be considered immutable. Instead of manipulating it directly, create a mutable wrapper view for any changes, and return an unmodifiable Collection type. This approach keeps the method pure and prevents any unintended changes the callee hasn't expected.

Following these common practices will make it easier to create immutable data structures from the start or gradually transition to a more immutable program state along the way.

Takeaways

- Immutability is a simple concept, but it requires a new mindset and approach to handling data and change.

- Lots of JDK types are already designed with immutability in mind.

- Records provide a new and concise way to reduce boilerplate for creating immutable data structures but deliberately lack a certain amount of flexibility in order to be as transparent and straightforward as possible.

- You can achieve immutability with the built-in tools of the JDK, and third-party libraries can provide simple solutions to the missing pieces.

- Introducing immutability into your code doesn't have to be an all-or-nothing approach. You can gradually apply common immutability practices to your existing code to reduce state-related bugs and ease refactoring efforts.

Working with Records

Java 14 introduced a new type of data structure as a preview[1] feature, which was finalized two releases later: *Records*. They are not just another typical Java type or technique you can use. Instead, Records are a completely new language feature providing you with a simple but feature-rich data aggregator with minimal boilerplate.

Data Aggregation Types

From a general point of view, *data aggregation* is the process of gathering data from multiple sources and assembling it in a format that better serves the intended purpose and more preferable usage. Perhaps the most well-known kind of data aggregation type is *tuples*.

Tuples

Mathematically speaking, a tuple is a "finite ordered sequence of elements." In terms of programming languages, a tuple is a data structure aggregating multiple values or objects.

There are two kinds of tuples. *Structural* tuples rely only on the order of the contained elements and are therefore accessible only via their indices, as seen in the following Python[2] code:

---

1 A JDK preview feature is a feature whose design, specification, and implementation are complete but is not permanent. It's supposed to gather feedback from the community to evolve further. Such a feature may exist in a different form or not at all in future releases.

2 Python has multiple sequence based types, as explained in more detail in its documentation (*https://oreil.ly/TaflY*).

```
apple = ("apple", "green")
banana = ("banana", "yellow")
cherry = ("cherry", "red")

fruits = [apple, banana, cherry]

for fruit in fruits:
  print "The", fruit[0], "is", fruit[1]
```

Nominal tuples don't use an index to access their data but use component names instead, as seen in the following Swift code:

```
typealias Fruit = (name: String, color: String)

let fruits: [Fruit] = [
  (name: "apple", color: "green"),
  (name: "banana", color: "yellow"),
  (name: "cherry", color: "red")]

for fruit in fruits {
  println("The \(fruit.name) is \(fruit.color)")
}
```

To demonstrate what Records have to offer, you'll first look at how to go from a classical POJO to an immutable one, and then I'll show you how to replicate the same functionality with a Record instead.

A Simple POJO

First, let's take a look at the "pre-Record" state of data aggregation in Java to better grasp what Records have to offer. As an example, we create a simple "user" type as a "classic" POJO, evolve it to an "immutable" POJO, and finally, a Record. It will be a simple type, with a username, an activity state, a last-login timestamp, and the usual boilerplate that comes along in typical Java code, as seen in Example 5-1.

Example 5-1. Simple User POJO

```
public final class User {

  private String username;
  private boolean active;
  private LocalDateTime lastLogin;

  public User() { } ❶

  public User(String username,
              boolean active,
              LocalDateTime lastLogin) { ❶
    this.username = username;
    this.active = active;
```

```java
    this.lastLogin = lastLogin;
  }

  public String getUsername() { ❷
    return this.username;
  }

  public void setUsername(String username) { ❸
    this.username = username;
  }

  public boolean isActive() { ❷
    return this.active;
  }

  public void setActive(boolean active) { ❸
    this.active = active;
  }

  public LocalDateTime getLastLogin() { ❷
    return this.lastLogin;
  }

  public void setLastLogin(LocalDateTime lastLogin) { ❸
    this.lastLogin = lastLogin;
  }

  @Override
  public int hashCode() { ❹
    return Objects.hash(this.username, this.active, this.lastLogin);
  }

  @Override
  public boolean equals(Object obj) { ❺
    if (this == obj) {
      return true;
    }

    if (obj == null || getClass() != obj.getClass()) {
      return false;
    }

    User other = (User) obj;
    return Objects.equals(this.username, other.username)
          && this.active == other.active
          && Objects.equals(this.lastLogin, other.lastLogin);
  }

  @Override
  public String toString() { ❺
    return new StringBuilder().append("User [username=")
                              .append(this.username)
```

```
                .append(", active=")
                .append(this.active)
                .append(", lastLogin=")
                .append(this.lastLogin)
                .append("]")
                .toString();
    }
}
```

❶ Constructors aren't strictly necessary but are added for convenience. If any constructor with arguments exists, an explicit "empty" constructor should be added, too.

❷ POJOs usually have getters instead of public fields.

❸ The first variant of the User type is still mutable due to its setter methods.

❹ Both the hashCode and equals method require dedicated implementations that depend on the actual structure of the type. Any changes to the type require both methods to adapt.

❺ The toString method is another convenience addition that isn't explicitly needed. Just like the previous methods, it has to be updated every time the type changes.

Including the empty lines and curly braces, that's over 70 lines for just holding three data fields. No wonder one of the most common complaints about Java is its verbosity and "too much ceremony" to do standard things!

Now, let's convert it into an immutable POJO.

From POJO to Immutability

Making the User POJO immutable reduces the required boilerplate slightly because you no longer need any setter methods, as shown in Example 5-2.

Example 5-2. Simple immutable User type

```
public final class User {

    private final String username; ❶
    private final boolean active;
    private final LocalDateTime lastLogin;

    public User(String username,
                boolean active,
                LocalDateTime lastLogin) { ❷
```

```
    this.username = username;
    this.active = active;
    this.lastLogin = lastLogin;
  }

  public String getUsername() { ❸
    return this.username;
  }

  public boolean isActive() { ❸
    return this.active;
  }

  public LocalDateTime getLastLogin() { ❸
    return this.lastLogin;
  }

  @Override
  public int hashCode() { ❹
    // UNCHANGED
  }

  @Override
  public boolean equals(Object obj) { ❹
    // UNCHANGED
  }

  @Override
  public String toString() { ❹
    // UNCHANGED
  }
}
```

❶ Without "setters," the fields can be declared `final`.

❷ Only a full "pass-through" constructor is possible because the fields must be set on object creation.

❸ The "getters" remain unchanged from the mutable variant.

❹ The supporting methods are also unchanged compared to the previous implementation.

By making the type immutable yourself, only the code of the setters and the empty constructor could be removed; everything else is still there. That's still a lot of code for holding three fields with not much additional functionality. Of course, we could remove more of the "ceremony" and use a simple class with three `public final` fields and a constructor. Depending on your requirements, that might be "just enough." The additional functionality, however, like equality comparison, and a correct `hashCode` so it can be used in a Set or HashMap, or a sensible toString output, are all desirable features.

From POJO to Record

Finally, let's take a look at a more general, less ceremonial, but still feature-rich solution using a Record instead:

```
public record User(String username,
                   boolean active,
                   LocalDateTime lastLogin) {
    // NO BODY
}
```

That's it.

The User Record has the same features as the immutable POJO. How it does so much with so little code will be explained in detail in the upcoming sections.

Records to the Rescue

Records are a way to define plain data aggregator types that access their data components by name in the vein of nominal tuples. Like nominal tuples, Records aggregate an ordered sequence of values and provide access via names instead of indices. Their data is shallowly immutable and transparently accessible. The typical boilerplate of other data classes is significantly reduced by generating accessors and data-driven methods like equals and hashCode. Even though the final version of JEP 395 (*https:// oreil.ly/ftGGN*) explicitly states that "war on boilerplate" is a non-goal, it's still a happy coincidence many developers will appreciate.

Being "plain" data aggregator types, there are some missing features compared to other options. This chapter will cover each missing feature and how to mitigate them, transforming Records into a more flexible solution for your data aggregation needs.

As seen in the previous section, Records use a new keyword—record—to delimit them from other classes and enums. The data components are declared like a constructor or method arguments directly after the Record's name:

```
public record User(String username,
                   boolean active,
                   LocalDateTime lastLogin) {
    // NO BODY
}
```

The general syntax for Records breaks down into two parts: a *header* defining the same properties as other types, plus its components and an optional *body* to support additional constructors and methods:

```
// HEADER
[visibility] record [Name][<optional generic types>]([data components]) {
  // BODY
}
```

The header is similar to a `class` or `interface` header and consists of multiple parts:

Visibility
> Like a `class`, `enum`, or `interface` definition, a Record supports Java's visibility keywords (`public`, `private`, `protected`).

The `record` keyword
> The keyword `record` distinguishes the header from other type declarations like `class`, `enum`, and `interface`.

Name
> Naming rules are identical to those of any other identifier, as defined in the *Java Language Specification*.[3]

Generic types
> Generic types are supported as with other type declarations in Java.

Data components
> The name is followed by a pair of parentheses containing the components of the Record. Each one translates into a `private final` field and a `public` accessor method behind the scenes. The components list also represents the constructor of the Record.

Body
> A typical Java body, like any other `class` or `interface`.

An effectively single line of code will be translated by the compiler to a class similar to Example 5-2 from the previous section. It extends `java.lang.Record` explicitly rather than `java.lang.Object` implicitly, just like enums do with `java.lang.Enum`.

Behind the Scenes

The generated class behind any Record gives you quite a lot of functionality without writing any additional code. It's time to take a deeper look at what's actually happening behind the scenes.

The JDK includes the command `javap`, which disassembles `.class` files and allows you to see the corresponding Java code for the bytecode. This way, it's easy to compare the actual difference between the POJO and Record version of the `User` type

---

3 See the Java Language Specification chapter 3.8 (*https://oreil.ly/zjrfS*) for the definition of valid Java identifier.

from "Data Aggregation Types" on page 77. The combined and cleaned-up output for both variants is shown in Example 5-3.

Example 5-3. Disassembled User.class file: POJO versus Record

```
// IMMUTABLE POJO
public final class User {
  public User(java.lang.String, boolean, java.time.LocalDateTime);
  public java.lang.String getUsername();
  public boolean isActive();
  public java.time.LocalDateTime getLastLogin();

  public int hashCode();
  public boolean equals(java.lang.Object);
  public java.lang.String toString();
}

// RECORD
public final class User extends java.lang.Record {
  public User(java.lang.String, boolean, java.time.LocalDateTime);
  public java.lang.String username();
  public boolean active();
  public java.time.LocalDateTime lastLogin();

  public final int hashCode();
  public final boolean equals(java.lang.Object);
  public final java.lang.String toString();
}
```

As you can see, the resulting classes are identical functionality-wise; only the naming of the accessor methods differ. But where did all those methods come from? Well, that's the "magic" of Records, giving you a full-fledged data aggregation type without writing more code than absolutely needed.

Record Features

Records are transparent data aggregators with specific guaranteed properties and well-defined behavior by *automagically*[4] providing functionality without needing to repeatedly write the following trivial boilerplate implementations:

- Component accessors
- Three types of constructors
- Object identity and description methods

---

4 "Automagically" describes an automatic process that's hidden from the user and therefore magic-like. Records provide automatic features without additional tools like annotation processors or extra compiler plugins.

That's a lot of functionality without requiring any additional code besides the Record declaration. Any missing pieces can be addressed by augmenting or overriding these features as necessary.

Let's check out Record's automatic features and how other typical Java features, like generics, annotations, and reflection, fit in.

Component accessors

All Record components are stored in `private` fields. Inside a Record, its fields are directly accessible. From the outside, you need to access them through the generated `public` accessor methods. The accessor method names correspond to their component name without the typical "getter" prefix `get`, as shown in the following code example:

```
public record User(String username,
                   boolean active,
                   LocalDateTime lastLogin) {
  // NO BODY
}

var user = new User("ben", true, LocalDateTime.now());

var username = user.username();
```

The accessor methods return the corresponding field's value as is. Though you can override any accessor method, as shown in the following code, I wouldn't recommend it:

```
public record User(String username,
                   boolean active,
                   LocalDateTime lastLogin) {

  @Override
  public String username() {
    if (this.username == null) {
      return "n/a";
    }

    return this.username;
  }
}

var user = new User(null, true, LocalDateTime.now());

var username = user.username();
// => "n/a"
```

Records are supposed to be immutable data holders, so making decisions while accessing their data could be considered a code smell. The creation of a Record defines its data, and that's where any validation or other logic should affect the data, as you will learn in the next section.

Canonical, compact, and custom constructors

A constructor identical to the Record's components definition is automatically available, called the *canonical* constructor. The Record's components are assigned to the corresponding fields "as is." Like component accessors, the canonical constructor is overridable to validate input, like null checks, or even manipulate data if necessary:

```
public record User(String username,
                   boolean active,
                   LocalDateTime lastLogin) {

    public User(String username,
                boolean active,
                LocalDateTime lastLogin) {

        Objects.requireNonNull(username);
        Objects.requireNonNull(lastLogin);

        this.username = username;
        this.active = active;
        this.lastLogin = lastLogin;
    }
}
```

That's a lot of additional lines for two actual null checks, including redeclaration of the constructor signature and assigning the components to the invisible fields.

Thankfully, a specialized *compact* form, shown in the following code example, is available, and it doesn't force you to repeat any boilerplate if you don't need it:

```
public record User(String username,
                   boolean active,
                   LocalDateTime lastLogin) {

    public User {  ❶
        Objects.requireNonNull(username);
        Objects.requireNonNull(lastLogin);

        username = username.toLowerCase();  ❷

            ❸
    }
}
```

❶ The constructor omits all arguments, including the parentheses.

❷ Field assignments aren't allowed in the compact canonical constructor, but you can customize or normalize data before it's assigned.

❸ The components will be assigned to their respective fields automatically, no additional code required.

At first, the syntax might look unusual because it omits all arguments, including the parentheses. This way, though, it's clearly distinguishable from an argument-less constructor.

The compact constructor is the perfect place to put any validation, as I will show you in "Record Validation and Data Scrubbing" on page 96.

Like with classes, you can declare additional constructors, but any custom constructor must start with an explicit invocation of the canonical constructor as its first statement. That's quite a restrictive requirement compared to classes. Still, this requirement serves an essential feature I'm going to discuss in "Component default values and convenience constructors" on page 91.

Object identity and description

Records provide a "standard" implementation for the object identity methods hashCode and equals based on data equality. Without an explicit implementation of the two object identity methods, you don't have to worry about updating your code if the Record's components change. Two instances of a Record type are considered equal if the data of their components are equal.

The object description method toString() is autogenerated from the components, too, giving you a sensible default output, for example:

```
User[username=ben, active=true, lastLogin=2023-01-11T13:32:16.727249646]
```

The object identity and description methods are overridable, too, like component accessors and constructors.

Generics

Records also support generics, which follow the usual rules:

```
public record Container<T>(T content, String identifier) {
  // NO BODY
}

Container<String> stringContainer = new Container<>("hello, String!",
                                                    "a String container");
String content = stringContainer.content();
```

Personally, I would advise against overusing generic Records. Using more specific Records that more closely match the domain model they represent gives you more expressiveness and reduces accidental misuse.

Annotations

Annotations behave a little differently than you might expect if used on a Record's components:

```
public record User(@NonNull String username,
                   boolean active,
                   LocalDateTime lastLogin) {
  // NO BODY
}
```

At first glance, `username` looks like a parameter, so a sensible conclusion would be that only annotations with `ElementType.PARAMETER` should be possible[5]. But with Records and their automagically generated fields and component accessors, some special considerations must be made. To support annotating these features, any annotations with the targets `FIELD`, `PARAMETER`, or `METHOD` are propagated to the corresponding locations if applied to a component.

In addition to the existing targets, the new target `ElementType.RECORD_COMPONENT` was introduced for more fine-grained annotation control in Records.

Reflection

To complement Java's reflection capabilities, Java 16 added the `getRecordComponents` method to `java.lang.Class`. In the case of a Record-based type, the call gives you an array of `java.lang.reflect.RecordComponent` objects, or `null` for any other type of `Class`. The components are returned in the same order that they are declared in the Record header, allowing you to look up the canonical constructor via the `getDeclaredConstructors` method on a Record's class.

Missing Features

Records are precisely what they are supposed to be: *plain, transparent, shallowly immutable data aggregators*. They provide a plethora of features without writing any line of code except their definition. Compared to other available data aggregators, they lack some features you might be used to, such as:

- Additional state
- Inheritance
- (Simple) default values
- Step-by-step creation

---

5 To learn more about annotations in general and how to use them, you should check out my article "Java Annotations Explained" (*https://oreil.ly/GHWWC*).

This section shows which features are "missing in action" and how to mitigate them if possible.

Additional state

Allowing any additional opaque state is an obvious omission from Records. They are supposed to be data aggregators representing a transparent state. That's why any additional field added to its body results in a compiler error.

 If you require more fields than what's possible with a Record's components alone, Records might not be the data structure you're looking for, and a custom POJO might work better.

For some scenarios at least, you could add *derived* state that's based on the existing components, by adding methods to the Records:

```
public record User(String username,
                   boolean active,
                   LocalDateTime lastLogin) {

  public boolean hasLoggedInAtLeastOnce() {
    return this.lastLogin != null;
  }
}
```

Methods can be added because they don't introduce additional state like a field. They have access to `private` fields, guaranteeing verbatim data access even if the component accessor is overridden. Which to choose—field or accessor—depends on how you design your Record and your personal preference.

Inheritance

Records are `final` types that already extend `java.lang.Record` behind the scenes, as previously seen in Example 5-3. Because Java doesn't allow inheriting more than one type, Records can't use inheritance. That doesn't mean they can't implement any interfaces, though. With interfaces, you can define Record templates and share common functionality with `default` methods.

Example 5-4 shows how to create Records for multiple shapes with the common concept of an origin and a surface area.

Example 5-4. Using interfaces with Records as templates

```java
public interface Origin {

  int x(); ❶
  int y(); ❶

  default String origin() { ❷
    return String.format("(%d/%d)", x(), y());
  }
}

public interface Area {
  float area(); ❸
}


// DIFFERENT RECORDS IMPLEMENTING INTERFACES

public record Point(int x, int y) implements Origin {
  // NO BODY
}

public record Rectangle(int x, int y, int width, int height)
  implements Origin, Area {

  public float area() { ❸
    return (float) (width() * height());
  }
}

public record Circle(int x, int y, int radius)
  implements Origin, Area {

  public float area() { ❸
    return (float) Math.PI * radius() * radius();
  }
}
```

❶ The interface defines the components of an implementing Record as simple methods with the correct names.

❷ Shared functionality is added with `default` methods.

❸ Method signatures in interfaces must not interfere with any implementing Record type.

Sharing behavior with interfaces and `default` methods is a straightforward approach, as long as all implementees share the interface contract. Interfaces can provide a few left-out pieces of the missing inheritance, and it might be tempting to create intricate hierarchies and interdependencies between Records. But structuring your record types this way will create cohesion between them that's not in the original spirit of Records being simple data aggregators defined by their state. The example is overengineered to illustrate the possibilities of multiple interfaces better. In the real world, you would most likely make `Origin` a Record, too, and use composition and additional constructors to achieve the same functionality.

Component default values and convenience constructors

Unlike many other languages, Java doesn't support default values for any constructor or method arguments. Records only provide their canonical constructor with all components automatically, which can become unwieldy, especially in the case of composed data structures, as seen in Example 5-5.

Example 5-5. Canonical constructors in composed data structures

```
public record Origin(int x, int y) {
  // NO BODY
}

public record Rectangle(Origin origin, int width, int height) {
  // NO BODY
}

var rectangle = new Rectangle(new Origin(23, 42), 300, 400);
```

To regain shorter constructor calls, you can add additional custom constructors for such composed data structures, which give you an easy way to have sensible default values, as shown in Example 5-6.

Example 5-6. Custom constructors for default values

```
public record Origin(int x, int y) {

  public Origin() {
    this(0, 0);
  }
}

public record Rectangle(Origin origin, int width, int height) {

  public Rectangle(int x, int y, int width, int height) { ❶
    this(new Origin(x, y), width, height);
```

```
  }

  public Rectangle(int width, int height) {  ❷
    this(new Origin(), width, height);
  }

  // ...
}

var rectangle = new Rectangle(23, 42, 300, 400);
// => Rectangle[origin=Origin[x=23, y=42], width=300, height=400]
```

❶ The first additional constructor mimics the components of Origin to provide a
  more convenient way to create a Rectangle.

❷ The second one is a convenience constructor by removing the necessity of providing an Origin.

Due to Java's naming semantics, not all combinations for default values might be
possible. For example, consider the following constructor signatures:

```
Rectangle(int x, float width, float height)

Rectangle(int y, float width, float height)
```

Both signatures differ only in their component names but not their types and are
therefore identical, which isn't allowed.

In this case, using static factory methods allows you to create any combination you
require:

```
public record Rectangle(Origin origin, int width, int height) {

  public static Rectangle atX(int x, int width, int height) {
    return new Rectangle(x, 0, width, height);
  }

  public static Rectangle atY(int y, int width, int height) {
    return new Rectangle(0, y, width, height);
  }

  // ...
}

var xOnlyRectangle = Rectangle.atX(23, 300, 400);
// => Rectangle[origin=Origin[x=23, y=0], width=300, height=400]
```

Using static factory methods is a more expressive alternative to custom constructors and the only resort for overlapping signatures.

In the case of argument-less constructors, a constant makes more sense:

```
public record Origin(int x, int y) {

    public static Origin ZERO = new Origin(0, 0);
}
```

First, your code is more expressive with meaningful names for constants. Second, only a single instance is created, which is constant anywhere because the underlying data structure is immutable.

Step-by-step creation

One of the advantages of immutable data structures is the lack of "half-initialized" objects. Still, not every data structure is initializable all at once. Instead of using a mutable data structure in such a case, you can use the *builder pattern* to get a mutable intermediate variable that's used to create an eventually immutable final result. Even though the builder pattern was incepted as a solution to recurring object creation problems in object-oriented programming, it's also highly beneficial for creating immutable data structures in a more functional Java environment.

The Builder Design Pattern

The *builder design pattern* was introduced in the book *Design Patterns: Elements of Reusable Object-Oriented Software*[6] by the "Gang of Four," referring to Erich Gamma, Richard Helm, Ralph Johnson, and John Vlissides.

This creational design pattern aims to provide a flexible solution for constructing complex data structures by separating the build process from the final representation of the data structure.

The main advantage of this pattern is the ability to create complex data structures step-by-step, allowing you to defer steps until the required data is available. It also fits into the *single responsibility principle*[7] of object-oriented design, defined as every class, module, or function in a program should have one responsibility/purpose in a program. In this case, the builder class is solely responsible for constructing a complex data structure, while the structure itself is responsible only for representing its data.

By separating the construction of the data structure from its representation, the data structure itself can be as simple as possible, making the pattern an excellent match for Records. Any required logic, or validation, is encapsulated into a (multistep-) builder.

---

6 Gamma, Helm, Johnson, and Vlissides, *Design Patterns: Elements of Reusable Object-Oriented Software* (Addison-Wesley Professional).

7 The *single responsibility principle* is the first of the *SOLID* principles for object-oriented programming. Its five principles intend to make OO designs more flexible, maintainable, and straightforward.

The previously used User Record can be complemented by a simple builder, as shown in Example 5-7.

Example 5-7. User Builder

```java
public final class UserBuilder {

  private final String username;

  private boolean active;
  private LocalDateTime lastLogin;

  public UserBuilder(String username) {
    this.username = username;
    this.active = true; ❶
  }

  public UserBuilder active(boolean isActive) { ❷
    if (this.active == false) { ❸
      throw new IllegalArgumentException();
    }

    this.active = isActive;
    return this; ❹
  }

  public UserBuilder lastLogin(LocalDateTime lastLogin) { ❺
    this.lastLogin = lastLogin;
    return this;
  }

  public User build() { ❻
    return new User(this.username, this.active, this.lastLogin);
  }
}

var builder = new UserBuilder("ben").active(false) ❼
                                    .lastLogin(LocalDateTime.now());

// ...

var user = builder.build(); ❽
```

❶ Explicit default values are possible, reducing the required code for creation.

❷ Field that can be changed during building need setter-like methods.

❸ Validation logic is bound to the specific setter-like method and not accumulated in any constructor.

❹ Returning this creates a fluent API for the builder.

❺ Optional fields can use their explicit types and change into an Optional only during the build method call.

❻ If you're done building, calling the build method will create the actual immutable User record. Usually, the builder should validate its state if necessary.

❼ The build process is fluent, and you can pass the builder around like any other variable.

❽ Finally, create the immutable object by calling the build method.

It's sensible to increase the adhesion between the type and its builder by placing the builder class directly in the corresponding type as a static nested class, as seen in Example 5-8.

Example 5-8. Nested Builder

```
public record User(long id,
                   String username,
                   boolean active,
                   Optional<LocalDateTime> lastLogin) {

  public static final class Builder {
    // ...
  }
}

var builder = new User.Builder("ben");
```

It might seem nonsensical to use a Record to achieve simplicity and immutability but still introduce the complexity of a builder. Why not use a full-fledged bean instead? Because even with the complexity of the builder, the concerns of creating and using the data are separate. The Record is still usable without the builder, but the builder provides an additional and flexible way to create a Record instance.

Use Cases and Common Practices

Records save you a lot of boilerplate code, and with a few additions you can supercharge them into an even more flexible and versatile tool.

Record Validation and Data Scrubbing

As shown in "Canonical, compact, and custom constructors" on page 86, Records support a *compact constructor* that behaves differently from a normal constructor. You have access to all components of the canonical constructor, but it doesn't have any arguments. It gives you a location to put any additional code required for the initialization process without needing to assign the components yourself. That makes it the perfect place to put any validation and data-scrubbing logic:

```java
public record NeedsValidation(int x, int y) {

  public NeedsValidation {
    if (x < y) {
      throw new IllegalArgumentException("x must be equal or greater than y");
    }
  }
}
```

Throwing Exceptions is one way to go. Another option is to *scrub* the data and adjust component values with sensible alternatives to form a valid Record:

```java
public record Time(int minutes, int seconds) {

  public Time {
    if (seconds >= 60) {
      int additionalMinutes = seconds / 60;
      minutes += additionalMinutes;
      seconds -= additionalMinutes * 60;
    }
  }
}

var time = new Time(12, 67);
// => Time[minutes=13, seconds=7]
```

Moving a certain degree of logic, like the normalization of out-of-range values, directly into a Record gives you more consistent data representations, regardless of the initial data. Another approach is requiring such data scrubbing beforehand and restricting a Record to do only *hard* validation by throwing a proper exception.

Record Validation with the Bean Validation API

Another validation option for Records is the *Bean Validation API* (JSR-380 (*https://oreil.ly/fBVJy*)). Records aren't JavaBeans *technically*, but they can still profit from the existing validation concept. The Bean Validation API gives you the tools to express and validate constraints with a multitude of annotations like @NonNull, @Positive, etc.

Implementing JSR-380-compatible constraints requires adding more dependencies to your project. Even then, the validation isn't run automatically. Bytecode manipulation is often used to mitigate this issue. The details of how to use the Bean Validation API are beyond the scope of this book, but the official Java Magazine has an excellent article (*https://oreil.ly/W8hVy*) that provides an overview of how to implement rudimentary Record validation with JSR-380.

Increasing Immutability

In "Immutable Collections" on page 65 you learned about the problem with shallow immutability in Collections. A shallowly immutable data structure has an immutable reference, but the data it refers to is still mutable. The same underlying problems of unexpected changes must also be considered with non-inherently immutable Record components. An easy way to minimize any changes in Record components is by trying to increase the level of immutability by copying or rewrapping them.

You can use the canonical constructor to create immutable copies of a component:

```java
public record IncreaseImmutability(List<String> values) {

  public IncreaseImmutability {
    values = Collections.unmodifiableList(values);
  }
}
```

The call to `Collections.unmodifiableList` creates a memory-wise lean but unmodifiable view of the original `List`. This prevents changes to the Record's component but can't control changes to the underlying `List` via the original reference. A greater level of immutability can be achieved by using the Java 10+ method `List.copyOf (Collection<? extends E> coll)` to create a deep copy independent of the original reference.

Creating Modified Copies

Even though the declaration of Records is as minimal as it gets, creating a slightly modified copy is a DIY job without any help from the JDK.

There are multiple approaches to creating modified copies if you don't want to do it completely manually:

- Wither methods
- Builder pattern
- Tool-assisted builder

Wither methods

Wither methods follow the name scheme `with[componentName]([Type] value)`. They're similar to setters but return a new instance instead of modifying the current one:

```java
public record Point(int x, int y) {

  public Point withX(int newX) {
    return new Point(newX, y());
  }

  public Point withY(int newY) {
    return new Point(x(), newY);
  }
}

var point = new Point(23, 42);
// => Point[x=23, y=42]

var newPoint = point.withX(5);
// => Point[x=5, y=42]
```

A nested Record is a handy way to separate the modification logic from the actual Record:

```java
public record Point(int x, int y) {

  public With with() {
    return new With(this);
  }

  public record With(Point source) {

    public Point x(int x) {
      return new Point(x, source.y());
    }

    public Point y(int y) {
      return new Point(source.x(), y);
    }
  }
}

var sourcePoint = new Point(23, 42);
// => Point[x=23, y=42]

var modifiedPoint = sourcePoint.with().x(5);
// => Point[x=5, y=42]
```

The original Record has only one additional method, and all mutator/copy methods are encapsulated in the `With` type.

The most obvious downside of wither methods, like default values in "Component default values and convenience constructors" on page 91, is the requirement to write a method for each component. Restricting your code to the most common scenarios is sensible, and only add new methods as required.

Builder pattern

The builder pattern, as introduced in "Step-by-step creation" on page 93, also allows for easier change management if you add a copy constructor. Such a constructor allows you to initialize the builder with an existing Record, make the appropriate changes, and create a new Record, as follows:

```java
public record Point(int x, int y) {

  public static final class Builder {

    private int x;
    private int y;

    public Builder(Point point) {
      this.x = point.x();
      this.y = point.y();
    }

    public Builder x(int x) {
      this.x = x;
      return this;
    }

    public Builder y(int y) {
      this.y = y;
      return this;
    }

    public Point build() {
      return new Point(this.x, this.y);
    }
  }
}

var original = new Point(23, 42);
// => Point[x=23, y=42]

var updated = new Point.Builder(original)
                    .x(5)
                    .build();
// => Point[x=5, y=42]
```

This approach shares the same problem as wither methods: strong cohesion between the components and code needed to create Record copies, making refactoring harder. To mitigate this, you can use a tool-assisted approach.

Tool-assisted builder

Instead of updating your Record builder classes each time a Record changes, you could use an annotation processor to do the work for you. A tool like RecordBuilder (*https://oreil.ly/0a35z*) generates a flexible builder for any Record, and all you have to do is add a single annotation:

```
@RecordBuilder
public record Point(int x, int y) {
  // NO BODY
}

// GENERAL BUILDER
var original = PointBuilder.builder()
                          .x(5)
                          .y(23)
                          .build();
// => Point[x=5, y=23]

// COPY BUILDER
var modified = PointBuilder.builder(original)
                          .x(12)
                          .build();
// => Point[x=12, y=23]
```

Any change to the Record's components will automatically be available in the generated builder. A wither-based approach is also possible but requires your Record to implement an additionally generated interface:

```
@RecordBuilder
public record Point(int x, int y) implements PointBuilder.With {
  // NO BODY
}

var original = new Point(5, 23);
// => Point[x=5, y=23]

// SINGLE CHANGE
var modified1 = original.withX(12);
// => Point[x=12, y=23]

// MULTI-CHANGE VIA BUILDER
var modified2 = original.with()
                       .x(12)
                       .y(21)
                       .build()
// => Point[x=12, y=21]

// MULTI-CHANGE VIA CONSUMER (doesn't require calling build())
var modified3 = original.with(builder -> builder.x(12).y(21));
// => Point[x=12, y=21]
```

Even though using an external tool to complement your Records, or any code, can save you a lot of typing, it also comes with some downsides. Depending on a tool for an essential part of your project that won't work without it creates a hard-to-break cohesion between them. Any bugs, security problems, or breaking changes may affect your code in unforeseen ways, often without the possibility of fixing it yourself. Annotation processors integrate themselves into your build tools, making them now interrelated, too. So make sure you evaluate such dependencies thoroughly[8] before adding them to your projects.

Records as Local Nominal Tuples

One type of construct prevalent in many functional programming languages is missing in Java: *dynamic tuples*. Programming languages usually use those as dynamic data aggregators without requiring an explicitly defined type. Java Records are simple data aggregators and can be considered *nominal tuples* in a sense. The most significant difference to most tuple implementations is that their contained data is held together by an umbrella type due to the Java type system. Records aren't as flexible or interchangeable as other languages' tuple implementations. Still, you can use them as localized *on-the-fly* data aggregators, thanks to an addition to Records in Java 15: *local Records*.

Contextually localized Records simplify and formalize data processing and bundle functionality. Imagine you have a list of music album titles of the 1990s, grouped by year as a `Map<Integer, List<String>>`, as follows:

```
Map<Integer, List<String>> albums =
  Map.of(1990, List.of("Bossanova", " Listen Without Prejudice"),
         1991, List.of("Nevermind", "Ten", "Blue lines"),
         1992, List.of("The Chronic", "Rage Against the Machine"),
         1993, List.of("Enter the Wu-Tang (36 Chambers)"),
         ...
         1999, List.of("The Slim Shady LP", "Californication", "Play"));
```

Working with such a nested and unspecific data structure is quite a hassle. Iterating Maps requires using the `entrySet` method, which returns `Map.Entry<Integer, List<String>>` instances in this case. Working with the entries might give you access to all the data but not in an expressive way.

The following code uses a Stream pipeline to create a filter method for the music album titles. Even without reading Chapter 6, which will explain Streams in detail, most of the code should be straightforward, but I'll guide you through it:

```
public List<String> filterAlbums(Map<Integer, List<String>> albums,
                                  int minimumYear) {
```

---

8 I've written an article about how to evaluate dependencies on my blog (*https://oreil.ly/vqCGu*).

```
        return albums.entrySet()
                .stream()
                .filter(entry -> entry.getKey() >= minimumYear) ❶
                .sorted(Comparator.comparing(Map.Entry::getKey)) ❷
                .map(Map.Entry::getValue) ❸
                .flatMap(List::stream) ❹
                .toList(); ❺
    }
```

❶ Filter the entries for albums that are from at least the minimum year.

❷ Sort the title lists by their respective years.

❸ Transform the entry to its actual value.

❹ The flatMap call helps to "flatten" the List<String> elements containing a year's titles to singular elements in the pipeline.

❺ Collect the elements to a List<String>.

Each Stream operation has to deal with getKey or getValue instead of expressive names representing the actual data in its context. That's why introducing a local Record as an intermediate type allows you to regain expressiveness in complex data processing tasks, like Stream pipelines, but any data processing can benefit from more expressiveness. You can even move parts of the logic into the Record to use method references or single calls for each operation.

Think about the form of the data you have, and how it should be represented, and design your Record accordingly. Next, you should refactor complex data processing tasks into Record methods.

Possible candidates are:

- Creating the Record from a Map.Entry instance
- Filtering by year
- Sorting by year

The following Record code shows implementations of these tasks:

```
public record AlbumsPerYear(int year, List<String> titles) { ❶

    public AlbumsPerYear(Map.Entry<Integer, List<String>> entry) { ❷
        this(entry.getKey(), entry.getValue());
    }

    public static Predicate<AlbumsPerYear> minimumYear(int year) { ❸
        return albumsPerYear -> albumsPerYear.year() >= year;
    }
```

```
  public static Comparator<AlbumsPerYear> sortByYear() { ❹
    return Comparator.comparing(AlbumsPerYear::year);
  }
}
```

❶ The Record components reflect how you want to access the data with more expressive names.

❷ An additional constructor allows using a method reference to create new instances.

❸ If a task depends on an out-of-scope variable, it should be defined as static helpers.

❹ Sorting should be done either by creating a static helper method returning a Comparator, or your Record could implement the Comparable interface instead if only a single sort needs to be supported.

The Record AlbumsPerYear is specifically designed for the Stream pipeline of the filterAlbums method and should only be available in its scope. The local context confines the Record, denying it access to surrounding variables. All nested Records are implicitly static to prevent state leaking into it through the surrounding class. Example 5-9 shows how the Record lives in the method and how the Record improves the overall code.

Example 5-9. Stream pipeline with localized Record

```
public List<String> filterAlbums(Map<Integer, List<String>> albums,
                                 int minimumYear) {

  record AlbumsPerYear(int year, List<String> titles) { ❶
    // ...
  }

  return albums.entrySet()
              .stream()
              .map(AlbumsPerYear::new) ❷
              .filter(AlbumsPerYear.minimumYear(minimumYear)) ❸
              .sorted(AlbumsPerYear.sortByYear()) ❸
              .map(AlbumsPerYear::titles) ❸
              .flatMap(List::stream) ❹
              .toList();
}
```

❶ The localized Record is directly declared in the method, restricting its scope. I didn't repeat the actual implementation for readability reasons.

❷ The first operation of the Stream pipeline is to transform the `Map.Entry` instance into the local Record type.

❸ Each subsequent operation uses an expressive method of the localized Record, either directly or as a method reference, instead of an explicit lambda expression.

❹ Some operations are harder to refactor, like `flatMap`, because the overall processing logic of the Stream dictates their use.

As you can see, using a local Record is an excellent way to improve the ergonomics and expressiveness of a declarative Stream pipeline without exposing the type outside of its apparent scope.

Better Optional Data Handling

Dealing with optional data and possible `null` values is the bane of every Java developer. One option is using the Bean Validation API, as shown in "Record Validation and Data Scrubbing" on page 96, and annotating each component with `@NonNull` and `@Nullable`, although this approach requires a dependency. If you want to stay within the JDK, Java 8 eased the pain of `null` handling by introducing the `Optional<T>` type, which you will learn more about in Chapter 9. For now, all you need to know is that it's a container type for possible `null` values, so even if the value is `null`, you can still interact with the container without causing a `NullPointerException`.

The `Optional` type clearly signifies that a component is not mandatory, but it requires a little more code than just changing the type to be an effective tool. Let's add a nonmandatory group to our `User` type example from earlier in this chapter:

```
public record User(String username,
                   boolean active,
                   Optional<String> group,
                   LocalDateTime lastLogin) {
    // NO BODY
}
```

Even though an `Optional<String>` is used to store the user's group, you still have to deal with the possibility of receiving `null` for the container itself. A better option would be accepting `null` for the value itself but still having an `Optional<String>` component. With Records reflecting their definition with their accessors 1:1, two additional steps are necessary to make Records safe and more convenient to use with `Optional`-based components.

Ensure non-null container

The first step to making Records safer and more convenient to use with `Optional`-based components is to ensure that the `Optional<String>` won't be `null` and, therefore, ruin the idea behind having it. The easiest way is to validate it with a compact constructor:

```
public record User(String username,
                   boolean active,
                   Optional<String> group,
                   LocalDateTime lastLogin) {

    public User {
      Objects.requireNonNull(group, "Optional<String> group must not be null");
    }
}
```

The most apparent problem is averted by moving a possible `NullPointerException` from using the component accessor to the moment of creating the Record itself, making it safer to use.

Add convenience constructors

The second way to make Records safer and more convenient to use is providing additional constructors with non-`Optional<T>`-based+ arguments and creating the container type yourself:

```
public record User(String username,
                   boolean active,
                   Optional<String> group,
                   LocalDateTime lastLogin) {

    public User(String username,
                boolean active,
                String group,
                LocalDateTime lastLogin) {
      this(username,
           active,
           Optional.ofNullable(group),
           lastLogin);
    }

    // ...
}
```

Code completion will show both constructors, indicating the optionality of the `group` component.

The combination of validation at Record creations and a convenience constructor gives flexibility to the creator of a Record and safer use to anyone consuming it.

Serializing Evolving Records

Records, like classes, are automatically serializable if they implement the empty marker interface `java.io.Serializable`. The serialization process of Records follows a more flexible and safer serialization strategy compared to classes, though, without requiring any additional code.

 The full serialization process consists of *serialization* (converting an object to a byte stream) and *deserialization* (reading an object from a byte stream). If not explicitly mentioned, serialization describes the whole process, not only the first aspect.

Serialization of ordinary, non-Record objects relies heavily on costly[9] reflection to access their private state. This process is customizable by implementing the `private` methods `readObject` and `writeObject` in a type. These two methods aren't provided by any interface but are still part of the Java Object Serialization Specification (*https://oreil.ly/S2YiO*). They're hard to get right and have led to many exploits in the past.[10]

Records are defined only by their immutable state, represented by their components. Without any code being able to affect the state after creation, the serialization process is quite simple:

- Serialization is based solely on the Record's components.
- Deserialization only requires the canonical constructor, not reflection.

Once the JVM derives the serialized form of a Record, a matching instantiator can be cached. Customizing that process isn't possible, which actually leads to a safer serialization process by giving the JVM control of the Record's serialized representation. This allows any Record type to evolve further by adding new components while still successfully deserializing from previously serialized data. Any unknown component encountered during deserialization without a value present will automatically use its *default value* (e.g., `null` for object-based types, `false` for `boolean`, etc.).

 Be aware that the code examples for serialization won't work as expected when using JShell. The internal class names won't be identical after replacing the Record definition, so the types won't match.

---

9 The word "cost" regarding reflection is associated with the incurred performance overhead and exposure to security problems. Reflection uses dynamically resolved type information, which prevents the JVM from utilizing all its possible optimizations. Consequently, reflection has slower performance than its nonreflective counterparts.

10 The method `readObject` can execute arbitrary code instead of simply reading the object. Some related CVEs: CVE-2019-6503 (*https://oreil.ly/-nsaI*), CVE-2019-12630 (*https://oreil.ly/dEFRd*), CVE-2018-1851 (*https://oreil.ly/F8LFk*).

Let's say you have a two-dimensional record `Point(float x, float y)` that you want to serialize. The following code doesn't hold any surprises:

```
public record Point(int x, int y) implements Serializable {
  // NO BODY
}

var point = new Point(23, 42);
// => Point[x=23, y=42]

try (var out = new ObjectOutputStream(new FileOutputStream("point.data"))) {
  out.writeObject(point);
}
```

As requirements change, you need to include the third dimension to the Record, z, as shown in the following code:

```
public record Point(int x, int y, int z) implements Serializable {
  // NO BODY
}
```

What will happen if you try to deserialize the `point.data` file into the changed Record? Let's find out:

```
var in = new ObjectInputStream(new FileInputStream("point.data"));

var point = in.readObject();
// => Point[x=23, y=42, z=0]
```

It just works.

The new component, which is missing from the serialized representation in `points.data` and therefore can't provide a value for the Record's canonical constructor, is initialized with the corresponding default value for its type, in this case, 0 (zero) for an `int`.

As mentioned in "Records" on page 72, Records are effectively nominal tuples, making them solely based on their components' names and types, not their exact order. That's why even changing the components' order won't break its deserialization capabilities:

```
public record Point(int z, int y, int x) implements Serializable {
  // NO BODY
}

var in = new ObjectInputStream(new FileInputStream("point.data"));

var point = in.readObject();
// => Point[z=0, y=42, x=23]
```

Removing components is also possible, as any missing component is ignored during deserialization.

One general caveat exists, though.

From the viewpoint of a single Record, it's solely defined by its components. For the Java serialization process, however, the type of what's serialized is relevant, too. That's why even if two Records have identical components, they're not interchangeable. You will encounter a `ClassCastException` if you try to deserialize into another type with identical components:

```
public record Point(int x, int y) implements Serializable {
  // NO BODY
}

try (var out = new ObjectOutputStream(new FileOutputStream("point.data"))) {
  out.writeObject(new Point(23, 42));
}

public record IdenticalPoint(int x, int y) implements Serializable {
  // NO BODY
}

var in = new ObjectInputStream(new FileInputStream("point.data"));
IdenticalPoint point = in.readObject();
// Error:
// incompatible types: java.lang.Object cannot be converted to IdenticalPoint
```

The incompatibility of serializing different types with identical components is a side effect of the "simpler but safer" serialization process used by Records. Without the possibility of manually affecting the serialization process, like traditional Java objects can do, you might need to migrate already serialized data. The most straightforward approach would be deserializing the old data into the old type, converting it to the new type, and serializing it as the new type.

Record Pattern Matching (Java 19+)

Even though this book is targeted at Java 11 while trying to be helpful with a few newer additions, I want to tell you about an upcoming feature still in development at the time of writing: *Record-based pattern matching* (JEP 405 (*https://oreil.ly/68o_a*)).

 JDK preview features are new features of the Java language, JVM, or the Java API that are fully specified, implemented, and yet impermanent. The general idea is to gather feedback on real-world use so that the feature might become permanent in a future release.

Java 16 introduced pattern matching for the `instanceof` operator,[11] thus removing the necessity of a cast after using the operator:

```
// PREVIOUSLY
if (obj instanceof String) {
  String str = (String) obj;
  // ...
}

// JAVA 16+
if (obj instanceof String str) {
    // ...
}
```

Java 17 and 18 expanded on the idea by enabling pattern matching for the `switch` expressions[12] as a preview feature:

```
// WITHOUT SWITCH PATTERN MATCHING
String formatted = "unknown";
if (obj instanceof Integer i) {
  formatted = String.format("int %d", i);
} else if (obj instanceof Long l) {
  formatted = String.format("long %d", l);
} else if (obj instanceof String str) {
  formatted = String.format("String %s", str);
}

// WITH SWITCH PATTERN MATCHING
String formatted = switch (obj) {
  case Integer i -> String.format("int %d", i);
  case Long l    -> String.format("long %d", l);
  case String s  -> String.format("String %s", s);
  default        -> "unknown";
};
```

Java 19+ includes both these features for Records, too, including destructuring[13], which means a Record's components are directly available as variables in the scope:

```
record Point(int x, int y) {
  // NO BODY
};

var point = new Point(23, 42);

if (point instanceof Point(int x, int y)) {
```

---

11 The extension of the `instanceof` operator to support *pattern matching* is summarized in JEP 394 (*https:// oreil.ly/tJ4EJ*).

12 Pattern Matching for `switch` is summarized in JEP 406 (*https://oreil.ly/dckrm*) and JEP 420 (*https://oreil.ly/ noIWq*).

13 Pattern Matching for Records is summarized in JEP 405 (*https://oreil.ly/FDBQZ*).

```
    System.out.println(x + y);
    // => 65
}

int result = switch (anyObject) {
    case Point(var x, var y) -> x + y;
    case Point3D(var x, var y, var z) -> x + y + z;
    default -> 0.0;
};
```

As you can see, the Records feature is still evolving, with exciting new features like pattern matching improving its feature set, making it a more versatile and flexible data aggregator type that simplifies your code.

Final Thoughts on Records

Java's new data aggregator type, Records, provides a great deal of simplicity with as little code as possible. It's achieved by adhering to specific rules and restrictions, which might seem arbitrary and confining initially, but it gives you safer and more consistent use. Records aren't supposed to be a one-size-fits-all solution for data storage and state to completely replace all POJOs or other preexisting data aggregator types. They're merely providing a new option fitting for a more functional and immutable approach.

The available feature set was chosen deliberately to create a new type of state representation, and *only* state. The simplicity of defining a new Record discourages the reuse of an abstraction type just because it might be more convenient than creating a new and more fitting one.

Records might not be as flexible as POJOs or custom types. But flexibility usually means more complexity, which often increases bug surface. The best way to deal with complexity is to reduce its surface as much as possible, and Records give you a lot of safe functionality "for free" and won't break as easily if their components evolve.

Takeaways

- Records are transparent data aggregator types solely defined by their components.

- Most features you're used to from classes, like implementing interfaces, generics, or annotations, are usable with Records, too.

- The typical boilerplate for a canonical constructor, component accessors, object identity, and object description is available in any Record type without additional code. If necessary, you can override each one of them.

- Records have certain restrictions to ensure their safe and simplistic use. Many of the missing features—at least compared to more flexible solutions like POJOs or JavaBeans—can be retrofitted with either JDK-only code or tools like annotation processing.
- Adhering to common practices like validation and a systematic approach to modified copies creates a consistent user experience.
- Records provide a safer and more flexible serialization solution than their class-based relatives.

CHAPTER 6

Data Processing with Streams

Almost any program has to deal with processing data, most likely in the form of Collections. An imperative approach uses loops to iterate over elements, working with each element in sequence. Functional languages, though, prefer a declarative approach and sometimes don't even have a classical loop statement to begin with.

The *Streams API*, introduced in Java 8, provides a fully declarative and lazily evaluated approach to processing data that benefits from Java's functional additions by utilizing higher-order functions for most of its operations.

This chapter will teach you the differences between imperative and declarative data processing. You will then have a visual introduction to Streams that highlights their underlying concepts and shows you how to get the most out of their flexibility to achieve a more functional approach to data processing.

Data Processing with Iteration

Processing data is an everyday task you've probably encountered a million times before and will continue to do in the future.

From a broad point of view, any type of data processing works like a pipeline, with a data structure like a Collection providing elements, one or more operations like filtering or transforming elements, and finally, delivering some form of a result. The result might be another data structure or even using it to run another task.

Let's start with a simple data processing example.

External Iteration

Say that we need to find the three science fiction books before 1970 sorted by title from a list of Book instances. Example 6-1 shows how to do this using a typical imperative approach with a for-loop.

Example 6-1. Finding books with a for-loop

```
record Book(String title, int year, Genre genre) {
    // NO BODY
}

// DATA PREPARATION

List<Book> books = ...; ❶

Collections.sort(books, Comparator.comparing(Book::title)); ❷

// FOR-LOOP

List<String> result = new ArrayList<>();

for (var book : books) {
    if (book.year() >= 1970) { ❸
        continue;
    }

    if (book.genre() != Genre.SCIENCE_FICTION) { ❸
        continue;
    }

    var title = book.title(); ❹
    result.add(title);

    if (result.size() == 3) { ❺
        break;
    }
}
```

❶ An unsorted Collection of books. It must be mutable, so it can be sorted in place in the next step.

❷ The List<Book> has to be sorted first, or the elements in result won't be the first three titles in alphabetical order.

❸ Ignore any unwanted books, like the ones not published before 1970 or not science fiction.

❹ The book `title` is all we are interested in.

❺ Restrict the found titles to a maximum of three.

Although the code works for what it needs to do, it has several shortcomings compared to other approaches. The most obvious downside is the amount of boilerplate code required for an iteration-based loop.

Loop statements, either a `for-` or `while`-loop, contain their data processing logic in their body, to create a new scope for each iteration. Depending on your requirements, the loop's body contains multiple statements, including decision-making about the iteration process itself in the form of `continue` and `break`. Overall, the data processing code is obscured by all this boilerplate and doesn't present itself fluently, nor is it easily followable, especially for a more complex loop than the previous example.

The origin of these problems is blending "what you are doing" (working with data) and "how it's done" (iterating over elements). This kind of iteration is called *external iteration*. Behind the scenes, the for-loop, in this case, the `for-each` variant, uses a `java.util.Iterator<E>` to traverse the Collection. The traversal process calls `hasNext` and `next` to control the iteration, as illustrated in Figure 6-1.

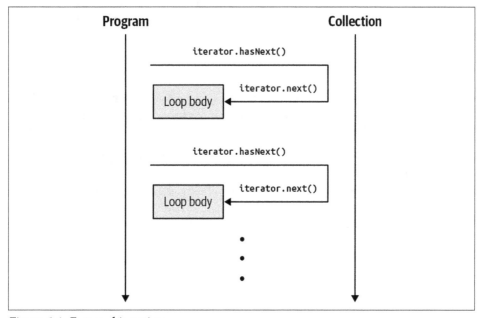

Figure 6-1. External iteration

In the case of a "traditional" for-loop, you have to manage going over the elements until an end condition is reached, which in a way is similar to an Iterator<E> and the hasNext and next method.

If you count the number of code lines that have to do with "what you're doing" and "how it's done," you'll notice that it spends more time on traversal management than data processing, as detailed in Table 6-1.

Table 6-1. Lines of code per data processing per task

Task	Lines of code
Data preparation Sorting the initial data and preparing a result Collection	2
Traversal process Looping and controlling the loop with continue and break	4
Data processing Choosing, transforming, and gathering the correct elements and data	4

However, requiring a lot of boilerplate code to traverse isn't the only drawback associated with external iteration. Another downside is the inherent serial traversal process. You need to rework the whole loop if you require parallel data processing, and you'll have to deal with all the associated gotchas, like the dreaded Concurrent ModificationException.

Internal Iteration

The opposite approach to external iteration is, you guessed it, *internal iteration*. With internal iteration, you give up explicit control of the traversal process and let the data source itself handle "how it's done," as illustrated in Figure 6-2.

Instead of using an iterator to control the traversal, the data processing logic is prepared beforehand to build a pipeline that does the iteration by itself. The iteration process becomes more opaque, but the logic influences which elements traverse the pipeline. This way, you can focus your energy and code on "what you want to do" rather than on the tedious and often repetitive details of "how it's done."

Streams are such data pipelines with internal iteration.

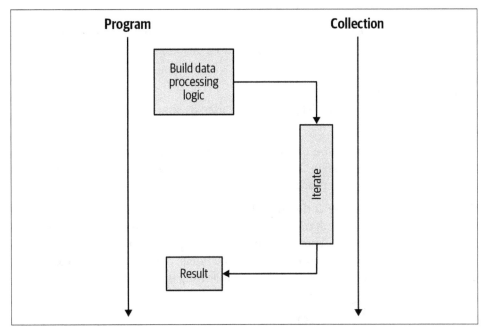

Figure 6-2. Internal iteration

Streams as Functional Data Pipelines

Streams, as a data processing approach, get the job done like any other, but have specific advantages due to having an internal iterator. These advantages are especially beneficial from a functional point of view. The advantages are:

Declarative approach
Build concise and comprehensible multistep data processing pipelines with a single fluent call chain.

Composability
Stream operations provide a scaffold made of higher-order functions to be filled with data processing logic. They can be mixed as needed. If you design their logic in a functional way, you automatically gain all their advantages, like composability.

Laziness
Instead of iteration over all elements, they get pulled one by one through the pipeline after the last operation is attached to it, reducing the required amount of operations to a minimum.

Performance optimization

Streams optimize the traversal process automatically depending on their data source and different kinds of operations used, including short-circuiting operations if possible.

Parallel data processing

Built-in support for parallel processing is used by simply changing a single call in the call chain.

In concept, Streams could be considered just another alternative to traditional loop constructs for data processing. In reality, though, Streams are special in *how* they go about providing those data processing capabilities.

The first thing to consider is the overall Stream workflow. Streams can be summed up as *lazy sequential data pipelines*. Such pipelines are a higher-level abstraction for traversing sequential data. They are sequences of higher-order functions to process their elements in a fluent, expressive, and functional way. The general workflow is illustrated in Figure 6-3 and explained in the following three steps.

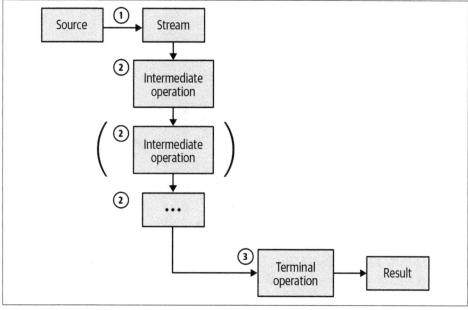

Figure 6-3. The basic concept of Java Streams

(1) Creating a Stream

The first step is creating a Stream out of an existing data source. Streams aren't limited to Collection-like types, though. Any data source that can provide sequential elements is a possible data source for a Stream.

(2) Doing the work

So-called *intermediate operations*—higher-order functions available as methods on the `java.util.stream.Stream<T>`—work on the elements passing through the pipeline, doing different tasks, like filtering, mapping, sorting, etc. Each one returns a new Stream, which can be connected with as many intermediate operations as needed.

(3) Getting a result

To finish the data processing pipeline, a final—*terminal*—operation is needed to get back a result instead of a Stream. Such a terminal operation completes the Stream pipeline blueprint and starts the actual data processing.

To see this in action, let's revisit the earlier task of finding three science fiction book titles before 1970. This time, instead of using a for-loop as we did in Example 6-1, we will use a Stream pipeline in Example 6-2. Don't worry too much about the Stream code yet; I'll explain the various methods shortly. Read through it, and you should be able to get the gist of it for now.

Example 6-2. Finding books with a Stream

```
List<Book> books = ...; ❶

List<String> result =
  books.stream()
        .filter(book -> book.year() < 1970) ❷
        .filter(book -> book.genre() == Genre.SCIENCE_FICTION) ❸
        .map(Book::title) ❹
        .sorted() ❺
        .limit(3L) ❻
        .collect(Collectors.toList()); ❼
```

❶ An unsorted collection of books.

❷ Only include books published before 1970.

❸ Only include science fiction books.

❹ Transform the element from the whole Book element to its title value.

❺ Sort the titles.

❻ Restrict the found titles to a maximum of three.

❼ Aggregate the titles into a new List<String> instance.

From a high-level point of view, implementations shown in both Examples 6-1 and 6-2 represent pipelines that elements can traverse, with multiple exit points for unwanted data. But notice how the functionality of the for-loop with its multiple statements is now condensed into a singular fluent Stream call.

This leads us to how Streams optimize the flow of their elements. You don't have to explicitly manage the traversal with continue or break because the elements will traverse the pipeline depending on the result of the operations. Figure 6-4 illustrates how the different Stream operations affect the element flow of Example 6-2.

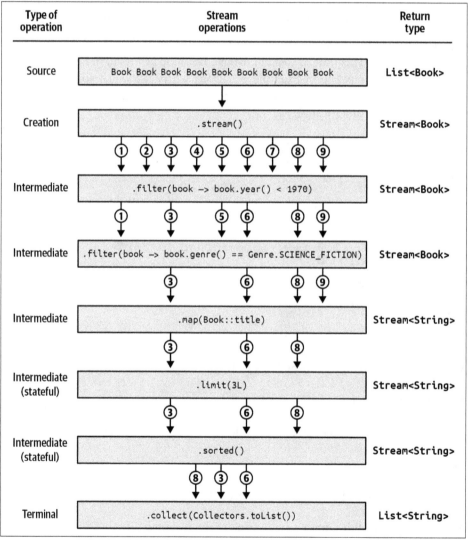

Figure 6-4. Flow of Book elements through the Stream pipeline

The elements flow one by one through the Stream and are funneled to the least amount needed to process the data.

Instead of needing to prepare the data beforehand and wrapping the processing logic in a loop statement's body, Streams are built with a fluent class of the different processing steps. Like other functional approaches, Stream code reflects "what" is happening in a more expressive and declarative fashion, without the typical verbiage of "how" it's actually done.

Stream Features

Streams are a functional API with specific behaviors and expectations built in. In a way, this confines their possibilities, at least compared to the blank canvas of traditional loops. By being nonblank canvases, though, they provide you with lots of predefined building blocks and guaranteed properties that you would have to create yourself with alternative approaches.

Lazy evaluation

The most significant advantage of Streams over loops is their laziness. Each time you call an intermediate operation on a Stream, it's not applied immediately. Instead, the call simply "extends" the pipeline further and returns a new lazily evaluated Stream. The pipeline accumulates all operations, and no work starts before you call its terminal operation, which will trigger the actual element traversal, as seen in Figure 6-5.

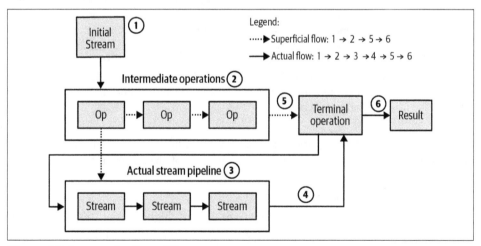

Figure 6-5. Lazy evaluation of Streams

Instead of providing all elements to a code block, like a loop, the terminal operation is asking for more data as needed, and the Stream tries to comply. Streams, as a data source, don't have to "overprovide" or buffer any elements if no one is requesting more elements. If you look back at Figure 6-4, that means not every element will traverse through every operation.

The flow of Stream elements follows a "depth-first" approach, reducing the required CPU cycles, memory footprint, and stack depth. This way, even infinite data sources are possible because the pipeline is responsible for requesting the required elements and terminating the Stream.

You can read more about the importance of laziness in functional programming in Chapter 11.

(Mostly) stateless and non-interfering

As you've learned in Chapter 4, an immutable state is an essential functional programming concept, and Streams do their best to adhere. Almost all intermediate operations are stateless and detached from the rest of the pipeline, having access only to the current element they're processing. Certain intermediate operations, however, require some form of state to fulfill their purpose, like limit or skip.

Another advantage of using Streams is their separation of the data source and the elements themselves. That way, operations won't affect the underlying data source in any way, nor does the Stream itself store any elements.

 Even though you can create Java stateful lambdas with side effects, you should strive to design the behavioral arguments of your data manipulation pipelines stateless and as pure functions. Any dependence on an out-of-scope state can severely impact safety and performance and make the whole pipeline nondeterministic and incorrect due to unintended side effects. One exception is certain terminal operations for doing "side-effect-only" code, which can help immensely to fit functional Stream pipelines in existing imperative designs.

Streams are *non-interfering* and *pass-through* pipelines that will let their elements traverse as freely as possible without interference, if not absolutely necessary.

Optimizations included

The internal iteration and fundamental design of higher-order functions allow Streams to optimize themselves quite efficiently. They utilize multiple techniques to improve their performance:

- Fusion[1] of (stateless) operations
- Removal of redundant operations
- Short-circuiting pipeline paths

Iteration-related code optimizations aren't restricted to Streams, though. Traditional loops get optimized by the JVM, too, if possible[2].

Also, loops like `for` and `while` are language features, and they can therefore be optimized to another degree. Streams are ordinary types with all the costs affiliated with them. They still need to be created by wrapping a data source, and the pipeline is a call chain requiring a new stack frame for each call. In most real-world scenarios, their general advantages outweigh the possible performance impact of such an overhead compared to a built-in statement like `for` or `while`.

Less boilerplate

As seen in Example 6-2, Streams condense data processing into a singular fluent method call chain. The call is designed to consist of small and on-point operations like `filter`, `map`, or `findFirst`, providing an expressive and straightforward scaffold around the data processing logic. Call chains should be easy to grasp, both visually and conceptually. Therefore, a Stream pipeline consumes as little visual real estate and cognitive bandwidth as necessary.

Non-reusable

Stream pipelines are single-use only. They're bound to their data source and traverse them exactly once after the terminal operation is called.

If you try to use a Stream again, an `IllegalStateException` gets thrown. You can't check if a Stream is already consumed, though.

As Streams don't change or affect their underlying data source, you can always create another Stream from the same data source.

Primitive streams

As with the functional interfaces introduced in Chapter 2, the Stream API contains specialized variants for dealing with primitives to minimize autoboxing overhead.

---

1 Brian Goetz, the Java Language Architect at Oracle, explains fusing operations on StackOverflow (*https://oreil.ly/vza0A*).

2 Chris Newland and Ben Evans, "Loop Unrolling: An elaborate mechanism for reducing loop iterations improves performance but can be thwarted by inadvertent coding," *Java Magazine* (2019) (*https://oreil.ly/Qo7wk*).

Both Stream and the specialized variants IntStream, LongStream, and DoubleStream, share a common base interface, BaseStream, as illustrated in Figure 6-6. Many of the available primitive Stream operations mirror their non-primitive counterparts, but not all of them.

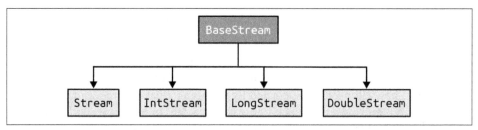

Figure 6-6. Stream type hierarchy

That's why I discuss in Chapter 7 when to use a primitive Stream and how to switch between non-primitive and primitive Streams with a single operation.

Easy parallelization

Data processing with traditional loop constructs is inherently serial. Concurrency is hard to do right and easy to do wrong, especially if you have to do it yourself. Streams are designed to support parallel execution from the ground up, utilizing the Fork/Join framework (*https://oreil.ly/fTN30*) introduced with Java 7.

Parallelizing a Stream is done by simply calling the parallel method at any point of the pipeline. However, not every Stream pipeline is a good match for parallel processing. The Stream source must have enough elements, and the operations have to be costly enough to justify the overhead of multiple threads. Switching threads—so-called context switches (*https://oreil.ly/kwBFq*)—is an expensive task.

In Chapter 8, you'll learn more about parallel Stream processing and concurrency in general.

(Lack of) Exception handling

Streams do a great job of reducing the verbosity of your code by introducing a functional approach to data processing. However, this doesn't make them immune to dealing with Exceptions in their operations.

Lambda expressions, and therefore the logic of Stream operations, don't have any special considerations or syntactic sugar to handle Exceptions more concisely than you're used to with try-catch. You can read more about the general problem of Exceptions in functional Java code and how to handle them in different ways in Chapter 10.

Spliterator, the Backbone of Streams

Just like the traditional *for-each* loop is built around the `Iterator<T>` type for traversing a sequence of elements, Streams have their own iteration interface: `java.util.Spliterator<T>`.

The `Iterator` type is based solely on the concept of "next" with only a few methods, which makes it a universal iterator for Java's Collection API. The concept behind `Spliterator`, however, is that it has the ability to split off a subsequence of its elements into another `Spliterator` based on certain characteristics. This particular advantage over the `Iterator` type makes it the core of the Stream API and allows Streams to process such subsequences in parallel and still be able to iterate over Java Collection API types.

Example 6-3 shows a simplified variant of `java.util.Spliterator`.

Example 6-3. The `java.util.Spliterator` interface

```java
public interface Spliterator<T> {

    // CHARACTERISTICS
    int characteristics();
    default boolean hasCharacteristics(int characteristics) {
        // ...
    }

    // ITERATION
    boolean tryAdvance(Consumer<? super T> action);
    default void forEachRemaining(Consumer<? super T> action) {
        // ...
    }

    // SPLITTING
    Spliterator<T> trySplit();

    // SIZE
    long estimateSize();
    default long getExactSizeIfKnown() {
        // ...
    }

    // COMPARATOR
    default Comparator<? super T> getComparator() {
        // ...
    }
}
```

The `boolean tryAdvance(Consumer action)` and `Spliterator<T> trySplit()` methods are the most important for the iteration process. Still, a Spliterator's characteristics decree the capabilities of all its operations.

Regarding Streams, the Spliterator's characteristics are responsible for how a Stream iterates internally and what optimizations it supports. There are eight combinable characteristics, defined as `static int` constants on the `Spliterator` type, as listed in Table 6-2. Even though it looks like the characteristics match expected Stream behavior, not all of them are actually used in the current Stream implementations.

Table 6-2. Spliterator characteristics

Characteristic	Description
CONCURRENT	The underlying data source can safely be concurrently modified during traversal. Affects only the data source itself and has no implications for Stream behavior.
DISTINCT	The data source contains only unique elements, like a `Set<E>`. Any pair of elements in a Stream is guaranteed to be `x.equals(y) == false`.
IMMUTABLE	The data source itself is immutable. No element can be added, replaced, or removed during traversal. Affects only the data source itself and has no implications for Stream behavior.
NONNULL	The underlying data source guarantees not to contain any `null` values. Affects only the data source itself and has no implications for Stream behavior.
ORDERED	There is a defined order for the elements of the data source. During traversal, the encountered elements will be in that particular order.
SORTED	If the `Spliterator<T>` is SORTED, its `getComparator()` method returns the associated `Comparator<T>`, or `null`, if the source is naturally sorted. SORTED `Spliterator`s must also be ORDERED.
SIZED	The data source knows its exact size. `estimateSize()` returns the actual size, not an estimate.
SUBSIZED	Signifies that all split-up chunks after calling `trySplit()` are also SIZED. Affects only the data source itself and has no implications for Stream behavior.

Stream characteristics don't have to be fixed and can depend on the underlying data source. `HashSet` is an example of a Spliterator with dynamic characteristics. It uses the nested `HashMap.KeySpliterator` class, which depends on the actual data, as seen in Example 6-4.

Example 6-4. Spliterator characteristics of `HashSet`

```
public int characteristics() {
    return (fence < 0 || est == map.size ? Spliterator.SIZED : 0) |
            Spliterator.DISTINCT;
}
```

The way `HashSet` creates its `KeySpliterator` shows that a Spliterator can use its surrounding context to make an informed decision about its capabilities.

You don't need to think much about a Stream's characteristics most of the time. Usually, the underlying capabilities of a data source won't change *magically* just because it's traversed with a Stream. A Set<E> will still provide distinct elements in an unordered fashion, regardless of being used with a for-loop or a Stream. So choose the most fitting data source for the task, no matter the form of traversal used.

When using Streams, you usually don't need to create a Spliterator yourself, as the convenience methods I'm going to discuss in the next chapter will do it behind the scenes for you. Still, if you need to create a Spliterator for a custom data structure, you don't necessarily have to implement the interface yourself, either. You can use one of the many convenience methods of java.util.Spliterators instead. The easiest variant is the following method:

```
<T> Spliterator<T> spliterator(Iterator<? extends T> iterator,
                               long size,
                               int characteristics)
```

The resulting Spliterator might not be the most optimized Spliterator, with only limited parallel support, but it's the simplest way to use existing Iterator-compatible data structures in Streams that don't support them out of the box.

Check out the official documentation (*https://oreil.ly/OPDTT*) for more information about the 20+ convenience methods provided by the java.util.Spliterators type.

Building Stream Pipelines

The Stream API is extensive, and a detailed explanation of each operation and possible use case could easily fill an entire book. Let's take a higher-level view of building Stream pipelines with the available higher-order functions instead. This overview still will help you replace many data processing tasks with Stream pipelines in your code, especially those following the *map/filter/reduce* philosophy.

Map/Filter/Reduce

Most data processing follows the same scheme and can be distilled to only three elemental kinds of operations:

Map
    Transforming data

Filter
    Choosing data

Reduce
    Deriving a result

In many functional languages, these three steps have more explicit meanings, though. They are readily available functions on Collection types and are the building blocks for any data processing.

The map/filter/reduce pattern treats a sequence of elements as a unit. It allows the removal of any control statements using internal iteration by combining self-contained, pure functions into a bigger chain of operations.

As you might have guessed from the description, Java Streams fit nicely into this pattern. Every single Stream operation falls into one of the three kinds. Intermediate operations represent map and filter steps, and terminal operations the reduce step.

The Stream API actually has operations named `map`, `filter`, and `reduce`. Still, it provides a lot more operations. The logic of most of these additional operations can be replicated by the three others, and internally, that's often the case. The extra operations give you a convenient way to avoid implementing common use cases yourself, with many different specialized operations readily available to you.

Creating a Stream

Every Stream pipeline starts with creating a new Stream instance from an existing data source. The most commonly used data sources are Collection types. That's why the three methods `Stream<E> stream()`, `Stream<E> parallelStream()`, and `Spliterator<E> spliterator()` were retrofitted to `java.util.Collection` with the introduction of Streams in Java 8, as seen in Example 6-5.

Example 6-5. Simplified Stream creation for `Collection<E>`-based types

```java
public interface Collection<E> extends Iterable<E> {

  default Stream<E> stream() {
    return StreamSupport.stream(spliterator(), false);
  }

  default Stream<E> parallelStream() {
    return StreamSupport.stream(spliterator(), true);
  }

  @Override
  default Spliterator<E> spliterator() {
    return Spliterators.spliterator(this, 0);
  }

  // ...
}
```

The `stream` method is the simplest way to create a new Stream instance from any `Collection`-based data structure, like `List` or `Set`. It utilizes an `IMMUTABLE` and `CONCURRENT` `Spliterator` as its default implementation. However, many `Collection` types provide their own implementations with optimized characteristics and behavior.

Even though the `stream` method on `Collection` might be the most convenient method to create a Stream, the JDK provides many other ways to create Streams as `static` convenience methods, like `Stream.of(T... values)`. In Chapter 7, you'll learn more ways to create Streams for different use cases, like infinite Streams or working with I/O.

Doing the Work

Now that you have a Stream, the next step is working with its elements.

Working with Stream elements is done by *intermediate operations*, which fall into three categories: transforming (*map*) elements, selecting (*filter*) elements, or modifying general Stream behavior.

 All Stream operations are aptly named and have ample documentation (*https://oreil.ly/uj3YQ*) and examples. Many methods use the "not yet a standard" addition to JavaDoc[3] `@implSpec` to refer to implementation-specific behavior. So make sure to check out either the online documentation or the JavaDoc itself in case your IDE isn't rendering all of the documentation correctly.

In this section, I will be using a simple `Shape` Record, shown in Example 6-6, to demonstrate the different operations.

Example 6-6. A simple Shape type

```
public record Shape(int corners) implements Comparable<Shape> {

  // HELPER METHODS

  public boolean hasCorners() {
    return corners() > 0;
  }

  public List<Shape> twice() {
```

---

3 Even though there are several new annotations used in JavaDoc since the release of Java 8, they aren't an *official* standard as of writing this book. The informal proposal is available at the official OpenJDK bug tracker as JDK-8068562 (*https://oreil.ly/1xIaS*).

```
    return List.of(this, this);
  }

  @Override
  public int compareTo(Shape o) {
    return Integer.compare(corners(), o.corners());
  }

  // FACTORY METHODS

  public static Shape circle() {
    return new Shape(0);
  }

  public static Shape triangle() {
    return new Shape(3);
  }

  public static Shape square() {
    return new Shape(4);
  }
}
```

There won't be a dedicated code example for every operation, as there are just too many. However, each operation and its element flow are illustrated.

Selecting elements

The first common task of data processing is selecting the correct elements, either by filtering with a `Predicate` or by choosing based on the number of elements.

`Stream<T> filter(Predicate<? super T> predicate)`
    The most straightforward way of filtering elements. If the `Predicate` evaluates to `true`, the element is considered for further processing. The `static` method `Predicate.not(Predicate<? super T> target)` allows for an easy negation of a Predicate without losing the advantage of method references. Common tasks, like `null` checks, are available via the `java.util.Objects` class and are usable as method references. See Figure 6-7.

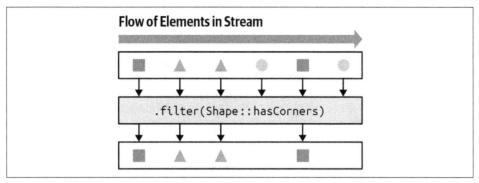

Figure 6-7. *Stream<T> filter(Predicate<? super T> predicate)*

Stream<T> dropWhile(Predicate<? super T> predicate)

Discards—or *drops*—any element passing through the operation as long as the Predicate evaluates to true. This operation is designed for ORDERED Streams. The dropped elements won't be deterministic if the Stream isn't ORDERED. For sequential Streams, dropping elements is a cheap operation. A parallel Stream, though, has to coordinate between the underlying threads, making the operation quite costly. The operation was introduced with Java 9. See Figure 6-8.

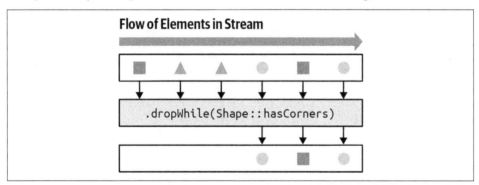

Figure 6-8. *Stream<T> dropWhile(Predicate<? super T> predicate)*

`Stream<T> takeWhile(Predicate<? super T> predicate)`

The antagonist to `dropWhile`, choosing elements until the `Predicate` evaluates to `false`. The operation was introduced with Java 9. See Figure 6-9.

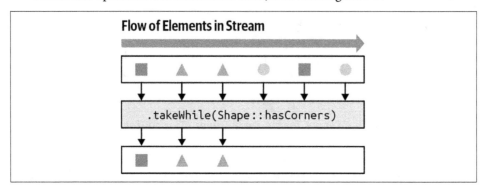

Figure 6-9. Stream<T> takeWhile(Predicate<? super T> predicate)

`Stream<T> limit(long maxSize)`

Limits the maximum number of elements passing through this operation to `maxSize`. See Figure 6-10.

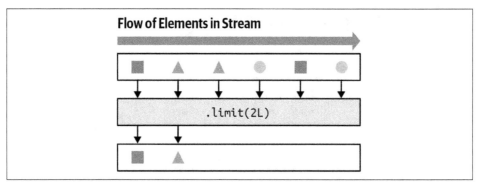

Figure 6-10. Stream<T> limit(long maxSize)

`Stream<T> skip(long n)`

The antagonist to `limit`, skipping n elements before passing all remaining elements to the subsequent Stream operations. See Figure 6-11.

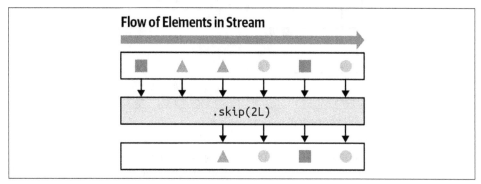

Figure 6-11. `Stream<T> skip(long n)`

`Stream<T> distinct()`

Compares elements with `Object#equals(Object)` to return only distinct elements. This operation needs to buffer all elements passing through to compare them. There's no integrated way to provide a custom `Comparator<T>` to determine distinctness. See Figure 6-12.

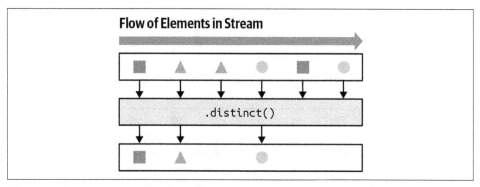

Figure 6-12. `Stream<T> distinct()`

`Stream<T> sorted()`

Sorts the elements in their natural order if they conform to `java.util.Comparable`. Otherwise, a `java.lang.ClassCastException` is thrown on Stream consumption. Figure 6-13 assumes the natural sorting for shapes is by their number of corners. This operation needs to buffer all elements passing through to sort them. See Figure 6-13.

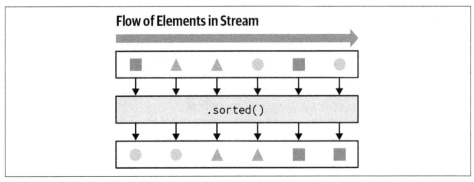

Figure 6-13. Stream<T> sorted()

`Stream<T> sorted(Comparator<? super T> comparator)`
  A more flexible version of `sorted` where you can provide a custom `comparator`.

Mapping elements

Another significant category of operation is *mapping*, or transforming, elements. Not many Streams and their elements start out in the desired form. Sometimes you need a different representation or are interested only in a subset of an element's properties.

Initially, only two mapping operations were available to Streams:

`Stream<R> map(Function<? super T, ? extends R> mapper)`
  The `mapper` function is applied to the elements, and the new element is returned down the Stream. See Figure 6-14.

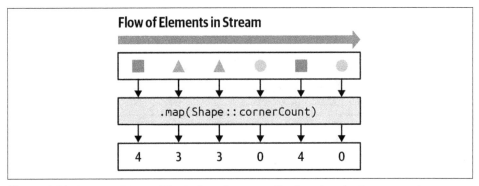

Figure 6-14. Stream<R> map(Function<? super T, ? extends R> mapper)

```
Stream<R> flatMap(Function<? super T, ? extends Stream<? extends R>>
mapper)
```
The mapper function is still applied to the elements. However, instead of returning a new element, a Stream<R> needs to be returned. If map were used, the result
would be a nested Stream<Stream<R>>, which is most likely not what you want.
The flatMap operation "flattens" a container-like element, like a Collection or
Optional, into a new Stream of multiple elements, which are used in subsequent
operations. See Figure 6-15.

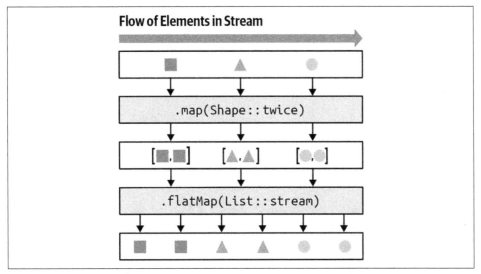

*Figure 6-15. Stream<R> flatMap(Function<? super T, ? extends Stream<?
extends R>> mapper)*

Java 16 introduced an additional mapping method (and its three primitive counterparts) that has a similar role as flatMap:

```
Stream<R> mapMulti(BiConsumer<? super T, ? super Consumer<R>> mapper)
```
The mapMulti operation doesn't require the mapper to return a Stream instance.
Instead, a Consumer<R> conveys the elements further down the Stream.

In its current form, the Shape type doesn't lead to cleaner code when the mapMulti
operation is used, as seen in Example 6-7.

Example 6-7. Shape flatMap versus mapMulti

```
// FLATMAP
Stream<Shape> flatMap =
  Stream.of(Shape.square(), Shape.triangle(), Shape.circle())
      .map(Shape::twice)
      .flatMap(List::stream);

// MAPMULTI
Stream<Shape> mapMulti =
  Stream.of(Shape.square(), Shape.triangle(), Shape.circle())
      .mapMulti((shape, downstream) -> shape.twice()
                                     .forEach(downstream::accept));
```

The winner in terms of conciseness and readability is clearly flatMap. Still, the main advantage of multiMap is that it condenses two operations, map and flatMap, into a single one.

The default implementation of mapMulti actually uses flatMap to create a new Stream for you, so your mapped elements don't need to know how to create a Stream themselves. By calling the downstream Consumer yourself, *you* decide which mapped elements belong to the new Stream, and the pipeline is responsible for creating it.

The mapMulti operation isn't supposed to replace flatMap. They are merely a complementary addition to Stream's repertoire of operations. However, there are use cases where mapMulti is preferable to flatMap:

- Only a small number of elements, or even zero, are mapped down the Stream pipeline. Using mapMulti avoids the overhead of creating a new Stream for every group of mapped elements, as done by flatMap.
- When an iterative approach to providing the mapped results is more straightforward than creating a new Stream instance. This gives you more freedom for the mapping process before feeding an element to the Consumer.

Peeking into a stream

One intermediate operation doesn't fit into the map/filter/reduce philosophy: peek.

The conciseness of Streams can pack a lot of functionality into a singular fluent call. Even though that's one of their main selling points, debugging them is way more challenging than traditional imperative loop constructs. To ease this pain point, the Stream API includes a particular operation, peek(Consumer<? super T> action), which, well, "peeks" into a Stream without interfering with the elements, as seen in Example 6-8.

Example 6-8. Peeking into a Stream

```
List<Shape> result =
  Stream.of(Shape.square(), Shape.triangle(), Shape.circle())
      .map(Shape::twice)
      .flatMap(List::stream)
      .peek(shape -> System.out.println("current: " + shape))
      .filter(shape -> shape.corners() < 4)
      .collect(Collectors.toList());

// OUTPUT:
// current: Shape[corners=4]
// current: Shape[corners=4]
// current: Shape[corners=3]
// current: Shape[corners=3]
// current: Shape[corners=0]
// current: Shape[corners=0]
```

The peek operation is mainly intended to support debugging. It might get skipped for optimizing the Stream if the operation isn't necessarily required for the final result, like counting elements, and the pipeline can get short-circuited.

The short-circuiting of operations will be explained more in "The Cost of Operations" on page 151.

Terminating the Stream

A *terminal* operation is the final step of a Stream pipeline that initiates the actual processing of the elements to produce a result or side effect. Unlike intermediate operations and their delayed nature, terminal operations evaluate eagerly.

The available terminal operations fall into four different groups:

- Reductions
- Aggregations
- Finding and matching
- Consuming

Reducing elements

Reduction operations, also known as *fold* operations, reduce the Stream's elements to a single result by repeatedly applying an *accumulator* operator. Such an operator uses the previous result to combine it with the current element to generate a new result, as shown in Figure 6-16. The accumulator is supposed to always return a new value without requiring an intermediate data structure.

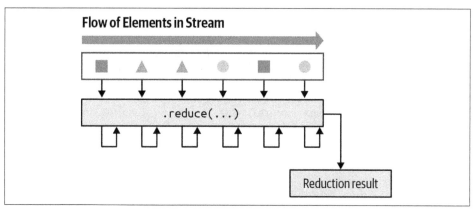

Figure 6-16. Reducing shapes by combining them next to each other

Like many functional tools, reductions often feel alien at first due to their nomenclature, especially if you come from an imperative background. The simplest way to better understand the general concept behind such tools is by looking at the involved parts and how they would work in a more familiar form.

In the case of reduction, three parts are involved:

The elements

Data processing is, well, about processing data elements. The familiar equivalent to a Stream would be any Collection type.

The initial value

The accumulation of data has to start somewhere. Sometimes this initial value is explicit, but certain reduction variants omit it by replacing it with the first element or allowing for an optional result if no element is present.

The accumulator function

The reduction logic works solely with the current element and the previous result or initial value. Depending only on its input to create a new value makes this a pure function.

Take finding the biggest value of a `Collection<Integer>` for an example. You have to go through each element and compare it with the next one, returning the greater number at each step, as shown in Example 6-9. All three parts of a reduction are represented.

Example 6-9. Finding the biggest number in a `Collection<Integer>`

```
Integer max(Collection<Integer> numbers) {
  int result = Integer.MIN_VALUE; ❶
```

```
  for (var value : numbers) { ❷
    result = Math.max(result, value); ❸
  }

  return result; ❹
}
```

❶ The initial value depends on the required task. In this case, comparing against the smallest possible `int` value is the logical choice to find the greatest number.

❷ The reduction logic has to be applied to each element.

❸ The actual reduction logic, representing the accumulator function.

❹ The reduced value.

To better reflect a reduction operation in general, the previous example allows you to derive a generic reduction operation as shown in Example 6-10.

Example 6-10. Reduce-like for-loop

```
<T> T reduce(Collection<T> elements,
             T initialValue,
             BinaryOperator<T> accumulator) {
  T result = initialValue;

  for (T element : elements) {
    result = accumulator.apply(result, element);
  }

  return result;
}
```

The generic variant again highlights that a functional approach separates *how* a task is done from *what* the task is actually doing. This way, the previous example of finding the maximum value can be simplified to a single method call by using the generic variant:

```
Integer max(Collection<Integer> numbers) {
  return reduce(elements,
                Integer.MIN_VALUE,
                Math::max);
}
```

The `max` method is also an example of why the Stream API provides more than just a `reduce` method: specialization to cover common use cases.

Even though all the specialized Stream operations can be implemented with one of the three available reduce methods—some of them actually are—the specialized variants create a more expressive fluent Stream call for typical reduction operations.

The Stream API has three different explicit reduce operations:

T reduce(T identity, BinaryOperator<T> accumulator)
> The identity is the seed—initial—value for the chain of accumulator operations. Although it's equivalent to Example 6-10, it's not constrained by the sequential nature of a for-loop.

Optional<T> reduce(BinaryOperator<T> accumulator)
> Instead of requiring a seed value, this operation picks the first encountered element as its initial value. That's why it returns an Optional<T>, which you will learn more about in Chapter 9. An empty Optional<T> is returned if the Stream doesn't contain any elements.

U reduce(U identity, BiFunction<U, ? super T, U> accumulator, BinaryOperator<U> combiner)
> This variant combines a map and reduce operation, which is required if the Stream contains elements of type T, but the desired reduced result is of type U. Alternatively, you can use an explicit map and reduce operation separately. Such a Stream pipeline might be more straightforward than using the combined reduce operations, as seen in Example 6-11 for summing up all characters in a Stream<String>.

Example 6-11. Three-arguments reduce operation versus map + two-arguments reduce

```
var reduceOnly = Stream.of("apple", "orange", "banana")
                       .reduce(0,
                               (acc, str) -> acc + str.length(),
                               Integer::sum);


var mapReduce = Stream.of("apple", "orange", "banana")
                      .mapToInt(String::length)
                      .reduce(0, (acc, length) -> acc + length);
```

Which to choose, a single reduce or separate map and reduce, depends on your preferences and if the lambda expressions can be generalized or refactored, in which case you could use method references instead.

As mentioned before, some typical reduction tasks are available as specialized operations, including any variants for primitive Streams, as listed in Table 6-3. The listed methods belong to IntStream but are also available for LongStream and DoubleStream with their related types.

Table 6-3. Typical reduction operations

Reduction operation	Description
Stream<T>	

`Optional<T> min(Comparator<? super T> comparator)`
 	
`Optional<T> max(Comparator<? super T> comparator)`
	Returns the minimum/maximum element of the Stream according to the provided `comparator`. An empty `Optional<T>` is returned if no elements reach the operation.

`long count()`	Returns the element count present at the end of the Stream pipeline. Be aware that certain Stream implementations may choose *not* to execute all intermediate operations if the count is determinable from the Stream itself, e.g., its characteristics contain `SIZED`, and no filtering is going on in the pipeline.
Primitive Streams	
`int sum()`	Sums up the elements of the Stream.
`OptionalDouble average()`	Calculates the arithmetic mean of the Stream elements. If the Stream contains no elements at the point of the terminal operation, an empty `OptionalDouble` is returned.
`IntSummaryStatistics summaryStatistics()`	Returns a summary of the Stream elements, containing the *count*, *sum*, *min*, and *max* of the Stream elements.

Even after migrating your code toward a more functional approach, reduction operations might not be your go-to operations for terminating a Stream. That's because there's another type of reduction operation available that feels more common to the ways you're used to: *aggregation operations*.

Aggregating elements with collectors

A ubiquitous step for every data processing task, be it Streams or an imperative approach with loops, is aggregating the resulting elements into a new data structure. Most commonly, you want the resulting elements in a new List, a unique Set, or some form of Map.

Reducing the elements to a new value, in this case, a Collection-like type, fits the bill of a reduction operation from the previous section, as shown in Example 6-12.

Example 6-12. Aggregate elements with a reduce operation

```
var fruits = Stream.of("apple", "orange", "banana", "peach")
                ...
                .reduce(new ArrayList<>(), ❶
                        (acc, fruit) -> {
                            var list = new ArrayList<>(acc); ❷
                            list.add(fruit);
                            return list;
                        },
```

```
                    (lhs, rhs) -> { ❸
                      var list = new ArrayList<>(lhs);
                      list.addAll(rhs);
                      return list;
                    });
```

❶ The three-argument reduce operation is used because the resulting type isn't the same type as the Stream elements.

❷ Reduce operations are supposed to return new values, so instead of using a shared ArrayList to aggregate the elements, a new ArrayList is created for each accumulation step.

❸ The combiner merges multiple ArrayList instances by creating a new one in the case of parallel processing.

That's quite a lot of verbose code to reduce a Stream down to a simple List, with new instances of ArrayList created for each element, plus additional ArrayList instances if run in parallel!

Of course, you could cheat and reuse the ArrayList acc variable in the aggregator function instead of creating and returning a new one. However, that would go against the general concept of reduce being an immutable reduction operation. That's why there's a better solution available: *aggregation operations*.

 Even though I call them "aggregation operations" throughout the chapter, technically, they're known as "mutable reduction operations" to differentiate them from reduction operations known as "immutable reduction operations."

The Stream terminal operation collect accepts a Collector to aggregate elements. Instead of reducing elements by combining Stream elements to a single result by repeatedly applying an *accumulator* operator, these operations use a *mutable results container* as an intermediate data structure, as seen in Figure 6-17.

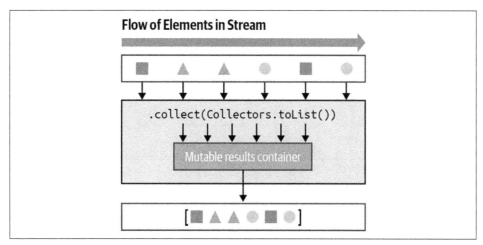

Figure 6-17. Collecting Stream elements

The Stream's elements are aggregated—or collected—with the help of the `java.util.stream.Collector<T, A, R>` type. The interface's generic types represent the different parts involved in the collection process:

- T: The *type* of Stream elements
- A: The *mutable result container* type
- R: The final *result type* of the collection process, which may differ from the intermediate container type

A `Collector` consists of multiple steps that match perfectly to its interface definition (*https://oreil.ly/GSgk7*), as illustrated in Figure 6-18 and explained in the following steps.

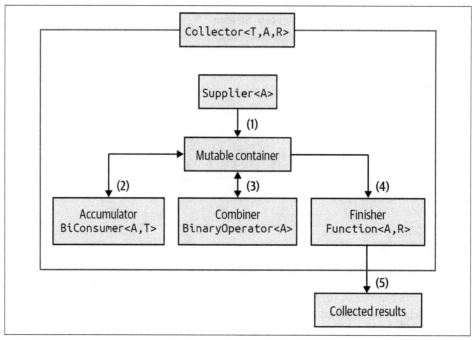

Figure 6-18. Inner workings of a `Collector<T, A, R>`

(1) `Supplier<A> supplier()`
The `Supplier` returns a new instance of the mutable result container used throughout the collection process.

(2) `BiConsumer<A, T> accumulator()`
The core of the `Collector`, as this `BiConsumer` is responsible for accumulating the Stream elements of type T into the container of type A by accepting the result container and the current element as its arguments.

(3) `BinaryOperator<A> combiner()`
In the case of parallel Stream processing, where multiple accumulators may do their work, the returned combiner `BinaryOperator` merges partial results containers into a single one.

(4) `Function<A, R> finisher()`
The finisher transforms the intermediate result container to the actual return object of type R. The necessity of this step depends on the implementation of the `Collector`.

(5) The final result
The collected instance, e.g., a `List`, a `Map`, or even a single value.

The JDK comes with the `java.util.Collectors` utility class, providing a variety of Collectors for many use cases. Listing and explaining them all in detail could fill another whole chapter. That's why I only introduce their particular use case groups here. Chapter 7 will have more examples and details about them and how you can create your own Collectors. Also, you should check out the official documentation (*https://oreil.ly/OXlWD*) for more details, including intended use cases and examples.

Collect into a `java.util.Collection` *type*

The most used variants for collecting Stream elements into a new `Collection`-based type include:

- `toCollection(Supplier<C> collectionFactory)`
- `toList()`
- `toSet()`
- `toUnmodifiableList()` (Java 10+)
- `toUnmodifiableSet()` (Java 10+)

The original `toList()` and `toSet()` methods have no guarantees on the returned Collection's underlying type, mutability, serializability, or thread safety. That's why the `Unmodifiable` variants were introduced in Java 10—to close that gap.

Collect into a `java.util.Map` *(key-value)*

Another frequently used `Collector` task is creating a `Map<K, V>` by mapping the key and value from the Stream's elements. That's why each variant must have at least a key and value mapper function: Key and value mapper functions must be provided.

- `toMap(…)` (3 variants)
- `toConcurrentMap(…)` (3 variants)
- `toUnmodifiableMap(…)` (2 variants, Java 10+)

Like the `toList` and `toList` methods, the original `toMap` variants do not guarantee the returned Map's underlying type, mutability, serializability, or thread safety. Concurrent variants are also available for a more efficient collection of parallel Streams.

Collect into a `java.util.Map` *(grouped)*

Instead of a simple key-value relationship, the following Collectors group the values by a key, usually with a Collection-based type as the value for the returned `Map`:

- `groupingBy(…)` (3 variants)
- `groupingByConcurrent(…)` (3 variants)

Collect into a `java.util.Map` *(partitioned)*

Partitioned maps group their elements based on a provided `Predicate`.

- `partitionBy(…)` (2 variants)

Arithmetic and comparison operations

There's a certain overlap between the reduction operations and Collectors, like the arithmetic- and comparison-related Collectors.

- `averagingInt(ToIntFunction<? super T> mapper)`

- `summingInt(ToIntFunction<? super T> mapper)`

- `summarizingInt(ToIntFunction<? super T> mapper)`

- `counting()`

- `minBy(Comparator<? super T> comparator)`

- `maxBy(Comparator<? super T> comparator)`

String operations

There are three variants for joining elements together to a singular `String`:

- `joining(…)` (3 variants)

Advanced use cases

In more advanced use cases, like multilevel reductions or complicated groupings/partitions, multiple collection steps are required with the help of "downstream" Collectors.

- `reducing(…)` (3 variants)

- `collectingAndThen(Collector<T,A,R> downstream, Function<R,RR> finisher)`

- `mapping(Function<? super T, ? extends U> mapper, Collector<? super U, A, R> downstream)` (Java 9+)

- `filtering(Predicate<? super T> predicate, Collector<? super T, A, R> downstream)` (Java 9+)

- `teeing(Collector<? super T, ?, R1> downstream1, Collector<? super T, ?, R2> downstream2, BiFunction<? super R1, ? super R2, R> merger)` (Java 12+)

Chapter 7 will detail how to use different Collectors and create complex collection workflows, including downstream collection.

Reducing versus collecting elements

The terminal operations reduce and collect are two sides of the same coin: both are reduction—or fold—operations. The difference lies in the general approach to recombining the results: *immutable* versus *mutable* accumulation. This difference leads to quite different performance characteristics.

The more abstract approach of *immutable* accumulation with the reduce operation is the best fit if subresults are cheap to create, like summing up numbers as shown in Example 6-13.

Example 6-13. Immutable accumulation of numbers with a Stream

```
var numbers = List.of(1, 2, 3, 4, 5, 6);

int total = numbers.stream()
                   .reduce(0, ❶
                           Integer::sum); ❷
```

❶   The initial value—the *seed*—is used for every parallel reduction operation.

❷   The method reference translates into a BiFunction<Integer, Integer, Integer> to accumulate the previous (or initial) value with the current Stream element.

Every reduction operation builds upon the previous one, as seen in Figure 6-19.

This approach isn't feasible for all scenarios, especially if creating an intermediate result is costly. Take the String type, for example. In Chapter 4, you learned about its immutable nature and why performing modifications can be costly. That's why it's generally advisable to use an optimized intermediate container, like StringBuilder or StringBuffer, to reduce the required processing power.

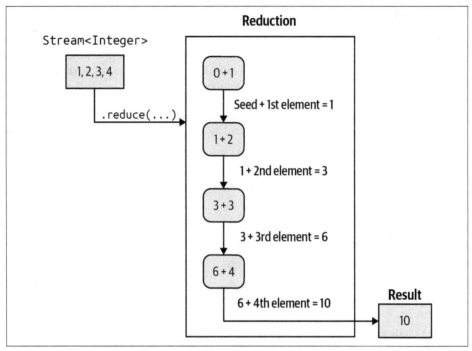

Figure 6-19. Immutable accumulation of numbers

Concatenating a list of `String` objects with an immutable reduction requires creating a new `String` for every step, leading to a runtime of $O(n^2)$ with n being the number of characters.

Let's compare an immutable and mutable variant of `String` concatenation in Example 6-14.

Example 6-14. Concatenating `String` elements: `reduce` versus `collect`

```
var strings = List.of("a", "b", "c", "d", "e");

// STREAM REDUCE
var reduced = strings.stream()
                  .reduce("", ❶
                          String::concat); ❷

// STREAM COLLECT - CUSTOM
var joiner = strings.stream()
                  .collect(Collector.of(() -> new StringJoiner(""), ❸
                                  StringJoiner::add, ❹
                                  StringJoiner::merge, ❺
                                  StringJoiner::toString)); ❻
```

```
// STREAM COLLECT - PREDEFINED
var collectWithCollectors = strings.stream()
                               .collect(Collectors.joining()); ❼
```

❶ The initial value is the first String creation.

❷ Every reduction step creates another new String, so the required processing
    power and memory scale with element count.

❸ The first argument specifies a Supplier<A> for the mutable container.

❹ The second argument is the reduction BiConsumer<A, T> accepting the con-
    tainer and the current element.

❺ The third argument defines a BinaryOperator<A> as to how to merge multiple
    containers in the case of parallel processing.

❻ And the last argument, a Function<A, R> tells the Collector how to build the
    final result of type R.

❼ The java.util.stream.Collectors utility class provides many ready-to-use
    Collectors, making Stream pipelines more reasonable than creating a Collector
    inline.

The Collector requires more arguments than an immutable reduction to do its
work. Still, these additional arguments allow it to use a mutable container and,
therefore, a different approach to reducing the Stream's elements in the first place.
For many common tasks, in this case concatenating Strings, you can use one of the
predefined Collectors available from java.util.stream.Collectors.

Which type of reduction to choose—immutable or mutable—depends highly on your
requirements. My personal rule of thumb is simple and stems from the names of
the actual methods: choose collect if the result is a Collection-based type, like List
or Map; choose reduce if the result is an accumulated single value. But don't forget
performance and memory considerations.

Chapter 7 goes into more detail about Collectors and how to create your own.

Aggregate elements directly

The Collector type is a powerful and versatile tool for collecting elements into new
data structures. Still, sometimes, a simpler solution would suffice. The Stream<T>
type provides more terminal aggregation operations for common tasks:

Returning a `List<T>`

Java 16 added the terminal operation `toList()` to simplify the most commonly used aggregation to create a new `List<T>`. It doesn't use a Collector-based workflow to aggregate the elements, leading to fewer allocations and requiring less memory. That makes it optimal to use when the stream size is known in advance, and a more concise alternative to `collect(Collectors.toList())`. There are no guarantees on the implementation type of the returned list or its serializability, just like with using `collect(Collectors.toList())`. Unlike that, however, the return list is an unmodifiable variant.

Returning an array

Returning the Stream's elements as an array doesn't require a reduction or Collector. Instead, you can use two operations:

- `Object[] toArray()`
- `A[] toArray(IntFunction<A[]> generator)`

The second variant of `toArray` allows you to create an array of a specific type instead of `Object[]` by providing an "array generator," which most likely is a method reference to the constructor:

```
String[] fruits = Stream.of("apple", "orange", "banana", "peach")
                  ...
                  .toArray(String[]::new);
```

Finding and matching elements

Besides aggregating Stream elements into a new representation, finding a particular element is another common task for Streams. There are multiple terminal operations available either to find an element or determine its existence:

`Optional<T> findFirst()`

Returns the first encountered element of the Stream. If the Stream is unordered, any element might be returned. Empty Streams return an empty `Optional<T>`.

`Optional<T> findAny()`

Returns any element of the Stream in a non-deterministic fashion. If the Stream itself is empty, an empty `Optional<T>` is returned.

As you can see, both methods have no arguments, so a prior `filter` operation might be necessary to get the desired element.

If you don't require the element itself, you should use one of the matching operations, which match the elements against a `Predicate<T>` instead:

`boolean anyMatch(Predicate<? super T> predicate)`

Returns `true` if *any* element of the Stream matches the `predicate`.

```
boolean allMatch(Predicate<? super T> predicate)
```
Returns `true` if *all* elements of the Stream match the `predicate`.

```
boolean noneMatch(Predicate<? super T> predicate)
```
Returns `true` if *none* of the elements matches the given `predicate`.

Consuming elements

The last group of terminal operations is *side-effects-only* operations. Instead of returning a value, the `forEach` methods only accept a `Consumer<T>`.

```
void forEach(Consumer<? super T> action)
```
Performs the `action` for each element. The execution order is explicitly nondeterministic to maximize the performance, especially for parallel Streams.

```
void forEachOrdered(Consumer<? super T> action)
```
The `action` is performed for every element in the encountered order if the Stream is `ORDERED`.

From a functional point of view, these operations seem out of place. As a developer trying to transition imperative code into a more functional direction, however, they can be quite useful.

Localized side effects aren't inherently harmful. Not all code is easily refactorable to prevent them, if even at all. Just like with all the other operations, the conciseness of the contained logic determines how straightforward and readable the Stream pipeline will be. If more than a method reference or a simple non-block lambda is needed, it's always a good idea to extract/refactor the logic into a new method and call it instead to maintain the conciseness and readability of the Stream pipeline.

The Cost of Operations

The beauty of Streams is their ability to concatenate multiple operations into a single pipeline, but you have to remember one thing: every operation might get called until an item gets rejected downstream.

Let's look at the simple Stream pipeline in Example 6-15.

Example 6-15. Fruit pipeline (naïve)

```
Stream.of("ananas", "oranges", "apple", "pear", "banana")
      .map(String::toUpperCase) ❶
      .sorted() ❷
      .filter(s -> s.startsWith("A")) ❸
      .forEach(System.out::println); ❹
```

❶ Process elements to the desired form.

❷ Sort naturally.

❸ Reject unwanted elements.

❹ Finally, work with the remaining elements.

In this fruit pipeline example, you have three intermediate and one terminal operation, for processing five elements. How many operation calls do you guess are done by this simple code? Let's count them!

The Stream pipeline calls `map` five times, `sorted` eight times, `filter` five times, and finally `forEach` two times. That's *20* operations to output *two* values! Even though the pipeline does what it's supposed to, that's ridiculous! Let's rearrange the operations to reduce the overall calls significantly, as seen in Example 6-16.

Example 6-16. Fruit pipeline (improved)

```
Stream.of("ananas", "oranges", "apple", "pear", "banana")
      .filter(s -> s.startsWith("a")) ❶
      .map(String::toUpperCase) ❷
      .sorted() ❸
      .forEach(System.out::println); ❹
```

❶ Reject unwanted elements first.

❷ Transform elements to the desired form.

❸ Sort naturally.

❹ Finally, work with the remaining elements.

By filtering first, the calls of the `map` operation and the work of the stateful `sorted` operation are reduced to a minimum: `filter` is called five times, `map` two times, `sorted` one time, and `forEach` two times, saving *50%* operations in total without changing the result.

Always remember that Stream elements are not being pushed through the Stream pipeline and its operations until they reach the terminal operation. Instead, the terminal operation pulls the elements through the pipeline. The fewer elements that flow through the pipeline, the better its performance will be. That's why some operations are considered *short-circuiting* in nature, meaning they can cut the Stream short. Essentially, short-circuiting operations, as listed in Table 6-4, are operations that might carry out their intended purpose without requiring the Stream to traverse all of its elements.

Table 6-4. Short-circuiting Stream operations

Intermediate Operations	Terminal Operations
limit	findAny
takeWhile	findFirst
	anyMatch
	allMatch
	noneMatch

This behavior even allows them to process an infinite Stream while an intermediate operation can still produce a finite Stream as its result, or a terminal operation can finish its task in finite time.

A non-short-circuiting operation with heavily optimized behavior is the terminal count operation. If the overall element count of a Stream terminated by count is derivable from the Stream itself, any prior operations that won't affect the count might get dropped, as the following code demonstrates:

```
var result = Stream.of("apple", "orange", "banana", "melon")
                .peek(str -> System.out.println("peek 1: " + str))
                .map(str -> {
                  System.out.println("map: " + str);
                  return str.toUpperCase();
                })
                .peek(str -> System.out.println("peek 2: " + str))
                .count();
// NO OUTPUT
```

Even though there are three operations with a System.out.println call in the pipeline, all of them are dropped. The reasoning behind this behavior is simple: map and peek operations don't inject or remove any elements in the Stream pipeline, so they don't affect the final count in any way; therefore, they aren't actually required.

Dropping operations is at the Stream's discretion if it deems it possible. For example, the preceding code runs all operations if a filter operation is added to the pipeline, shown as follows:

```
var result = Stream.of("apple", "orange", "banana", "melon")
                .filter(str -> str.contains("e"))
                .peek(str -> System.out.println("peek 1: " + str))
                .map(str -> {
                  System.out.println("map: " + str);
                  return str.toUpperCase();
                })
                .peek(str -> System.out.println("peek 2: " + str))
                .count();
```

```
// OUTPUT:
// peek 1: apple
// map: apple
// peek 2: APPLE
// peek 1: orange
// map: orange
// peek 2: ORANGE
// peek 1: melon
// map: melon
// peek 2: MELON
```

That doesn't mean every kind of Stream pipeline will drop "unnecessary" operations, either. If you require side effects in your Stream pipeline, you should use one of the two forEach terminal operation variants, which are intended as side-effects-only operations.

Modifying Stream Behavior

A Stream's characteristics, as explained in "Spliterator, the Backbone of Streams" on page 125, are initially set on its creation. Not every Stream operation is a good match for every characteristic, though. Especially in parallel Streams, the encountered order of elements might significantly impact performance. For example, selecting elements with the filter operation is an easily parallelizable task, but takeWhile needs to synchronize between tasks if run in parallel. That's why particular Stream characteristics can be switched by the intermediate operations listed in Table 6-5, which return an equivalent Stream with changed traits.

Table 6-5. Modifying Stream Behavior

Operation	Description
parallel()	Enables parallel processing. May return this if the Stream is already parallel.
sequential()	Enables sequential processing. May return this if the Stream is already sequential.
unordered()	Returns a Stream with unordered encounter order. May return this if the Stream is already unordered.
onClose(Runnable closeHandler)	Adds an additional close handler to be called after the Stream is finished.

Switching Stream behavior is just a single method call away. However, that doesn't mean it's always a good idea. In fact, switching to parallel processing is often a bad idea if the pipeline and the underlying Stream aren't designed to run in parallel in the first place.

See Chapter 8 to learn how to make an informed decision about using parallel processing for Stream pipelines.

To Use a Stream, or Not?

Streams are an excellent way to make your data processing more expressive and utilize many of the functional features available in Java. You may feel a strong urge to (over)use Streams for all kinds of data processing. I know I certainly overdid it at first. You have to keep in mind, though, that not every data processing pipeline benefits equally from becoming a Stream.

Your decision to use a Stream—or not to use one—should always be an informed decision based on the following intertwined factors:

How complex is the required task?
> A simple loop that's a few lines long won't benefit much from being a Stream with one or two small operations. It depends on how easy it is to fit the whole task and required logic into a mental model.

> If I can grasp what's happening with ease, a simple for-each loop might be the better choice. On the other hand, compressing a multi-page-long loop into a more accessible Stream pipeline with well-defined operations will improve its readability and maintainability.

How functional is the Stream pipeline?
> Stream pipelines are mere scaffolds to be filled with your logic. If the logic isn't a good fit for a functional approach, like side-effect-laden code, you won't get all the benefits and safety guarantees that Streams have to offer.

> Refactoring or redesigning code to be more functional, pure, or immutable is always a good idea and makes it a better match for the Stream API. Still, forcing your code to fit into a Stream pipeline without the actual need is deciding on a solution without really understanding the problem first. A certain degree of adapting your code to enable new features that benefit productivity, reasonability, and maintainability is good.

> However, it should be a conscious decision on what's best for your code and project in the long run, not just a "requirement" to use a feature.

How many elements are processed?

The overhead of creating the scaffold that holds the Stream pipeline together diminishes with the number of processed elements. For small data sources, the relation between the required instances, method calls, stack frames, and memory consumption is not as negligible as for processing more significant quantities of elements.

In a direct comparison of raw performance, a "perfectly optimized" for-loop wins out over a sequential Stream for a simple reason. Traditional Java looping constructs are implemented at the language level, giving the JVM more optimization possibilities, especially for small loops. On the other hand, Streams are implemented as ordinary Java types, creating an unavoidable runtime overhead. That doesn't mean their execution won't be optimized, though! As you've learned in this chapter, a Stream pipeline can short-circuit or fuse operations to maximize pipeline throughput.

None of these factors in isolation should affect your decision to use a Stream, only in tandem. Especially, the most common concern of many developers—performance—is seldom the most significant criterion for designing code and choosing the right tools.

Your code could always be more performant. Dismissing a tool out of performance anxiety before measuring and verifying the actual performance might deprive you of a better solution for your actual problem.

Sir Tony Hoare[4] once said, "We should forget about small efficiencies, say about 97% of the time: premature optimization is the root of all evil."

This advice can be applied when deciding whether to use Streams or loops. Most of the time—around 97%—you do not need to concern yourself with raw performance, and Streams may be the most simple and straightforward solution for you with all the benefits the Stream API offers. Once in a while—the 3%—you will need to focus on raw performance to achieve your goals, and Streams might not be the best solution for you, although in Chapter 8 you will learn how to improve processing performance by leveraging parallel Streams.

When deciding whether or not to use Streams, you might think about how willing you are to use something new and unfamiliar. When you first learned to program, I bet all the loop constructs you're now quite familiar with appeared to be complicated. Everything seemed hard at first until, over time and with repeated use, you became

---

4 Sir Charles Antony Richard Hoare is a British computer scientist and recipient of the Turing Award—regarded as the highest distinction in the field of computer science—who has made foundational contributions to programming languages, algorithms, operating systems, formal verification, and concurrent computing.

familiar and more comfortable with using those loop contracts. The same is going to be true for using Streams. Learning the ins and outs of the Steam API will take some time, but it will become easier and more obvious when and how to use Streams efficiently to create concise and straightforward data processing pipelines.

Another thing you have to keep in mind is that the primary goal of Streams isn't to achieve the best raw performance possible or to replace all other looping constructs. Streams are supposed to be a more declarative and expressive way of processing data. They give you the equivalent of the classical map/filter/reduce pattern backed by Java's strong type system but also designed with all the powerful functional techniques introduced in Java 8 in mind. Designing a functional Stream pipeline is the most straightforward and concise way to apply functional code to a sequence of objects.

Finally, the general idea of combining pure functions with immutable data leads to a looser coupling between data structures and their data processing logic. Each operation only needs to know how to handle a single element in its current form. This decoupling enables greater reusability and maintainability of smaller domain-specific operations that can be composed into bigger, more sophisticated tasks if necessary.

Takeaways

- The Stream API provides a fluent and declarative way to create map/filter/reduce-like data processing pipelines without the need for external iteration.
- Concatenable higher-order functions are the building blocks for a Stream pipeline.
- Streams use internal iteration, which entrusts more control over the traversal process to the data source itself.
- Many common and specialized operations are available besides the classical map/filter/reduce operations.
- Streams are lazy; no work is done until a terminal operation is called.
- Sequential processing is the default, but switching to parallel processing is easy.
- Parallel processing might not be the best approach to all data processing problems and usually needs to be verified to solve the problem more efficiently.

Working with Streams

Streams utilize many of the functional features introduced in Java 8 to provide a declarative way to process data. The Stream API covers many use cases, but you need to know how the different operations and available helper classes work to make the most of them.

Chapter 6 concentrated on showing you the foundation of Streams. This chapter will build on that and teach you different ways to create and work with Streams for various use cases.

Primitive Streams

In Java, generics only work with object-based types (yet[1]). That's why Stream<T> can't be used for sequences of primitive values like int. There are only two options for using primitive types with Streams:

- Autoboxing
- Specialized Stream variants

Java's autoboxing support—the automatic conversion between primitive types and their object-based counterparts like int and Integer—may seem like a simple workaround because it automagically works, as shown as follows:

```
Stream<Long> longStream = Stream.of(5L, 23L, 42L);
```

---

[1] *Project Valhalla*, as discussed in "Project Valhalla and Specialized Generics" on page 46, will allow value-based types, like primitives, to be used as generic type boundaries. Unfortunately, though, at the point of writing this book, no targeted availability date is known.

Autoboxing introduces multiple problems, though. For one, there's the overhead associated with the conversion from primitive values to objects compared to using primitive types directly. Usually, the overhead is negligible. Still, in a data processing pipeline, the overhead of such frequent creation of wrapper types accumulates and can degrade overall performance.

Another nonissue with primitive wrappers is the possibility of null elements. The direct conversion from primitive to object type never results in null, but any operation in the pipeline might return null if it has to deal with the wrapper type instead of a primitive.

To mitigate this, the Stream API, like other functional features of the JDK, has specialized variants for primitive types int, long, and double without relying on autoboxing, as listed in Table 7-1.

Table 7-1. Primitive Streams and their equivalents

Primitive Type	Primitive Stream	Boxed Stream
int	IntStream	Stream<Integer>
long	LongStream	Stream<Long>
double	DoubleStream	Stream<Double>

The available operations on primitive Streams are similar to their Generic counterpart but use primitive functional interfaces. For example, an IntStream provides a map operation for transforming elements, just like Stream<T>. Unlike Stream<T>, the required higher-order function to do so is the specialized variant IntUnaryOperator, which accepts and returns an int, as the following simplified interface declaration shows:

```
@FunctionalInterface
public interface IntUnaryOperator {

    int applyAsInt(int operand);

    // ...
}
```

Operations accepting higher-order functions on primitive Streams use specialized functional interfaces, like IntConsumer or IntPredicate, to stay within the confines of the primitive Stream. That reduces the number of available operations compared to Stream<T>. Still, you can easily switch between a primitive Stream and the corresponding Stream<T> by mapping to another type or converting the primitive Stream to its boxed variant:

- `Stream<Integer> boxed()`
- `Stream<U> mapToObj(IntFunction<? extends U> mapper)`

The other way around, from `Stream<T>` to a primitive Stream, is also supported, with `mapTo-` and `flatMapTo-` operations available on `Stream<T>`:

- `IntStream mapToInt(ToIntFunction<? super T> mapper)`
- `IntStream flatMapToInt(Function<? super T, ? extends IntStream> mapper)`

Besides the usual intermediate operations, primitive Streams have a set of self-explanatory arithmetic terminal operations for common tasks:

- `int sum()`
- `OptionalInt min()`
- `OptionalInt max()`
- `OptionalDouble average()`

These operations don't need any arguments because their behavior is nonnegotiable for numbers. The returned types are the primitive equivalents you expect from similar `Stream<T>` operations.

As with primitive Streams in general, doing arithmetic with Streams has its use cases, like highly optimized parallel processing of humongous amounts of data. For simpler use cases, though, switching to primitive Streams compared to existing processing structures usually won't be worth it.

Iterative Streams

Stream pipelines and their internal iteration usually deal with existing sequences of elements or data structures readily convertible to sequences of elements. Compared to traditional looping constructs, you have to let go of controlling the iteration process and let the Stream take over. If you require more control, though, the Stream API still has you covered with its `static iterate` methods available on the `Stream` type and the primitive variants:

- `<T> Stream<T> iterate(T seed, UnaryOperator<T> f)`
- `IntStream iterate(int seed, IntUnaryOperator f)`

Java 9 added two additional methods, including a `Predicate` variant to have an end condition:

- `<T> Stream<T> iterate(T seed, Predicate<T> hasNext, UnaryOperator<T> next)`
- `IntStream iterate(int seed, IntPredicate hasNext, IntUnaryOperator next)`

Primitive `iterate` variants are available for `int`, `long`, and `double` on their corresponding Stream variants.

The iterative approach to Streams produces an *ordered* and potentially infinite sequence of elements by applying a `UnaryOperator` to a seed value. In other words, the Stream elements will be [`seed, f(seed), f(f(seed)), …`], and so on.

If the general concept feels familiar, you're right! It's a Stream equivalent to a for-loop:

```
// FOR-LOOP
for (int idx = 1; ❶
     idx < 5; ❷
     idx++) { ❸
  System.out.println(idx);
}

// EQUIVALENT STREAM (Java 8)
IntStream.iterate(1, ❶
                  idx -> idx + 1) ❸
         .limit(4L) ❷
         .forEachOrdered(System.out::println);

// EQUIVALENT STREAM (Java 9+)
IntStream.iterate(1, ❶
                  idx -> idx < 5, ❷
                  idx -> idx + 1) ❸
         .forEachOrdered(System.out::println);
```

❶ The seed, or initial iteration value.

❷ The termination condition.

❸ The incrementation of the iteration value. The for-loop needs an assignment where the Stream requires a return value instead.

Both loop and Streams variants produce the same elements for the loop body/subsequent Stream operations. Java 9 introduced an `iterate` variant that includes a limiting `Predicate`, so no additional operations are needed to restrict the overall elements.

The most significant advantage of an iterative Stream over a `for`-loop is that you can still use a loop-like iteration but gain the benefits of a lazy functional Stream pipeline.

The end condition doesn't have to be defined on Stream creation. Instead, a later intermediate Stream operation, like `limit`, or a terminal condition, like `anyMatch`, may provide it.

The characteristics of an iterative Stream are `ORDERED`, `IMMUTABLE`, and in the case of primitive Streams, `NONNULL`. If the iteration is number-based and the range is known beforehand, you can benefit from more Stream optimizations, like short-circuiting, by using the `static range-` methods for Stream creation available on `IntStream` and `LongStream` instead:

- `IntStream range(int startInclusive, int endExclusive)`
- `IntStream rangeClosed(int startInclusive, int endInclusive)`
- `LongStream range(long startInclusive, long endExclusive)`
- `LongStream rangeClosed(long startInclusive, long endInclusive)`

Even though the same results are achievable with `iterate`, the main difference is the underlying `Spliterator`. The returned Stream's characteristics are `ORDERED`, `SIZED`, `SUBSIZED`, `IMMUTABLE`, `NONNULL`, `DISTINCT`, and `SORTED`.

Choosing between iterative or ranged Stream creation depends on what you want to achieve. The iterative approach gives you more freedom for the iteration process, but you lose out on Stream characteristics enabling the most optimization possibilities, especially in parallel Streams.

Infinite Streams

The lazy nature of Streams allows for infinite sequences of elements as they are processed on-demand, and not all at once.

All available Stream interfaces in the JDK—`Stream<T>` and its primitive relatives `IntStream`, `LongStream`, and `DoubleStream`—have `static` convenience methods to create infinite Streams either based on an iterative approach or an unordered generative one.

While the `iterate` methods from the previous section start with a *seed* and rely on applying their `UnaryOperator` on the current iteration value, the `static generate` methods only rely on a `Supplier` to generate their next Stream element:

- `<T> Stream<T> generate(Supplier<T> s)`
- `IntStream generate(IntSupplier s)`

- `LongStream generate(LongSupplier s)`

- `DoubleStream generate(DoubleSupplier s)`

The lack of a starting seed value affects the Stream's characteristics, making it UNORDERED, which can be beneficial for parallel use. An unordered Stream created by a `Supplier` is helpful for constant non-interdependent sequences of elements, like random values. For example, creating a UUID Stream factory is quite simple:

```
Stream<UUID> createStream(long count) {
  return Stream.generate(UUID::randomUUID)
               .limit(count);
}
```

The downside of unordered Streams is that they won't guarantee that a `limit` operation will pick the first n elements in a parallel environment. That may result in more calls to the element-generating `Supplier` than are actually necessary for the result of the Stream.

Take the following example:

```
Stream.generate(new AtomicInteger()::incrementAndGet)
      .parallel()
      .limit(1_000L)
      .mapToInt(Integer::valueOf)
      .max()
      .ifPresent(System.out::println);
```

The expected output of the pipeline is `1000`. The output, though, will most likely be greater than `1000`.

This behavior is expected from an unordered Stream in a parallel execution environment. Under most circumstances, it won't matter much, but it highlights the necessity of choosing the right Stream type with favorable characteristics to gain maximum performance and the fewest invocations possible.

Random Numbers

The Stream API has special considerations for generating an infinite Stream of random numbers. Although it's possible to create such a Stream with `Stream.generate` using, for example, a `java.util.Random` instance, there's an easier way available.

Three different random-number-generating types are capable of creating Streams:

- `java.util.Random`

- `java.util.concurrent.ThreadLocalRandom`

- `java.util.SplittableRandom`

All three provide multiple methods to create Streams of random elements:

```
IntStream ints()
IntStream ints(long streamSize)
IntStream ints(int randomNumberOrigin,
               int randomNumberBound)
IntStream ints(long streamSize,
               int randomNumberOrigin,
               int randomNumberBound)

LongStream longs()
LongStream longs(long streamSize)
LongStream longs(long randomNumberOrigin,
                 long randomNumberBound)
LongStream longs(long streamSize,
                 long randomNumberOrigin,
                 long randomNumberBound)

DoubleStream doubles()
DoubleStream doubles(long streamSize)
DoubleStream doubles(double randomNumberOrigin,
                     double randomNumberBound)
DoubleStream doubles(long streamSize,
                     double randomNumberOrigin,
                     double randomNumberBound)
```

Technically, the Streams are only *effectively infinite*, as it's stated in their documentation.[2] If no `streamSize` is provided, the resulting Stream contains `Long.MAX_VALUE` elements. The upper and lower bounds are set with the `randomNumberOrigin` (inclusive) and `randomNumberBound` (exclusive).

General usage and performance characteristics will be discussed in "Example: Random Numbers" on page 208.

Memory Isn't Infinite

The most important thing to remember when using infinite Streams is that your memory is quite finite. Limiting your infinite Streams isn't just important, it's an absolute necessity! Forgetting to put a restricting intermediate or terminal operation will inevitably use up all memory available to the JVM and eventually throw an `OutOfMemoryError`.

The available operations to restrict any Stream are listed in Table 7-2.

---

2 For example, the documentation of `Random#ints()` (*https://oreil.ly/gxC39*) states that the method is implemented to be an equivalent of `Random.ints(Long.MAX_VALUE)`.

Table 7-2. Stream-restricting operations

Operation	Description
Intermediate Operations	
`limit(long maxSize)`	Limits a Stream to `maxSize` elements
`takeWhile(Predicate<T> predicate)`	Takes elements until `predicate` evaluates `false` (Java 9+)
Terminal Operations (guaranteed)	
`Optional<T> findFirst()`	Returns the first element of the Stream
`Optional<T> findAny()`	Returns a single, non-deterministic Steam element
Terminal Operations (non-guaranteed)	
`boolean anyMatch(Predicate<T> predicate)`	Returns whether *any* Stream elements match `predicate`
`boolean allMatch(Predicate<T> predicate)`	Returns whether *all* Stream elements match `predicate`
`boolean noneMatch(Predicate<T> predicate)`	Returns whether *no* Stream element matches `predicate`

The most straightforward choice is `limit`. Choice-based operations using a `Predicate` like `takeWhile` must be crafted with diligence, or you might still end up with a Stream consuming more memory than needed. For terminal operations, only the `find-` operations are guaranteed to terminate the Stream.

The `-Match` operations suffer from the same problem as `takeWhile`. If the predicate doesn't match according to their purpose, the Stream pipeline will process an *infinite* number of elements and, therefore, all the available memory.

As discussed in "The Cost of Operations" on page 151, the position of the restricting operation in the Stream also makes a difference in how many elements will pass through. Even if the final result might be identical, restricting the flow of Stream elements as early as possible will save you more memory and CPU cycles.

From Arrays to Streams and Back

Arrays are a particular type of object. They're a Collection-like structure, holding elements of their *base type*, and they only provide a method to access a specific element by its index, and the overall length of the array, besides the *usual* methods inherited from `java.lang.Object`. They're also the only way to have a collection of primitive types until *Project Valhalla* becomes available in the future.[3]

However, two characteristics make arrays a good match for Stream-based processing. First, their length is set on their creation and won't change. Second, they're an ordered sequence. That's why there are multiple convenience methods available on

---

3 See the sidebar "Project Valhalla and Specialized Generics" on page 46 for more information about *Project Valhalla*.

`java.util.Arrays` to create an appropriate Stream for different base types. Creating
an array from a Stream is done with an appropriate terminal operation.

Object-Type Arrays

Creating a typical `Stream<T>` is supported by two `static` convenience methods on
`java.util.Arrays`:

- `<T> Stream<T> stream(T[] array)`
- `<T> Stream<T> stream(T[] array, int startInclusive,
  int endExclusive)`

As you can see, creating a `Stream<T>` from an array is quite self-explanatory.

The other way around, from `Stream<T>` to `T[]`, is done by using one of these two
terminal operations:

- `Object[] toArray()`
- `<A> A[] toArray(IntFunction<A[]> generator)`

The first variant can only return an `Object[]` array regardless of the actual element
type of the Stream due to how arrays are created by the JVM. If you need an array of
the Stream's elements type, you need to provide the Stream with a way to create an
appropriate array. That's where the second variant comes in.

The second variant requires an `IntFunction` that creates the array of the provided
size. The most straightforward way is to use a method reference:

```
String[] fruits = new String[] { "Banana", "Melon", "Orange" };

String[] result = Arrays.stream(fruits)
                        .filter(fruit -> fruit.contains("a"))
                        .toArray(String[]::new);
```

 There is no static type checking for using the created array in
`toArray`. Types are checked at runtime when an element is stored
in the allocated array, throwing an `ArrayStoreException` if the
types aren't compatible.

Primitive Arrays

The three primitive Stream specializations, `IntStream`, `LongStream`, and `Double
Stream`, all have dedicated variants of the `static` method `Arrays.stream`:

- `IntStream stream(int[] array)`

- `IntStream stream(int[] array, int startInclusive, int endExclusive)`

The LongStream and DoubleStream variants differ only in the array type and the returned primitive Stream.

Because the element type is fixed in a primitive Stream, they have only a singular toArray method that doesn't require an IntFunction:

```
int[] fibonacci = new int[] { 0, 1, 1, 2, 3, 5, 8, 13, 21, 34 };

int[] evenNumbers = Arrays.stream(fibonacci)
                          .filter(value -> value % 2 == 0)
                          .toArray();
```

Low-Level Stream Creation

So far, all Stream creation methods I've discussed were quite high-level, creating a Stream from another data source, iteration, generation, or arbitrary object. They are directly available on their respective types, with as few arguments needed as possible. The auxiliary type java.util.stream.StreamSupport has also several low-level static convenience methods available for creating Streams directly from a Spliterator. This way, you can create a Stream representation for your own custom data structures.

The following two methods accept a Spliterator to create a new Stream:

`Stream<T> stream(Spliterator<T> spliterator, boolean parallel)`
> The easiest way to create a sequential or parallel Stream from any source that is representable by a Spliterator<T>.

`Stream<T> stream(Supplier<? extends Spliterator<T>> supplier,`
`int characteristics, boolean parallel)`
> Instead of using the Spliterator right away, the Supplier gets called once and only after the terminal operation of the Stream pipeline is invoked. That relays any possible interference with the source data structure to a smaller timeframe, making it safer for non-IMMUTABLE or non-CONCURRENT eager-bound Streams.

It's strongly recommended that the Spliterators used to create a Stream<T> are either IMMUTABLE or CONCURRENT to minimize possible interference or changes to the underlying data source during the traversal.

Another good option is using a *late-binding* Spliterator, meaning the elements aren't fixed at the creation of the Spliterator. Instead, they're bound on first use, when the Stream pipeline starts processing its elements after calling a terminal operation.

Low-level Stream creation methods also exist for the primitive Spliterator variants.

If you don't have a `Spliterator<T>` but a `Iterator<T>`, the JDK's got you covered. The type `java.util.Spliterators` has multiple convenience methods for creating Spliterators, with two methods designated for `Iterator<T>`:

```
Spliterator<T> spliterator(Iterator<? extends T> iterator,
                           long size,
                           int characteristics)

Spliterator<T> spliteratorUnknownSize(Iterator<? extends T> iterator,
                                      int characteristics)
```

You can use the created `Spliterator<T>` instance in the previously discussed `Stream<T> stream(Spliterator<T> spliterator, boolean parallel)` method to finally create a `Stream<T>`.

Working with File I/O

Streams aren't only for Collection-based traversal. They also provide an excellent way to traverse the filesystem with the help of the `java.nio.file.Files` class.

This section will look at several use cases for file I/O and Streams. Contrary to other Streams, I/O-related Streams must be explicitly closed by calling `Stream#close()` after you are finished using them. The `Stream` type conforms to the `java.lang.Auto Closeable` interface, so the examples will use a `try-with-resources`-block, which will be explained in "Caveats of File I/O Streams" on page 175.

All examples in this section use the files in the book's code repository (*https://github.com/benweidig/a-functional-approach-to-java*) as their source. The following filesystem tree represents the overall structure of the files used in the examples:

```
├── README.md
├── assets
│   └── a-functional-approach-to-java.png
├── part-1
│   ├── 01-an-introduction-to-functional-programming
│   │   └── README.md
│   ├── 02-functional-java
│   │   ├── README.md
│   │   ├── java
│   │   └── ...
└── part-2
    ├── 04-immutability
    │   ├── ...
```

```
|    └── jshell
|        ├── immutable-copy.java
|        ├── immutable-math.java
|        ├── unmodifiable-list-exception.java
|        └── unmodifiable-list-modify-original.java
├── ...
```

Reading Directory Contents

Listing the contents of a directory can be done by calling the method `Files.list` to create a lazily populated `Stream<Path>` of the provided `Path`:

```
static Stream<Path> list(Path dir) throws IOException
```

Its argument must be a directory, or else it will throw a `NotDirectoryException`. Example 7-1 shows how to list a directory.

Example 7-1. Listing a directory

```
var dir = Paths.get("./part-2/04-immutability/jshell");

try (var stream = Files.list(dir)) {
  stream.map(Path::getFileName)
        .forEach(System.out::println);
} catch (IOException e) {
  // ...
}
```

The output lists the files of the directory `jshell` for Chapter 4:

```
unmodifiable-list-exception.java
unmodifiable-list-modify-original.java
immutable-copy.java
immutable-math.java
```

The order of retrieved content isn't guaranteed, which I will go into more detail about in "Caveats of File I/O Streams" on page 175.

Depth-First Directory Traversal

The two `walk` methods do, as their name suggests, "walk" the whole file tree from a specific starting point. The lazily populated `Stream<Path>` traverses *depth-first*, meaning if an element is a directory, it will be entered and traversed first before the next element in the current directory.

The difference between the two `walk` variants in `Files` is the maximum directory depth they're going to traverse:

```
static Stream<Path> walk(Path start,         ❶
                         int maxDepth,        ❷
                         FileVisitOption... options)   ❸
                         throws IOException

static Stream<Path> walk(Path start,         ❶
                         FileVisitOption... options)   ❸
                         throws IOException
```

❶ The starting point of the traversal.

❷ The maximum number of directory levels to traverse. The value 0 (zero) restricts the Stream to the starting level. The second variant without maxDepth has no depth limit.

❸ Zero or more options on how to traverse the filesystem. So far, only FOLLOW_LINKS exists. Be aware that by following links, a possible cyclic traversal might occur. If the JDK detects this, it throws a FileSystemLoopException.

You can walk the filesystem as shown in Example 7-2.

Example 7-2. Walking the filesystem

```
var start = Paths.get("./part-1");

try (var stream = Files.walk(start)) {
  stream.map(Path::toFile)
        .filter(Predicate.not(File::isFile))
        .sorted()
        .forEach(System.out::println);
} catch (IOException e) {
  // ...
}
```

The traversal generates the following output:

```
./part-1
./part-1/01-an-introduction-to-functional-programming
./part-1/02-functional-java
./part-1/02-functional-java/java
./part-1/02-functional-java/jshell
./part-1/02-functional-java/other
./part-1/03-functional-jdk
./part-1/03-functional-jdk/java
./part-1/03-functional-jdk/jshell
```

The Stream will have at least one element, the starting point. If it's not accessible, an IOException is thrown. As with list, the Stream elements' encounter order isn't guaranteed; I will go into more detail in "Caveats of File I/O Streams" on page 175.

Searching the Filesystem

Although you can search for a particular `Path` with `walk`, you could use the method `find` instead. It bakes a `BiPredicate` with access to the `BasicFileAttribute` of the current element directly into the Stream creation, making the Stream more focused on your task's requirements:

```
static Stream<Path> find(Path start, ❶
                    int maxDepth, ❷
                    BiPredicate<Path, BasicFileAttributes> matcher, ❸
                    FileVisitOption... options) ❹
                    throws IOException
```

❶   The starting point of the search.

❷   The maximum number of directory levels to traverse. The value 0 (zero) restricts it to the starting level. Unlike `Files.walk`, no method variant without `maxDepth` exists.

❸   Criteria for including a `Path` in the Stream.

❹   Zero or more options on how to traverse the filesystem. So far, only `FOLLOW_LINKS` exists. Be aware that by following links, a possible cyclic traversal might occur. If the JDK detects this, it throws a `FileSystemLoopException`.

With it, Example 7-2 can be implemented without needing to map the `Path` to a `File`, as shown in Example 7-3.

Example 7-3. Finding files

```
var start = Paths.get("./part-1");

BiPredicate<Path, BasicFileAttributes> matcher =
  (path, attr) -> attr.isDirectory();

try (var stream = Files.find(start, Integer.MAX_VALUE, matcher)) {
    stream.sorted()
          .forEach(System.out::println);
} catch (IOException e) {
  // ...
}
```

The output is equivalent to using `walk`, and the same assumptions—depth-first and non-guaranteed encounter order—apply to `find`, too. The real difference is the access to the `BasicFileAttributes` of the current element, which may affect performance. If you need to filter or match by file attributes, using `find` will save you reading the file attributes explicitly from the `Path` element, which could be slightly more performant. However, if you require only the Path element and no access to its file attributes, the walk method is just as good an alternative.

Reading Files Line-By-Line

The common task of reading a file and processing it line-by-line is a breeze with Streams, which provides the lines method. There are two variants, depending on the file's Charset:

```
static Stream<String> lines(Path path, Charset cs) throws IOException

static Stream<String> lines(Path path) throws IOException
```

The second variant defaults to StandardCharsets.UTF_8.

Even though you can use any Charset you want, it will make a performance difference in parallel processing. The lines method is optimized for UTF_8, US_ASCII, and ISO_8859_1.

Let's look at a simple example of counting the words in *War and Peace* by Tolstoy, as seen in Example 7-4.

Example 7-4. Counting words in "War and Peace"

```
var location = Paths.get("war-and-peace.txt"); ❶

// CLEANUP PATTERNS ❷
var punctuation = Pattern.compile("\\p{Punct}");
var whitespace  = Pattern.compile("\\s+");
var words       = Pattern.compile("\\w+");

try (Stream<String> stream = Files.lines(location)) { ❸

  Map<String, Integer> wordCount =
          // CLEAN CONTENT ❹
    stream.map(punctuation::matcher)
          .map(matcher -> matcher.replaceAll(""))
          // SPLIT TO WORDS ❺
          .map(whitespace::split)
          .flatMap(Arrays::stream)
          // ADDITIONAL CLEANUP ❻
          .filter(word -> words.matcher(word).matches())
          // NORMALIZE ❼
          .map(String::toLowerCase)
          // COUNTING ❽
          .collect(Collectors.toMap(Function.identity(),
                                word -> 1,
```

```
                            Integer::sum));
} catch (IOException e) {
  // ...
}
```

❶ The plain text version of *War and Peace* from Project Gutenberg[4] is used, so no formatting might get in the way of counting words.

❷ The regular expressions are precompiled to prevent recompilation for each element. Such optimizations are essential because the overhead of creating a Pattern for each element and map operation will quickly compound and affect the overall performance.

❸ The lines call returns a Stream<String> with the file's lines as elements. The try-with-resources block is required because the I/O operation must be closed explicitly, which you'll learn more about in "Caveats of File I/O Streams" on page 175.

❹ The punctuation needs to be removed, or identical words directly next to any punctuation will be counted as different words.

❺ The cleaned line is now split on whitespace characters, which creates a Stream<String[]>. To actually count the words, the flatMap operation will flatten the Stream to a Stream<String>.

❻ The "word" matcher is an additional cleanup and selection step to count only the actual words.

❼ Mapping the element to lowercase ensures differently-cased words are counted as one.

❽ The terminal operation creates a Map<String, Integer> with the word as its key and the occurrence count as its value.

The Stream pipeline does what it was set out to do, taking over the task of reading the file and providing you with its content line-by-line so that you can concentrate your code on the processing steps. We will revisit this particular example in Chapter 8 to take another look at how such a common task can be improved immensely by using a parallel Stream.

---

4 Project Gutenberg provides multiple versions of *War and Peace* (*https://oreil.ly/AXag1*) for free.

Caveats of File I/O Streams

Working with Streams and file I/O is pretty straightforward. However, there are three unusual aspects I mentioned before. They aren't a big deal and don't diminish the usability or usefulness of using Stream-based file I/O, although you need to be aware of them:

- Closing the Streams is required
- Directory contents are weakly consistent
- Non-guaranteed element order

These aspects stem from dealing with I/O in general and are found in most I/O-related code, not only Stream pipelines.

Explicit closing of the stream

Dealing with resources in Java, like file I/O, typically requires you to close them after use. An unclosed resource can *leak*, meaning the garbage collector can't reclaim its memory after the resource is no longer required or used. The same is true for dealing with I/O with Streams. That's why you need to close I/O-based Streams explicitly, at least compared to non-I/O Streams.

The `Stream<T>` type extends `java.io.AutoClosable` through `BaseStream`, so the most straightforward way to close it is to use a `try-with-resources` block, as seen throughout the "Working with File I/O" section and in the following code:

```
try (Stream<String> stream = Files.lines(location)) {
  stream.map(...)
       ...
}
```

All Stream-related methods on `java.nio.file.Files` throw an `IOException` according to their signatures, so you need to handle that Exception in some form. Combining a `try-with-resources` block with an appropriate `catch` block can solve both requirements in one fell swoop.

Weakly consistent directory content

The `list`, `walk`, and `find` methods on `java.nio.file.Files` are *weakly consistent* and lazily populated. That means the actual directory content isn't scanned once on Stream creation to have a fixed snapshot during traversal. Any updates to the filesystem may or may not be reflected after the `Stream<Path>` is created or traversed.

The reasoning behind this constraint is most likely due to performance and optimization considerations. Stream pipelines are supposed to be lazy sequential pipelines with no distinction of their elements. A fixed snapshot of the file tree would require gathering all possible elements on Stream creation, not lazily on the actual Stream processing triggered by a terminal operation.

Non-guaranteed element order

The lazy nature of Streams creates another aspect of file I/O Streams you might not expect. The encounter order of file I/O Streams isn't guaranteed to be in natural order —in this case, alphabetically—which is why you might need an additional `sorted` intermediate operation to ensure consistent element order. That's because the Stream is populated by the filesystem, which isn't guaranteed to return its files and directories in an ordered fashion.

Dealing with Date and Time

Dealing with dates is always a challenge, with many edge cases. Thankfully, a new *Date & Time API*[5] was introduced in Java 8. Its immutable nature fits nicely in any functional code and provides some Stream-related methods, too.

Querying Temporal Types

The new Date and Time API provides a flexible and functional query interface for arbitrary properties. Like with most Stream operations, you inject the actually required logic to do your task into the method via its arguments, making the methods themselves more general scaffolds with greater versatility:

```
<R> R query(TemporalQuery<R> query);
```

The generic signature allows querying for any type, making it quite flexible:

```
// TemporalQuery<Boolean> == Predicate<TemporalAccessor>
boolean isItTeaTime = LocalDateTime.now()
                            .query(temporal -> {
                                var time = LocalTime.from(temporal);
                                return time.getHour() >= 16;
                            });

// TemporalQuery<LocalTime> == Function<TemporalAccessor, Localtime>
LocalTime time = LocalDateTime.now().query(LocalTime::from);
```

The utility class `java.time.temporal.TemporalQueries` provides predefined queries, shown in Table 7-3, to eliminate the need to create common queries yourself.

---

5 The Java *Date & Time API* (JSR310) (*https://oreil.ly/l1oV8*) set out to replace `java.util.Date` with a comprehensive set of types allowing for a consistent and complete way to deal with date- and time-related types in an immutable fashion.

Table 7-3. Predefined `TemporalQuery<T>` in `java.time.temporal.TemporalQueries`

`static` Method	Return Type
`chronology()`	`Chronology`
`offset()`	`ZoneOffset`
`localDate()`	`LocalDate`
`localTime()`	`LocalTime`
`precision()`	`TemporalUnit`
`zoneId()`	`ZoneId`
`zone()`	`ZoneId`

Obviously, not all Time API types support each query type. For example, you can't get a `ZoneId`/`ZoneOffset` from a `Local-` type. Each method is documented[6] quite well with their supported types and intended use cases.

LocalDate-Range Streams

Java 9 introduced Stream capabilities for a single JSR 310 type, `java.time.Local Date`, to create a consecutive range of `LocalDate` elements. You don't have to worry about all the intricacies and edge cases of different calendar systems and how the date calculations are actually performed. The Date and Time API will handle them for you by giving you a consistent and easy-to-use abstraction.

Two `LocalDate` instance methods create an ordered and consecutive Stream:

- `Stream<LocalDate> datesUntil(LocalDate endExclusive)`
- `Stream<LocalDate> datesUntil(LocalDate endExclusive, Period step)`

Their implementation won't overflow, meaning that any element plus `step` *must* be before `endExclusive`. The direction of the dates isn't future-only, too. If `endExclusive` is in the past, you must provide a negative `step` to create a Stream going toward the past.

Measuring Stream Performance with JMH

Throughout the book, I mention how Java's functional techniques and tools, like Streams, incur a certain overhead compared to a traditional approach and that you have to consider it. This is why measuring the performance of Stream pipelines with benchmarks can be crucial. Streams aren't an easy target for benchmarking because

---

6 The official documentation of `java.time.temporal.TemporalQueries` (*https://oreil.ly/ibSAv*) lists in detail which types are supported by each predefined `TemporalQuery`.

they are complex pipelines of multiple operations with many optimizations behind the scenes that depend on their data and operations.

The JVM and its *just-in-time* compiler can be tricky to benchmark and determine the actual performance. That's where the *Java Micro-Benchmarking Harness* (JMH) comes in to help.

The JMH (*https://oreil.ly/a6UN4*) takes care of JVM warm-up, iterations, and code optimizations that might dilute the results, making them more reliable and, therefore, a better baseline for evaluation. It's the de facto standard for benchmarking and got included in the JDK with version 12.[7]

Plugins are available for IDEs and build systems like Gradle (*https://oreil.ly/w3ZAg*), IntelliJ (*https://oreil.ly/5PcfZ*), Jenkins (*https://oreil.ly/s1VY9*), or TeamCity (*https://oreil.ly/TDFe6*).

The JMH GitHub repository sample directory (*https://oreil.ly/zXe-w*) has a myriad of well-documented benchmarks explaining the intricacies of its usage.

I won't talk further about how to benchmark Streams or lambdas in general because it is out of scope for this chapter and it could easily consume the space of an entire book. In fact, I recommend you check out *Optimizing Java* by Benjamin J Evans, James Gough, and Chris Newland[8] and *Java Performance* by Scott Oaks[9] to learn more about benchmarking and how to measure performance in Java.

More about Collectors

Chapter 6 introduced Collectors and the corresponding terminal operation `collect` as a powerful tool to aggregate a Stream pipeline's elements into new data structures. The utility type `java.util.stream.Collectors` has a plethora of `static` factory methods to create Collectors for almost any task, from simple aggregation into a new `Collection` type, or even more complex, multistep aggregation pipelines. Such more complex Collectors are done with the concept of *downstream Collectors*.

The general idea of Collectors is simple: collect elements into a new data structure. That's a pretty straightforward operation if you want a `Collection`-based type like `List` or `Set`. In the case of a `Map`, however, you usually need complex logic to get a correctly formed data structure that fulfills your goal.

---

7 JMH is also supported for Java versions before 12, but you need to include its two dependencies manually: JMH Core (*https://oreil.ly/vdrjs*) and the JMH Generators: Annotation Processors (*https://oreil.ly/xwzUT*).

8 Benjamin J. Evans, James Gough, and Chris Newland, *Optimizing Java* (*https://oreil.ly/pnUYh*) (O'Reilly, 2018).

9 Scott Oaks, *Java Performance* (*https://oreil.ly/A3vJQ*), 2nd ed. (O'Reilly, 2018).

Collecting a sequence of elements to a key-value-based data structure like Map can be done in various ways, each with its own challenges. For example, even with a simple key-value mapping where each key has only one value, there's already the problem of key collisions to be dealt with. But if you want to further transform the Map's value part, like grouping, reducing, or partitioning, you need a way to manipulate the collected values. That's where downstream Collectors come into play.

Downstream Collectors

Some of the predefined Collectors available via `java.util.stream.Collectors` factory methods accept an additional Collector to manipulate downstream elements. Basically, this means that after the primary Collector has done its job, the downstream Collector makes further changes to the collected values. It's almost like a secondary Stream pipeline working on the previously collected elements.

Typical tasks for downstream Collectors include:

- Transforming
- Reducing
- Flattening
- Filtering
- Composite Collector operations

All examples of this section will use the following User Record and users data source:

```
record User(UUID id,
            String group,
            LocalDateTime lastLogin,
            List<String> logEntries) { }

List<User> users = ...;
```

Transforming elements

Grouping Stream elements into simple key-value Map's is easy with the `Collec tors.groupingBy` methods. The value part of a key-value mapping, though, might not be represented in the form you need and thus require additional transformation.

For example, grouping a Stream<User> by its group creates a Map<String, List<User>>:

```
Map<String, List<User>> lookup =
  users.stream()
       .collect(Collectors.groupingBy(User::group));
```

Simple enough.

What if you don't want the whole User and only its id in its place? You can't use an intermediate map operation to transform the elements before collecting them because you wouldn't have access to the User anymore to actually group them. Instead, you can use a downstream Collector to transform the collected elements. That's why multiple groupingBy methods are available, like the one we're going to use in this section:

```
static <T, K, A, D> Collector<T, ?, Map<K, D>>
groupingBy(Function<? super T, ? extends K> classifier,
           Collector<? super T, A, D> downstream)
```

Although the different generic types in this method signature might look intimidating, don't fret! Let's break the signature down into its parts to get a better understanding of what's happening.

The four types involved are listed in Table 7-4.

Table 7-4. Generic types of groupingBy

Generic Type	Used for
T	The Stream's elements type before collecting
K	The Map result's key type
D	The type of the result Map value part that is created by the downstream Collector
A	The accumulator type of the downstream Collector

As you can see, each type of the method signature represents a part of the overall process.

- The classifier creates the keys by mapping the elements of type T to the key type K.

- The downstream Collector aggregates the elements of type T to the new result type D.

- The overall result will therefore be a Map<K, D>.

 Java's type inference will usually do the heavy lifting of matching the correct types for you, so you don't have to think much about the actual generic signatures if you only want to use such complex generic methods and not write them yourself. If a type mismatch occurs and the compiler can't deduct the types automatically, try to refactor the operation logic into dedicated variables with the help of your IDE to see the inferred types. It's easier to tweak smaller blocks of code than an entire Stream pipeline at once.

In essence, each Collector accepting an additional downstream Collector consists of the original logic—in this case, the key-mapper—and a downstream Collector, affecting the values mapped to a key. You can think of the downstream collecting process as working like another Stream that's collected. Instead of all elements, though, it only encounters the values associated with the key by the primary Collector.

Let's get back to the lookup Map for `User` groups. The goal is to create a `Map<String, Set<UUID>>`, mapping the `User` groups to a list of distinct `id` instances. The best way to create a downstream Collector is to think about the particular steps required to achieve your goal and which factory methods of `java.util.stream.Collectors` could achieve them.

First, you want the `id` of a `User` element, which is a mapping operation. The method `Collector<T, ?, R> mapping(Function<? super T, ? extends U> mapper, Collector<? super U, A, R> downstream)` creates a Collector that maps the collected elements before passing them down to another Collector. The reasoning behind requiring another downstream Collector is simple; the mapping Collector's sole purpose is, as you might have guessed, *mapping* the elements. The actual collection of mapped elements is outside its scope and therefore delegated to the downstream Collectors.

Second, you want to collect the mapped elements into a `Set`, which can be done using the `Collectors.toSet` method.

By writing the Collectors separately, their intent and hierarchy become more visible:

```
// COLLECT ELEMENTS TO SET
Collector<UUID, ?, Set<UUID>> collectToSet = Collectors.toSet();

// MAP FROM USER TO UUID
Collector<User, ?, Set<UUID>> mapToId =
  Collectors.mapping(User::id, collectToSet);

// GROUPING BY GROUP
Collector<User, ?, Map<String, Set<UUID>>> groupingBy =
  Collectors.groupingBy(User::group, mapToId);
```

As I said before, you can usually let the compiler infer the types and use the `Collectors` factory methods directly. If you import the class statically, you can even forgo the repetitive `Collectors.` prefix. Combining all the Collectors and using them in the Stream pipeline leads to a straightforward collection pipeline:

```
import static java.util.stream.Collectors.*;

Map<String, Set<UUID>> lookup =
  users.stream()
       .collect(groupingBy(User::group,
                           mapping(User::id, toSet())));
```

The result type is inferable by the compiler, too. Still, I prefer to explicitly state it to communicate better what kind of type is returned by the Stream pipeline.

An alternative approach is keeping the primary downstream Collector as a variable to keep the collect call simpler. The downside of this is the necessity to help the compiler infer the correct types if it's not obvious, like in the case of using a lambda expression instead of a method reference:

```
// METHOD REFERENCE
var collectIdsToSet = Collectors.mapping(User::id, ❶
                                    Collectors.toSet());

// LAMBDA ALTERNATIVE
var collectIdsToSetLambda = Collectors.mapping((User user) -> user.id(), ❷
                                    Collectors.toSet());

Map<String, Set<UUID>> lookup =
  users.stream()
       .collect(Collectors.groupingBy(User::group,
                                    collectIdsToSet)); ❸
```

❶ The method reference tells the compiler which type the Stream's elements are, so the downstream Collector knows it, too.

❷ The lambda variant of mapper needs to know the type to work with. You can either provide an explicit type to the lambda argument or replace var with the more complicated generic Collector<T, A , R> signature.

❸ The collect call is still expressive thanks to the variable name. If certain aggregation operations are commonly used, you should consider refactoring them into an auxiliary type with factory methods, similar to java.util.stream. Collectors.

Reducing elements

Sometimes, a reduction operation is needed instead of an aggregation. The general approach to designing a reducing downstream Collector is identical to the previous section: define your overall goal, dissect it into the necessary steps, and finally, create the downstream Collector.

For this example, instead of creating a lookup Map for id by group, let's count the logEntries per User.

The overall goal is to count the log entries per User element. The required steps are getting the log count of a User and summing them up to the final tally.

You could use the Collectors.mapping factory method with another downstream Collector to achieve the goal:

```
var summingUp = Collectors.reducing(0, Integer::sum);

var downstream =
  Collectors.mapping((User user) -> user.logEntries().size(), summingUp);

Map<UUID, Integer> logCountPerUserId =
  users.stream()
       .collect(Collectors.groupingBy(User::id, downstream));
```

Instead of requiring a mapping and reducing downstream Collector working in tandem, you could use one of the other `Collector.reduce` variants, which includes a mapper:

```
Collector<T, ?, U> reducing(U identity,
                            Function<? super T, ? extends U> mapper,
                            BinaryOperator<U> op)
```

This `reduce` variant needs, in addition to a seed value (`identity`) and the reduction operation (`op`), a `mapper` to transform the `User` elements into the desired value:

```
var downstream =
  Collectors.reducing(0,                                       // identity
                      (User user) -> user.logEntries().size(), // mapper
                      Integer::sum);                           // op

Map<UUID, Integer> logCountPerUserId =
  users.stream()
       .collect(Collectors.groupingBy(User::id, downstream));
```

Like the `reduce` intermediate operation, a reducing Collector for downstream operations is an incredibly flexible tool, being able to combine multiple steps into a single operation. Which method to choose, multi-downstream Collectors or single reduction, depends on personal preferences and the overall complexity of the collection process. If you only need to sum up numbers, though, the `java.util.stream.Collectors` type also gives you more specialized variants:

```
var downstream =
  Collectors.summingInt((User user) -> user.logEntries().size());

Map<UUID, Integer> logCountPerUserId =
  users.stream()
       .collect(Collectors.groupingBy(User::id, downstream));
```

The `summing` Collector is available for the usual primitive types (`int`, `long`, `float`). Besides summing up numbers, you can calculate averages (prefixed with `averaging`) or simply count the elements with the help of the `Collectors.counting` method.

Flattening collections

Dealing with Collection-based elements in Streams usually requires a `flatMap` intermediate operation to "flatten" the Collection back into discrete elements to work with further down the pipeline, or you'll end up with nested Collections like `List<List<String>>`. The same is true for the collecting process of a Stream.

Grouping all `logEntries` by their `group` would result in a `Map<String, List<List<String>>>`, which most likely won't be what you want. Java 9 added a new predefined Collector with built-in flattening capabilities:

```
static Collector<T, ?, R> flatMapping(Function<T, Stream<U>> mapper,
                                      Collector<U, A, R> downstream)
```

Like the other added Collector, `Collectors.filtering`, which I discuss in "Filtering elements" on page 184, it doesn't provide any advantages over an explicit `flatMap` intermediate operation if used as the sole Collector. But, used in a multilevel reduction, like `groupingBy` or `partitionBy`, it gives you access to the original Stream element *and* allows for flattening the collected elements:

```
var downstream =
  Collectors.flatMapping((User user) -> user.logEntries().stream(),
                         Collectors.toList());

Map<String, List<String>> result =
  users.stream()
       .collect(Collectors.groupingBy(User::group, downstream));
```

Similar to transforming and reducing Collectors, you will get the hang of when to use a flattening downstream Collector. If the result type of the Stream pipeline doesn't match your expectations, you likely need a downstream Collector to remedy the situation, either by using `Collectors.mapping` or `Collectors.flatMapping`.

Filtering elements

Filtering Stream elements is an essential part of almost any Stream pipeline, done with the help of the intermediate `filter` operation. Java 9 added a new predefined Collector with built-in filtering capabilities, moving the step of filtering elements to directly before the accumulation process:

```
static <T, A, R> Collector<T, ?, R> filtering(Predicate<T> predicate,
                                              Collector<T, A, R> downstream)
```

On its own, it's no different from an intermediate `filter` operation. As a downstream Collector, though, its behavior is quite different from `filter`, easily seen when grouping elements:

```
import static java.util.stream.Collectors.*;

var startOfDay = LocalDate.now().atStartOfDay();

Predicate<User> loggedInToday =
  Predicate.not(user -> user.lastLogin().isBefore(startOfDay));
```

```
// WITH INTERMEDIATE FILTER

Map<String, Set<UUID>> todaysLoginsByGroupWithFilterOp =
  users.stream()
       .filter(loggedInToday)
       .collect(groupingBy(User::group,
                           mapping(User::id, toSet()))));


// WITH COLLECT FILTER

Map<String, Set<UUID>> todaysLoginsByGroupWithFilteringCollector =
  users.stream()
       .collect(groupingBy(User::group,
                           filtering(loggedInToday,
                                     mapping(User::id, toSet())))));
```

You might expect an equivalent result, but the order of operations leads to different results:

Intermediate filter first, grouping second
   Using an intermediate `filter` operation removes any undesired element before any collection occurs. Therefore, no groups of users that haven't logged in today are included in the resulting `Map`, as illustrated in Figure 7-1.

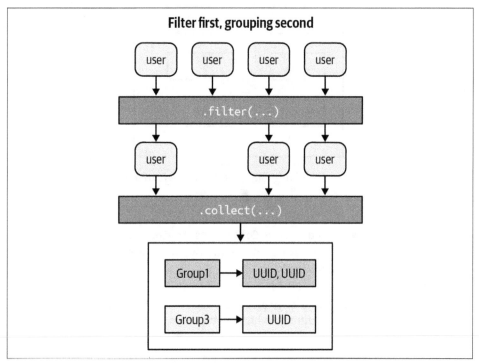

Figure 7-1. Grouping elements with "filter first, grouping second"

Group first, filter downstream

Without an intermediate `filter` operation, the `groupingBy` Collector will encounter all `User` elements, regardless of their last login date. The downstream Collector, `Collectors.filtering`, is responsible for filtering the elements, so the returned `Map` still includes all user groups, regardless of the last login. The flow of elements is illustrated in Figure 7-2.

Which approach is preferable depends on your requirements. Filtering first returns the least number of key-value pairs possible, but grouping first grants you access to all `Map` keys and their (maybe) empty values.

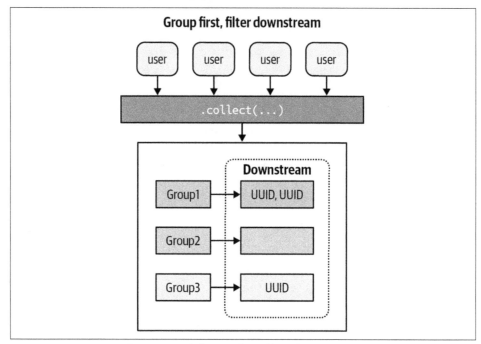

Figure 7-2. Grouping elements with "group first, filter downstream"

Composite collectors

The last Collector I want to discuss is `Collectors.teeing`, which was added in Java 12. It differs from the others because it accepts two downstream Collectors at once and combines both results into one.

> The name *teeing* originates from one of the most common pipe fittings—the T-fitting—which has the shape of a capital letter T.

The Stream's elements first pass through both downstream Collectors, so a BiFunction can merge both results as the second step, as illustrated in Figure 7-3.

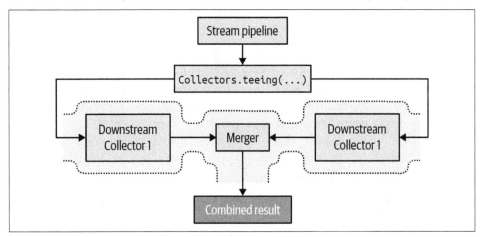

Figure 7-3. Teeing Collector flow of elements

Imagine you want to know how many users you have and how many of them never logged in. Without the `teeing` operation, you would have to traverse the elements twice: once for the overall count and another time for counting the never-logged-in users. Both counting tasks can be represented by dedicated Collectors, `counting` and `filtering`, so you need to traverse the elements only once and let `teeing` do the two counting tasks at the end of the pipeline. The results are then merged with a `BiFunction<Long, Long>` into the new data structure `UserStats`. Example 7-5 shows how to implement it.

Example 7-5. Finding min and max login dates

```
record UserStats(long total, long neverLoggedIn) { ❶
  // NO BODY
}

UserStats result =
  users.stream()
      .collect(Collectors.teeing(Collectors.counting(), ❷
              Collectors.filtering(user -> user.lastLogin() == null, ❸
                            Collectors.counting()),
              UserStats::new)); ❹
```

❶   A local Record type is used as the result type because Java lacks dynamic tuples.

❷   The first downstream Collector counts all elements.

❸ The second downstream Collector filters first and uses an additional downstream Collector to count the remaining elements.

❹ A method reference to the UserStats constructor serves as the merge function of the two downstream Collector results.

Like many functional additions, the teeing Collector might initially seem strange if you're coming from a mainly object-oriented background. On its own, a for-loop with two out-of-body variables to count could achieve the same result. The difference lies in how the teeing Collector benefits from the Stream pipeline and its overall advantages and functional possibilities, not just the terminal operation itself.

Creating Your Own Collector

The auxiliary type java.util.stream.Collectors gives you more than 44 predefined factory methods in the current LTS Java version 17 at the time of writing this book. They cover most general use cases, especially if used in tandem. There may be times when you need a custom, more context-specific Collector that's more domain-specific and easier to use than a predefined one. That way, you can also share such specific Collectors in a custom auxiliary class, like Collectors.

Recall from Chapter 6 that Collectors aggregate elements with the help of four methods:

- Supplier<A> supplier()
- BiConsumer<A, T> accumulator()
- BinaryOperator<A> combiner()
- Function<A, R> finisher()

A method of the Collector interface I haven't mentioned is Set<Characteristics> characteristics(). Like Streams via their underlying Spliterator, Collectors have a set of characteristics that allow for different optimization techniques. The three currently available options are listed in Table 7-5.

Table 7-5. Available java.util.Collector.Characteristics

Characteristic	Description
CONCURRENT	Supports parallel processing.
IDENTITY_FINISH	The finisher is the identity function, returning the accumulator itself. In this case, only a cast is required instead of calling the finisher itself.
UNORDERED	Indicates that the order of Stream elements isn't necessarily preserved.

To better understand how these parts fit together, we're going to recreate one of the existing Collectors, Collectors.joining(CharSequence delimiter), which joins CharSequence elements, separated by the delimiter argument. Example 7-6 shows how to implement the Collector<T, A, R> interface with a java.util.String Joiner to achieve the required functionality.

Example 7-6. Custom Collector for joining String elements

```java
public class Joinector implements Collector<CharSequence, // T
                                            StringJoiner, // A
                                            String> {     // R

  private final CharSequence delimiter;

  public Joinector(CharSequence delimiter) {
    this.delimiter = delimiter;
  }

  @Override
  public Supplier<StringJoiner> supplier() {
    return () -> new StringJoiner(this.delimiter); ❶
  }

  @Override
  public BiConsumer<StringJoiner, CharSequence> accumulator() {
    return StringJoiner::add; ❷
  }

  @Override
  public BinaryOperator<StringJoiner> combiner() {
    return StringJoiner::merge; ❸
  }

  @Override
  public Function<StringJoiner, String> finisher() {
    return StringJoiner::toString; ❹
  }

  @Override
  public Set<Characteristics> characteristics() {
    return Collections.emptySet(); ❺
  }
}
```

❶ The StringJoiner type is the perfect mutable results container due to its public API and delimiter support.

❷ The accumulation logic for adding new elements to the container is as simple as using the proper method reference.

❸ The logic for combining multiple containers is also available via method reference.

❹ The last step, transforming the results container to the actual result, is done with the container's `toString` method.

❺ The `Joinector` doesn't have any of the available Collector characteristics, so an empty `Set` is returned.

Simple enough, but it's still a lot of code for very little functionality consisting mostly of returning method references. Thankfully, there are convenience factory methods called of available on `Collector` to simplify the code:

```
Collector<CharSequence, StringJoiner, String> joinector =
   Collector.of(() -> new StringJoiner(delimiter), // supplier
              StringJoiner::add,                    // accumulator
              StringJoiner::merge,                  // combiner
              StringJoiner::toString);              // finisher
```

This shorter version is equivalent to the previous full implementation of the interfaces.

The last argument of the `Collector.of` method isn't always visible, if not set; it's a vararg of the Collector's characteristics.

Creating your own Collectors should be reserved for custom-result data structures or to simplify domain-specific tasks. Even then, you should first try to achieve the results with the available Collectors and a mix of downstream Collectors. The Java team has invested a lot of time and knowledge to give you safe and easy-to-use generic solutions that can be combined into quite complex and powerful solutions. Then, if you have a working Collector, you can still refactor it into an auxiliary class to make it reusable and easier on the eyes.

Final Thoughts on (Sequential) Streams

The Java Streams API is, in my opinion, an absolute game changer, and that's why it's important to know about the multitude of available operations and ways to use Streams for different tasks. Streams give you a fluent, concise, and straightforward approach to data processing, with an option to go parallel if needed, as you'll learn more about in Chapter 8. Still, they aren't designed to replace preexisting constructs like loops, merely to complement them.

The most important skill you as a Java developer should acquire regarding Streams is finding the balance between using just enough Stream pipelines to improve the readability and reasonability of your code without sacrificing performance by ignoring traditional looping constructs.

Not every loop needs to be a Stream. However, not every Stream would be better off being a loop, either. The more you get used to using Streams for data processing, the easier you will find a healthy balance between the two approaches to data processing.

Takeaways

- The Stream API provides a wide range of possibilities to create Streams, from iterative approaches that are similar to traditional looping constructs to specialized variants for certain types like file I/O or the new Date and Time API.

- Like functional interfaces, most Streams and their operations support primitive types via specialized types to reduce the amount of autoboxing. These specialized variants can give you a performance-wise edge if needed but will restrict the available operations. But you can always switch between primitive and non-primitive Streams in a pipeline to gain the benefits of both worlds.

- Downstream Collectors can affect the collection process in multiple ways, like transforming or filtering, to manipulate the result into the representation required for your task.

- If a combination of downstream Collectors cannot fulfill your task, you can fall back on creating your own Collector instead.

CHAPTER 8

Parallel Data Processing with Streams

Our world is overwhelmingly concurrent and parallel; we can almost always do more than one thing at once. Our programs need to solve more and more problems, and that's why data processing often benefits from being parallel, too.

In Chapter 6, you've learned about Streams as data processing pipelines built of functional operations. Now it's time to go parallel!

In this chapter, you will learn about the importance of concurrency and parallelism, how and when to use parallel Streams, and when not to. Everything you learned in the previous two chapters about data processing with Streams so far also applies to using them for parallel processing. That's why this chapter will concentrate on the differences and intricacies of parallel Streams.

Concurrency versus Parallelism

The terms *parallelism* and *concurrency* often get mixed up because the concepts are closely related. Rob Pike, one of the co-designers of the programming language *Go* (*https://go.dev*), defined the terms nicely:

> Concurrency is about *dealing* with a lot of things at once. Parallelism is about *doing* a lot of things at once. The ideas are, obviously, related, but one is inherently associated with structure, and the other is associated with execution. Concurrency is structuring things in a way that might allow parallelism to actually execute them simultaneously. But parallelism is not the goal of concurrency. The goal of concurrency is good structure and the possibility to implement execution modes like parallelism.
>
> —Rob Pike, "Concurrency Is Not Parallelism" at Waza 2012 (*https://oreil.ly/iS_oL*)

Concurrency is the general concept of multiple tasks running in overlapping time periods competing over the available resources. A single CPU core interleaves them by scheduling and switching between tasks as it sees fit. Switching between tasks is relatively easy and fast. This way, two tasks can figuratively run on a single CPU core simultaneously, even though they literally don't. Think of it like a juggler using only one hand (single CPU core) with multiple balls (tasks). They can hold only a single ball at any time (doing the work), but which ball it is changes over time (interrupting and switching to another task). Even with only two balls, they have to juggle the workload.

Parallelism, on the other hand, isn't about managing interleaved tasks but their simultaneous execution. If more than one CPU core is available, the tasks can run in parallel on different cores. The juggler now uses both hands (more than one CPU core) to hold two balls at once (doing the work simultaneously).

See Figure 8-1 for a more visual representation of how thread scheduling differs between the two concepts.

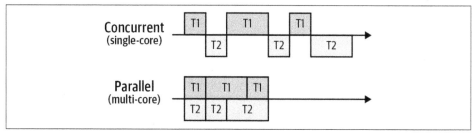

Figure 8-1. Concurrent versus parallel thread execution

Concurrency and parallelism in Java share the same goal: taking care of multiple tasks with threads. Their difference lies in the challenge of doing it efficiently, with ease, and doing it right and safely.

Concurrency and Parallelism in the Real World

A real-world example of the distinction between concurrency and parallelism is walkie-talkies. On a single channel, people can talk concurrently, one at a time. They manage the context switching by saying "over" so the other person can talk. If you introduce multiple walkie-talkie channels, people can talk in parallel. Each channel is still concurrent, requiring a locking mechanism. But on different channels, people can talk simultaneously without requiring coordination between channels.

Both multitasking concepts aren't mutually exclusive and are often used together.

One thing to consider when using multiple threads is that you can no longer easily follow or debug the actual flow of your application as you could do in a single-threaded one. To use data structures in concurrent environments, they have to be "thread-safe," usually requiring coordination with locks, semaphores, etc., to work correctly and guarantee safe access to any shared state. Executing code in parallel usually lacks such coordination because it's focused on the execution itself. This makes it safer, more natural, and easier to reason with.

Streams as Parallel Functional Pipelines

Java provides an easy-to-use data processing pipeline with parallel processing capabilities: *Streams*. As discussed in Chapter 6, they process their operations in sequential order by default. However, a single method call switches the pipeline into "parallel mode," either the intermediate Stream operation `parallel`, or the `parallelStream` method available on `java.util.Collection`-based types. Going back to a sequentially processed Stream is possible by calling the intermediate operation `sequential`.

 Switching between execution modes by calling either the `parallel` or `sequential` method affects a Stream pipeline as a whole regardless of the position in the pipeline. The last one called before the terminal operation dictates the mode for the whole pipeline. There's no way to run a certain part of the Stream in a different execution mode from the rest.

Parallel Streams use the concept of *recursive decomposition*, meaning they *divide and conquer* the data source by splitting up the elements with the underlying Spliterator to process chunks of elements in parallel. Each chunk is processed by a dedicated thread and may even be split up again, recursively, until the Stream API is satisfied that the chunks and threads are a good match for the available resources.

You don't have to create or manage these threads or use an explicit `ExecutorService`. Instead, the Stream API uses the common `ForkJoinPool` internally to spin-off and manage new threads.

ForkJoinPool

A `ForkJoinPool` executes threads in a *work-stealing* manner. That means that worker threads that have finished their own tasks can "steal" tasks from other threads waiting to be processed, and therefore utilize idle threads more efficiently.

The *common* `ForkJoinPool` is a lazily initialized `static` thread pool managed by the runtime itself. It's configured with sensible defaults to utilize the available resources the best way possible, e.g., not using up all CPU cores at once. If the defaults don't fit your requirements, you can configure certain aspects via system properties, as explained in its documentation (*https://oreil.ly/VUL8g*).

Two major concurrent features use the common ForkJoinPool: parallel Streams, and asynchronous Tasks with CompletableFutures, which you'll learn more about in Chapter 13.

These chunks of elements and their operations are forked into multiple threads. Finally, the subresults of the threads are joined again to derive a final result, as shown in Figure 8-2.

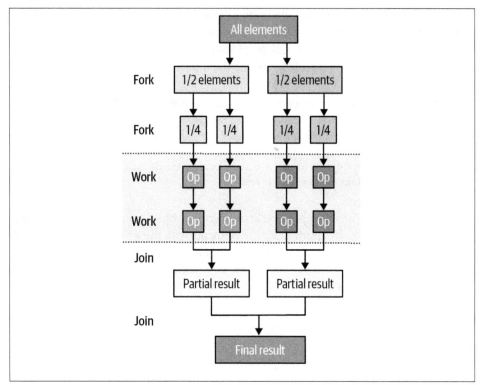

Figure 8-2. Parallel Stream Fork/Join

The size of the chunks varies, depending on the Stream's data source underlying Spliterator characteristics. "Choosing the Right Data Source" on page 200 goes over the different characteristics and data sources and their affinity for proficiency in splitting elements into chunks.

Parallel Streams in Action

To illustrate how to process a Stream in parallel, we're going to count the occurrences of distinct words in Tolstoy's *War and Peace*,[1] as was previously done. First, a rough approach should be outlined as a blueprint for the necessary steps that need to be translated into Stream operations:

- Loading the content of *War and Peace*
- Cleaning the content by removing punctuation, etc.
- Splitting the content to create words
- Counting all distinct words

Instead of using the `Files.lines` method, as used with serial Stream processing in "Reading Files Line-By-Line" on page 173, a more naïve sequential approach, as shown in Example 8-1, is chosen to better represent the improvements the right data source and parallel Streams can have.

Example 8-1. Sequentially counting words in War and Peace

```
var location = Paths.get("war-and-peace-text.txt");

// CLEANUP PATTERNS ❶
var punctuation = Pattern.compile("\\p{Punct}");
var whitespace  = Pattern.compile("\\s+");
var words       = Pattern.compile("\\w+");

try {
  // LOAD CONTENT ❷
  var content = Files.readString(location);

  Map<String, Integer> wordCount =
    Stream.of(content)
          // CLEAN CONTENT ❸
          .map(punctuation::matcher)
          .map(matcher -> matcher.replaceAll(""))
          // SPLIT TO WORDS ❹
          .map(whitespace::split)
          .flatMap(Arrays::stream)
          .filter(word -> words.matcher(word).matches())
          // COUNTING ❺
          .map(String::toLowerCase)
          .collect(Collectors.toMap(Function.identity(),
                                    word -> 1,
```

---

1 Project Gutenberg provides multiple versions of Tolstoy's *War and Peace* (*https://oreil.ly/AXag1*) for free. The plain-text version is used so no additional formatting affects the process of counting words.

```
                                    Integer::sum));
} (IOException e) {
  // ...
}
```

❶ Multiple precompiled Pattern instances are used to clean up the content.

❷ The content is read in one swoop.

❸ The cleanup patterns remove all punctuation.

❹ The lines are split on whitespace and the resulting String[] array is flat-mapped to a Stream of String elements, which are further filtered to be actually "words."

❺ Counting words in a case-insensitive fashion is done simply by converting all words to lowercase and letting a Collector do the actual work.

Counting is done with the help of Collectors.toMap, which takes the words as keys by calling Function.identity(), which is a shortcut to create a Function<T, T> that returns its input argument. If a key collision occurs, meaning a word is encountered more than once, the Collector merges the existing value with the new value, 1, by evaluating Integer::sum with both values.

On my computer with a 6-core/12-thread CPU, the sequential version runs in ~140 ms.

 Threads, in the case of a CPU, refer to *simultaneous multithreading* (SMT), not Java threads. It's often referred to as *hyperthreading*, which is the proprietary implementation of SMT by Intel.

This initial Stream pipeline might solve the problem of counting words in *War and Peace* but it leaves quite some room for improvement. Making it parallel wouldn't change much because the data source provides only a singular element, so only later operations can be forked off. So how can the pipeline be redesigned to gain performance from a parallel approach?

If you think back to Figure 8-2, parallel Streams fork pipelines of operations that are merged back together to create a result. Right now, the pipeline counts words for a singular String, which is the whole book. The pipeline could easily count words in any String element flowing through it and let the terminal collect operation merge the results just as easily.

For a good parallel performance of all operations, the Stream pipeline needs a data source with multiple elements. Instead of using Files.readString, the convenience type also has a Stream-creating method that reads a file line-by-line: static Stream<String> lines(Path path) throws IOException. Even though processing more elements will result in more clean-up operation calls in total, the tasks are distributed to multiple threads run in parallel to use the available resources most efficiently.

Another important change must be done to the collect operation. To ensure no ConcurrentModificationException occurs, the thread-safe variant Collectors.toConcurrentMap is used with the same arguments as before.

 As Collectors share a mutable intermediate results container, they're susceptible to concurrent modifications from multiple threads during the combiner step. That's why you should always check the documentation of the Collector used in a parallel pipeline for thread safety, and choose an appropriate alternative if necessary.

All these small adaptions to switch to a parallel approach accumulate in the code shown in Example 8-2.

Example 8-2. Parallel counting words in War and Peace

```
// ...

// LOAD CONTENT ❶
try (Stream<String> stream = Files.lines(location)) {

  Map<String, Integer> wordCount =
    stream.parallel()
          // CLEAN LINES ❷
          .map(punctionaction::matcher)
          .map(matcher -> matcher.replaceAll(""))
          .map(whitespace::split)
          // SPLIT TO WORDS ❷
          .flatMap(Arrays::stream)
          .filter(word -> words.matcher(word).matches())
          // COUNTING ❸
          .map(String::toLowerCase)
          .collect(Collectors.toConcurrentMap(Function.identity(),
                                              word -> 1,
                                              Integer::sum));
}
```

❶ The Files.lines call requires you to close the Stream. Using it in a try-with-resources-block delegates the work to the runtime, so you don't have to close it manually.

❷ All previous steps—cleaning and splitting the lines—are unchanged.

❸ Counting is done the same way but with a thread-safe Collector variant instead.

By using an optimized data source and adding a `parallel` operation call into the pipeline, the required time decreases to ~25 ms.

That's a performance increase of over 5x! So why don't we always use parallel Streams?

When to Use and When to Avoid Parallel Streams

Why use a sequential Stream if a parallel Stream can provide a performance boost with a single method call and a few considerations to the data source and terminal operation? The simple answer: any performance gains aren't guaranteed and are affected by many factors. Using parallel Streams is primarily a performance optimization and should always be a conscious and informed decision, not just because it's *easy* thanks to a single method call.

There are no *absolute* rules about choosing parallel over sequential data processing. The criteria depend on many different factors, like your requirements, the task at hand, available resources, etc., and all influence each other. That's why there is no easy answer to the question "when should I use parallel Streams?", neither *quantitative* nor *qualitative*. Still, there are certain *informal* guidelines that provide a good starting point to decide.

Let's take a look at them in order of how a Stream pipeline is built, from creating a Stream to adding intermediate operations and finishing the pipeline by adding the terminal operation.

Choosing the Right Data Source

Every Stream—sequential or parallel—begins with a data source handled by a Spliterator.

In a sequential Stream, the Spliterator behaves like a simple Iterator, supplying the Stream with one element after another. For parallel Streams, however, the data source gets split up into multiple chunks. Ideally, these chunks are of roughly equivalent size, so the work is distributed evenly, but that isn't always possible, depending on the data source itself. This splitting process is called *decomposing the data source*. It can be cheap and favorable for parallel processing, or complicated and costly.

For example, an array-based data source, like `ArrayList`, knows its exact size and easily decomposes because the location of all elements is known, so equally large chunks are easily obtainable.

A linked list, on the other hand, is a fundamentally sequential data source, with each of its elements effectively knowing only their direct neighbors. Finding a specific position means you have to traverse all beforehand. Java's implementation, LinkedList, cheats by keeping track of the size, which creates the more favorable Spliterator characteristics SIZED and SUBSIZED. Nevertheless, it's not a preferred data source for parallel Streams.

Table 8-1 lists different common data sources and their decomposability for parallel use.

Table 8-1. Parallel decomposability

Data source	Parallel Decomposability
IntStream.range / .rangeClosed	+++
Arrays.stream (primitives)	+++
ArrayList	++
Arrays.stream (objects)	++
HashSet	+
TreeSet	+
LinkedList	--
Stream.iterate	--

The degree of efficient decomposability isn't the only factor regarding data sources and their possible performance in parallel Streams. A more technical aspect that's easy to overlook is *data locality*.

Besides more cores, modern computers feature a myriad of caches to improve performance at a memory level. Where memory is stored depends on the decisions made by the runtime and the CPU itself. Reading from an L1 cache is ~100 times faster than RAM; L2 cache ~25 times. The "closer" the data is to actual processing, the better performance can be achieved.

Usually, JDK implementations store object fields and arrays in adjacent memory locations. This design allows for prefetching "near" data and speeding up any task.

Arrays and lists of reference types, a List<Integer> or an Integer[], store a collection of pointers to the actual values, compared to an array of primitives—int[]— which stores its values next to each other. If there's a cache miss because the required next value isn't prefetched, the CPU has to wait for the actual data to be loaded, and is therefore wasting resources. That doesn't mean that only primitive arrays are a good match for parallel processing, though. Data locality is just one of many criteria that might affect your decision to choose the right data source for going parallel. Compared to the other criteria, though, it's quite a minuscule one and slightly out of your direct control of how the runtime and JDK store data.

Number of Elements

There's no definitive number of elements that will give you the best parallel performance, but one thing is clear: the more elements a parallel Stream has to process, the better, so it can offset the overhead of coordinating multiple threads.

To process elements in parallel, they must be partitioned, processed, and joined again for the final result. These operations are all related, and finding a sensible balance is a *must-have*. This balance is represented by the *NQ model*.

N represents the number of elements, while Q is the cost of a single task. Their product—$N * Q$—indicates the likeliness of getting a speedup from parallel processing. A general overview of weighing the different aspects can be seen in Figure 8-3.

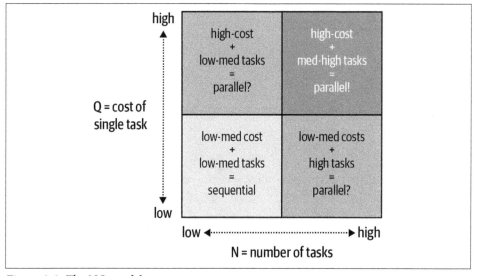

Figure 8-3. The NQ model

As you can see, a higher number of elements is always a good indicator for possible speedup by parallel processing compared to a lower number. Long-running tasks also profit from being run in parallel and might even outweigh the lack of enough elements. But the best-case scenario is having both: lots of elements *and* high-cost tasks.

Stream Operations

After choosing the right data source, the operations are the next puzzle piece. The main goal of designing your parallel operations is to achieve the same final result as with a sequential Stream. That's why most of the design choices for intermediate operations are universal.

In the case of parallel Streams, though, issues that aren't a big deal in sequential Streams can accumulate quickly. So adhering to more functional principles and parallel-friendly operations is important.

Pure lambdas

Lambda expressions used in Stream operations should always be *pure*, meaning they shouldn't rely on *non-local* mutable state or emit any side effects. To mitigate the most apparent non-local state issues, any captured variables must be effectively final, as explained in "Effectively final" on page 21, which affects only the reference itself.

Reading immutable state isn't an issue either. The real problem arises from a thread that changes non-local state, so any access requires synchronization between them, or you end up with non-deterministic behavior, like *race conditions*.

The Origin of Race Conditions

Involving more than one thread in a task introduces a new set of challenges. The most common and urgent is dealing with *state access*. A so-called *race condition* can occur when two or more threads try to access the same shared state.

Reading from multiple threads isn't an issue as long as none of the threads can change the state. Changing the state is a problem, though, because the access order is non-deterministic if it's not (manually) synchronized. The actual access order depends on how the threads are scheduled, and other optimizations are done *behind the scenes*.

The JVM employs the optimizations technique of *reordering* memory access, described in JSR-133 (*https://oreil.ly/EBYLE*), executing it in a different order than that defined in your code. But possible reordering doesn't stop at the JVM. The CPU itself can also execute its instructions in any order and store its memory as it deems best.

The easiest way to prevent any non-deterministic behavior is to make sure that any non-local state is deeply immutable. This way, the lambda stays pure and can't be affected by other threads running the same lambda.

Parallel-friendly operations

Not all Stream operations are a good fit for parallel processing. The simplest way to judge an operation is its reliance on a specific encounter order for the Stream's elements.

For example, the limit, skip, or distinct intermediate operations rely heavily on encounter order to provide a deterministic—or *stable*—behavior for ordered Streams, meaning they always choose or dismiss the same items.

This stability, however, comes at a price in parallel Streams: synchronization across all threads and increased memory needs. For example, to guarantee that the limit operation produces the same results in parallel use as in sequential Streams, it must wait for all preceding operations to finish in encounter order and buffer all elements until it's known if they are needed.

Luckily, not all pipelines require a fixed encounter order. Calling the unordered operation on a Stream pipeline changes the resulting Stream's characteristics to UNORDERED, and therefore, stable operations become unstable. In many cases, it doesn't matter which distinct elements are picked, as long as the final result contains no duplicates. For limit, it's a little trickier and depends on your requirements.

There are also two stable terminal operations that depend on the encounter order of the data source, findFirst and forEach. Both provide an unstable variant, too, as listed in Table 8-2. They should be preferred for parallel Streams if your requirements allow it.

Table 8-2. Stable versus unstable terminal operations

Stable operations	Unstable operations
findFirst()	findAny()
forEachOrdered(Consumer<? super T> action)	forEach(Consumer<? super T> action)

Even with fully parallelized intermediate operations, the final applicative terminal operation in a Stream pipeline is sequential to achieve a singular result or emit a side effect. Just like with unstable intermediate operations, the terminal operations findAny and forEach can profit immensely from being unconstrained from encounter order and having to wait for other elements from other threads.

Reduce versus collect

The terminal operations reduce and collect are two sides of the same coin: both are *reduction*, or *fold*, operations.

In functional programming, *fold* operations combine elements by applying a function to the elements and recombine the results recursively to build up a return value. The difference lies in the general approach on how to recombine the results: immutable versus mutable accumulation.

As discussed in "Reducing versus collecting elements" on page 147, a *mutable* accumulation is more akin to how you would approach the problem in a for-loop, as seen in Example 8-3.

Example 8-3. Mutable accumulation with a for-loop

```
var numbers = List.of(1, 2, 3, 4, 5, 6, ...);

int total = 0;

for (int value : numbers) {
  total += value;
}
```

For a sequentially processed problem, this is a straightforward approach. Using non-local and mutable state, however, is a contraindicator for parallel processing.

Functional programming favors immutable values, so the accumulation depends only on the previous result and current Stream element to produce a new and immutable result. This way, the operations can easily be run in parallel, as seen in Figure 8-4.

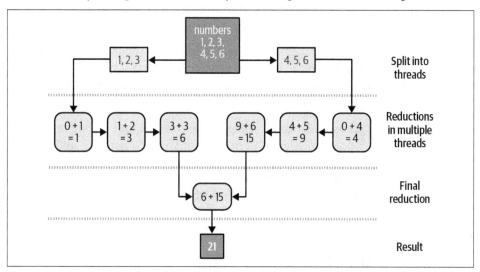

Figure 8-4. Immutable accumulation of numbers

The flow still has the same elements as before: an initial value 0 for each summation of values. Instead of accumulating the results in a single value, each step returns a new value as the left operand for the next summation. The simplest Stream form is shown in Example 8-4.

Example 8-4. Immutable accumulation of numbers with a Stream

```
int total = Stream.of(1, 2, 3, 4, 5, 6, ...)
                .parallel()
                .reduce(0, ❶
                        Integer::sum); ❷
```

❶ The initial value—or *identity*—is used for every parallel reduction operation.

❷ The method reference translates into a BiFunction<Integer, Integer, Integer> to accumulate the previous (or initial) value with the current Stream element.

This more abstract form of reduction is easily parallelizable if it's *associative* and without any shared state. A reduction is associative if the order or grouping of the accumulator arguments is irrelevant to the final result.

Even though immutable reduction is more amenable to parallel processing, it's not the only reduction option in town. Depending on your requirements, a mutable reduction might be a more fitting solution because creating a new immutable result for every accumulation step could be costly. With enough elements, such costs accumulate over time, affecting performance and memory requirements.

A mutable reduction mitigates this overhead by using a mutable results container. The accumulation function receives this container instead of only the prior result, and it doesn't return any value, unlike a reduce operator. To create the final result, the combiner merges all containers.

The factors that a decision between using reduce or collect in sequential and parallel Streams boil down to what kind of element you have and the usability and straightforwardness of the terminal fold operation. There are times when you might need every bit of performance available to you to improve your data processing and a more complicated fold operation. Many other factors affect performance in general, so having an easier-to-understand and maintainable terminal operation might outweigh the downside of sacrificing a little bit more memory and CPU cycles.

Stream Overhead and Available Resources

Compared to traditional looping structures, a Stream always creates an unavoidable overhead, regardless of being sequential or parallel. Their advantage lies in providing a declarative way of defining data processing pipelines and utilizing many functional principles to maximize their ease of use and performance. In most real-world scenarios, though, the overhead is negligible compared to their conciseness and clarity.

In the case of parallel Streams, though, you start with a more significant initial handicap compared to sequential Streams. Besides the overhead of the Stream scaffold itself, you have to think about data source decomposition costs, thread management by the ForkJoinPool, and recombining the final result, to get the full picture of all moving parts. And all those parts must have the resources—CPU cores and memory available to actually run them in parallel.

Coined by the computer scientist Gene Amdahl in 1967, *Amdahl's law*[2] provides a way to calculate the theoretical latency speedup in parallel executions for constant workloads. The law takes the *parallel portion* of a single task and the *number of tasks* running in parallel into account, as shown in Figure 8-5.

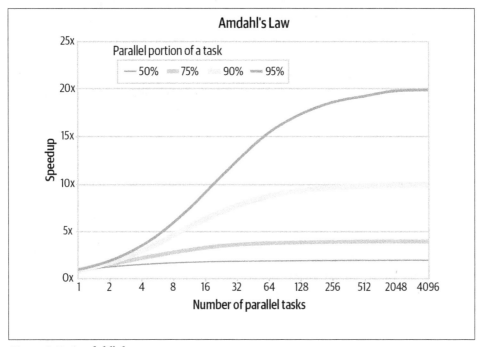

Figure 8-5. Amdahl's law

As you can see, the maximum performance gains have a ceiling depending on the count of parallel tasks that can be run simultaneously. There is no benefit in easily parallelizable tasks if the runtime can't actually run them in parallel due to the lack of adequate resources and is forced to interleave the tasks instead.

Example: War and Peace (revisited)

With all these criteria for parallel Stream performance in mind, let's analyze the previous example of counting the distinct words of Tolstoy's *War and Peace* again to

---

2 The Wikipedia entry on Amdahl's law (*https://oreil.ly/Q-hOb*) describes the actual formula in detail.

better understand why this particular Stream pipeline is a great match for parallel processing.

Data source characteristics
> The Stream is created from a UTF-8 plain text file with the help of the `Files.lines` method, which has quite good parallel characteristics according to its documentation.[3]

Number of elements
> The text file contains over 60,000 lines; therefore, more than 60,000 elements flow through the pipeline. That's not much for modern computers, but it's also not a negligible number of elements.

Intermediate operations
> Each Stream operation works on a single line, completely independent from another, without any shared or outside state that requires coordination. The regular expressions are precompiled and read-only.

Terminal operation
> The Collector can gather the results independently and merges them with a simple arithmetic operation.

Available resources
> My computer has 12 CPU threads available at most, and therefore ~5,000 lines per thread if all of them are utilized.

It looks like the example hit the *parallelism jackpot*, even if not all criteria were matched perfectly. That's why the performance gain for even such a simple task was quite high and near the expected speedup of Amdahl's law for highly parallelizable operations. Looking back at Figure 8-5, the 5x improvement on my setup with 6 cores/12 threads suggests a parallelizability of ~90%.

Example: Random Numbers

This simplistic but deliberately chosen example of counting words in *War and Peace* showed that parallel Streams could provide enormous performance gains that scale with the available resources. But that's not always the case for every workload, especially for more complex ones.

Let's look at another example, working with random numbers, and how `IntStream`—sequential and parallel—compares to a simple `for`-loop, as shown in Example 8-5.

---

3 The call is delegated to `Files.lines(Path path, CharSet cs)`. Its documentation (*https://oreil.ly/Kyqmg*) states possibly good parallel performance due to its `Spliterator` splitting in an optimal ratio under normal circumstances.

Example 8-5. Random number statistics

```java
var elementsCount = 100_000_000; ❶

IntUnaryOperator multiplyByTwo = in -> in * 2; ❷

var rnd = new Random(); ❸

// FOR-LOOP ❹
var loopStats = new IntSummaryStatistics();
for(int idx = 0; idx < elementsCount; idx++) {
  var value = rnd.nextInt();
  var subResult = multiplyByTwo.applyAsInt(value);
  var finalResult = multiplyByTwo.applyAsInt(subResult);
  loopStats.accept(finalResult);
}

// SEQUENTIAL IntStream ❺
var seqStats = rnd.ints(elementsCount)
                  .map(multiplyByTwo)
                  .map(multiplyByTwo)
                  .summaryStatistics();

// PARALLEL IntStream ❻
var parallelStats = rnd.ints(elementsCount)
                  .parallel()
                  .map(multiplyByTwo)
                  .map(multiplyByTwo)
                  .summaryStatistics();
```

❶ 100 million elements should be enough elements to reach the (non-definite) threshold to gain a performance boost from parallel processing.

❷ To do at least some work, the elements will be multiplied by 2 twice with the help of a shared lambda.

❸ The default source for pseudorandom numbers, `java.util.Random`, is used.

❹ The `for`-loop version tries to mimic a Stream as well as possible, including using the same logic for collecting the results.

❺ The sequential Stream is as straightforward as possible: Stream creation, two mapping functions, and then the collection of the results in the form of summary statistics.

❻ The parallel variant only needs to add a `parallel` operation to the Stream pipeline.

Is the summarizing of random numbers a good match for the criteria of parallel processing? Let's analyze!

Data source characteristics

Even though Random is thread-safe, explicitly mentioned in its documentation[4] is that repeated use from different threads will impact performance negatively. Instead, the ThreadLocalRandom type is recommended.

Number of elements

100 million elements should be enough to get a performance gain from parallel processing, so no worries there.

Intermediate operations

No local or shared state. Another plus point for possible parallel performance. But the example might be too simplistic to offset the parallel overhead.

Terminal operation

The IntSummaryStatistics collector holds only four integers and can combine subresults with simple arithmetics. It shouldn't impact parallel performance negatively.

The scorecard for parallel processing doesn't look too bad. The most obvious problem is the data source itself. A more fitting data source might increase performance compared to the default Random number generator.

Besides Random and ThreadLocalRandom, there's also SplittableRandom, which is specially designed for Streams. After measuring the elapsed time of the for-loop as the baseline compared to the other options, the necessity of choosing a favorable data source and measuring the Stream's performance is quite obvious. The factor of increased time between the different data sources, at least on my particular hardware setup, is listed in Table 8-3.

Table 8-3. Elapsed time for different random number generators

Data source	for-loop	Sequential Stream	Parallel Stream
Random	1.0x	1.05x	27.4x
SplittableRandom	1.0x	2.1x	4.1x
ThreadLocalRandom	1.0x	2.3x	0.6x

---

4 Usually, the documentation of a type, like for java.util.Random (*https://oreil.ly/SMnyu*), gives indications about its use in multi-threaded environments.

Even though there should be enough elements in the pipeline, enabling parallel processing can be counterproductive and decrease the performance manifold. That's why making Streams parallel must be a conscious and informed decision.

Better performance is a worthwhile goal, but it depends on the context and your requirements if a parallel Stream is preferable to sequential data processing. You should always start with a sequential Stream and go parallel only if the requirements dictate it and you've measured the performance gain. Sometimes, a "good old" for-loop might do the job just as well, or even better.

Parallel Streams Checklist

Example 8-5 exposed the problem of unfavorable data sources for parallel processing. But it's not the only indicator for non-parallelizable workflows. Based on the criteria in "When to Use and When to Avoid Parallel Streams" on page 200, a checklist can be established as a quick indicator to favor a parallel Stream, or not, as seen in Table 8-4.

Table 8-4. Parallel Stream checklist

Criteria	Considerations
Data source	• Cost of decomposability • Evenness/predictability of split chunks • Data locality of elements
Number of elements	• Total number of elements • NQ model
Intermediate operations	• Interdependence between operations • Necessity of shared state • Parallel-friendly operations • Encounter order
Terminal operation	• Cost of merging the final result • Mutable or immutable reduction
Available resources	• CPU count • Memory • Common ForkJoinPool or customized

Any of these criteria affect parallel Stream performance and should influence your decision. No single one of them is an absolute deal-breaker, though.

Your code could *always* be more performant. Running Streams in parallel adds the complexity and overhead of coordinating multiple threads with possibly little gain or even decreased performance if not used correctly or in unfavorable environments. However, if used for fitting data sources and parallelizable tasks, using parallel Streams is an easy-to-use optimization technique for introducing a more efficient way of data processing into your pipelines.

Takeaways

- Hardware evolves in the direction of more cores, not necessarily faster ones. Concurrency and parallelism play an important role in utilizing all available resources.

- Sequential processing is defined by its textual order in the code. Parallel code execution may overlap, making it harder to follow, analyze, and debug.

- Going parallel with Streams is easy, but their inherent complexity is hidden.

- Concurrent and parallel code introduces a whole new set of requirements and possible problems and caveats. Parallel processing is an optimization technique and should be treated as such: if you don't need it, don't do it; it's a hard problem.

- Most functionally preferred techniques, like *pure functions* and *immutability*, are beneficial, if not a requirement, for error-free and performant parallelized code. Adhering to these techniques early on, even in sequential code, allows an easier transition to parallel processing, if needed.

- Kent Beck's famous quote applies to parallel Streams, too: "First make it work, then make it right, and, finally, make it fast."[5] Start with a sequential Stream to fulfill your data processing needs. Improve it by optimizing its operations. Only if necessary and proven beneficial, make it fast by going parallel.

- Read the documentation of your data source, operations, etc., to see if they are a good fit for parallel execution. It often provides the reasoning behind implementation details, performance indications, examples, and sometimes even alternative approaches.

---

5 Kent Beck is an American software engineer and the creator of *extreme programming*. The quote is usually attributed to him, even though the gist of it has existed for a long time; for example, as described in B. W. Lampson, "Hints for Computer System Design," in *IEEE Software*, Vol. 1, No. 1, 11-28 (Jan. 1984).

CHAPTER 9

Handling null with Optionals

As a Java developer, you've likely encountered your share of NullPointerExceptions, and then some. Many people call the null reference a *billion-dollar mistake*. Actually, the inventor of null itself originally coined that phrase:

> I call it my billion-dollar mistake.
>
> It was the invention of the null reference in 1965. At that time, I was designing the first comprehensive type system for references in an object-oriented language (ALGOL W). My goal was to ensure that all use of references should be absolutely safe, with checking performed automatically by the compiler. But I couldn't resist the temptation to put in a null reference simply because it was so easy to implement.
>
> This has led to innumerable errors, vulnerabilities, and system crashes, which have probably caused a billion dollars of pain and damage in the last forty years.
>
> —Sir Charles Antony Richard Hoare, (QCon London 2009)

Although there is no absolute consensus on how to deal with this "mistake," many programming languages have a proper and idiomatic way of handling null references, often directly integrated into the language itself.

This chapter will show you how Java handles null references and how to improve it in your code with the Optional<T> type and its functional API, and learn how, when, and when not to use Optionals.

The Problem with null References

Java's handling of the absence of a value depends on the type. All primitive types have default values, e.g., a zero equivalent for numeric types and false for boolean. Non primitive types, like classes, interfaces, and arrays, use null as their default value if unassigned, meaning the variable isn't referencing any object.

The concept of reference types may seem similar to C/C++ pointers, but Java references are a specialized type inside the JVM called reference. The JVM strictly controls them to ensure type safety and safeguarding memory access.

A null reference isn't just "nothing"; it's a *special state*, because null is a generalized type that can be used for any object reference, regardless of the actual type. If you attempt to access a null reference, the JVM will throw a NullPointerException, and the current thread will crash if you don't handle it appropriately. This is usually mitigated by a defensive programming approach, requiring null checks *everywhere* at runtime, as seen in Example 9-1.

Example 9-1. A minefield of possible nulls

```
record User(long id, String firstname, String lastname) {

    String fullname() {
      return String.format("%s %s", ❶
                           firstname(),
                           lastname());
    }

    String initials() {
      return String.format("%s%s",
                           firstname().substring(0, 1), ❷
                           lastname().substring(0, 1)); ❷
    }
}

var user = new User(42L, "Ben", null);

var fullname = user.fullname();
// => Ben null ❶

var initials = user.initials();
// => NullPointerException ❷
```

❶ String.format accepts null values as long it's not the sole value for arguments[1] after the format string. It translates to the string "null," regardless of the chosen format specifier, even for numeric ones.

---

1 Varargs don't accept null as a sole argument because it's an inexact argument type, because it might represent Object or Object[]. To pass a single null to a vararg you need to wrap it in an array: new Object[]{ null }.

❷ Using null as an argument in a method call might not crash the current thread. However, calling a method on a null reference certainly does.

The previous example highlights two major problems in dealing with null.

First, null references are valid values for variables, arguments, and return values. That doesn't mean that null is the expected, correct, or even acceptable value for each of them and might not be handled correctly down the line.

For example, calling fullname on user in the previous example worked fine with a null reference for lastname, but the output—"Ben null"—is most likely not what's intended. So even if your code and data structures can handle null values superficially, you still might need to check for them to ensure a correct outcome.

The second problem with null references is one of their main features: type ambiguity. They can represent any type without actually being that particular type. That unique property is necessary, so a single keyword can represent the generalized concept of "absence of value" throughout your code without resorting to different types or keywords for different object types. Even though a null reference is usable just like the type it represents, it still *isn't* the type itself, as seen in Example 9-2.

Example 9-2. null type ambiguity

```
// "TYPE-LESS" NULL AS AN ARGUMENT

methodAcceptingString(null); ❶

// ACCESSING A "TYPED" NULL

String name = null;

var lowerCaseName = name.toLowerCase(); ❷
// => NullPointerException


// TEST TYPE OF NULL

var notString = name instanceof String; ❸
// => false

var stillNotString = ((String) name) instanceof String; ❸
// => false
```

❶ null can represent any object type and, therefore, is a valid value for any non-primitive argument.

❷ A variable referencing `null` is like any other variable of that type, except that any call on it will result in a `NullPointerException`.

❸ Testing a variable with `instanceof` will always evaluate to `false` regardless of the type. Even if it's explicitly cast into the required type, the `instanceof` operator tests the underlying value itself. Therefore, it tests against the typeless value `null`.

These are the most apparent sore points with `null`. Not to worry; there are ways to ease the pain.

How to Handle null in Java (Before Optionals)

Dealing with `null` in Java is an essential and necessary part of every developer's work, even if it can be cumbersome. Encountering an unexpected and unhandled `NullPointerException` is the root cause of many problems and must be dealt with accordingly.

Other languages, like Swift (*https://oreil.ly/FWgxV*), provide dedicated operators and idioms in the form of a safe navigation[2] or `null` coalesce operator[3] to make dealing with `null` easier. Java doesn't provide such built-in tools to handle `null` references, though.

There were three different ways to deal with `null` references before Optionals:

- Best practices
- Tool-assisted `null` checks
- Specialized types similar to Optional

As you will see later, handling `null` references shouldn't rely solely on Optionals. They are a great addition to the prior techniques by providing a standardized and readily available specialized type within the JDK. Still, they're not the final thought on how to manage `null` throughout your code, and knowing about all available techniques is a valuable addition to your skills toolkit.

---

2 Many programming languages have a dedicated operator to safely call fields or methods on possible `null` references. The Wikipedia article on the safe navigation operator (*https://oreil.ly/hC2lu*) has an in-depth explanation and examples in many languages.

3 The `null` coalescing operator is like a shortened ternary operator. The expression `x != null ? x : y` is shortened to `x ?: y`, with `?:` (question-mark colon) being the operator. Not all languages use the same operator, though. The Wikipedia article (*https://oreil.ly/wtnzw*) gives an overview of different programming languages supporting which operator form.

Best Practices for Handling null

If a language doesn't provide integrated null handling, you must resort to *best practices* and *informal rules* to null-proof your code. That's why many companies, teams, and projects develop their own coding style or adapt existing ones to their needs to provide guidelines to write consistent and safer code, not only regarding null. By adhering to these self-imposed practices and rules, they're able to write more predictable and less error-prone code consistently.

You don't have to develop or adapt a full-blown style guide defining every aspect of your Java code. Instead, following these four rules is a good starting point for handling null references. In the following sections, I'll cover four rules to follow as a good starting point for handling null references.

Don't initialize a variable to null

Variables should always have a non-null value. If the value depends on a decision-making block like an if-else statement, you should consider either refactoring it into a method or, if it's a simple decision, using the ternary operator:

```
// DON'T

String value = null;

if (condition) {
  value = "Condition is true";
} else {
  value = "Fallback if false";
}

// DO

String asTernary = condition ? "Condition is true"
                             : "Fallback if false";

String asRefactored = refactoredMethod(condition);
```

The additional benefit is that it makes the variable effectively final if you don't reassign it later, so you can use them as out-of-body variables in lambda expressions.

Don't pass, accept, or return null

As variables shouldn't be null, so should any arguments and return values avoid being null. Nonrequired arguments being null can be avoided by overloading a method or constructor:

```
public record User(long id, String firstname, String lastname) {

  // DO: Additional constructor with default values to avoid null values
```

```
    public User(long id) {
        this(id, "n/a", "n/a");
    }
}
```

If method signatures clash due to identical argument types, you can always resort to `static` methods with more explicit names instead.

After providing specific methods and constructors for nonmandatory values, you shouldn't accept `null` in the original ones if it's appropriate. The easiest way to do this is using the `static requireNonNull` method available on `java.util.Objects`:

```
public record User(long id, String firstname, String lastname) {

    // DO: Validate arguments against null
    public User {
        Objects.requireNonNull(firstname);
        Objects.requireNonNull(lastname);
    }
}
```

The `requireNonNull` call does the `null` check and throws a `NullPointerException` if appropriate. Since Java 14, any `NullPointerException` includes the name of the variable that was `null`, thanks to JEP 358 (*https://oreil.ly/8nUOO*). If you want to include a specific message or target a previous Java version, you can add a `String` as the second argument to the call.

Check everything outside your control

Even if you adhere to your own rules, you can't rely on others to do, too. Using nonfamiliar code, especially if not stated explicitly in the documentation, should always be assumed to be possibly `null` and needs to be checked.

null is acceptable as an implementation detail

Avoiding `null` is essential for the `public` surface of your code but is still sensible as an implementation detail. Internally, a method might use `null` as much as needed as long as it won't return it to the callee.

When and when not to follow the rules

These rules aim to reduce the general use of `null` whenever possible if code is intersecting, like API surfaces, because less exposure leads to fewer required `null` checks and possible `NullPointerExceptions`. But that doesn't mean you should avoid `null` altogether. For example, in isolated contexts, like local variables or non-public APIs, using `null` isn't as problematic and might even simplify your code as long as it's used deliberately and with care.

You can't expect everyone to follow the same rules as you or be as diligent, so you need to be defensive with code, especially outside of your control. This is all the more reason to consistently stick to your best practices and also encourage others to do the same. This will improve your overall code quality, regardless of null. But it's not a silver bullet and requires discipline among your team to gain the most benefits. Manually handling null and adding a few null checks is preferable to getting an unwelcome surprise in the form of a NullPointerException because you assumed something could "never" be null. The JIT compiler[4] will even perform "+null+ check elimination" to remove many explicit null checks from optimized Assembly code thanks to its greater knowledge at runtime.

Tool-Assisted null Checks

A logical extension of the best practices and informal rules approach is to use third-party tools to enforce them automatically. For null references in Java, an established best practice is to use annotations to mark variables, arguments, and method return types as either @Nullable or @NonNull.

Before such annotations, the only place to document nullability was JavaDoc. With these annotations, static code analysis tools can find possible problems with null at compile time. Even better, adding these annotations to your code gives your method signatures and type definitions a more evident intent of how to use them and what to expect, as seen in Example 9-3.

Example 9-3. null handling with annotations

```
interface Example {

    @NonNull List<@Nullable String> getListOfNullableStrings(); ❶

    @Nullable List<@NonNull String> getNullableListOfNonNullStrings(); ❷

    void doWork(@Nullable String identifier); ❸
}
```

❶ Returns a non-null List of possible null String objects.

❷ Returns a possible null List containing non-null String objects.

❸ The method argument identifier is allowed to be null.

---

4 Java's just-in-time (JIT) compiler performs a myriad of optimizations to improve the executed code. If necessary, it recompiles code when more information about how it's executed becomes available. An overview of possible optimization is available on the Open JDK Wiki (*https://oreil.ly/TlDD6*).

The JDK doesn't include these annotations, though, and the corresponding JSR 305 (*https://oreil.ly/vMsKa*) state has been "dormant" since 2012. Nevertheless, it's still the de facto community standard and is widely adopted by libraries, frameworks, and IDEs. Several libraries[5] provide the missing annotations, and most tools support multiple variants of them.

 Even though the behavior of @NonNull and @Nullable seems evident on the surface, the actual implementation might differ between tools, especially in edge cases.[6]

The general problem with a tool-assisted approach is the reliance on the tool itself. If it's too intrusive, you might end up with code that won't run without it, especially if the tool involves code generation "behind the scenes." In the case of null-related annotations, however, you don't have to worry much. Your code will still run without a tool interpreting the annotations, and your variables and method signatures will still clearly communicate their requirements to anyone using them, even if unenforced.

Specialized Types Like Optional

A tool-assisted approach gives you compile-time null checks, whereas specialized types give you safer null handling at runtime. Before Java introduced its own Optional type, this gap in missing functionality was bridged by different libraries, like the rudimentary Optional type provided by the Google Guava framework (*https://oreil.ly/7JA1E*) since 2011.

Even though there's now an integrated solution available in the JDK, Guava doesn't plan to deprecate the class in the foreseeable future.[7] Still, they gently recommend that you prefer the new, standard Java Optional whenever possible.

---

5 The most common libraries to provide the marker annotation are FindBugs (*https://oreil.ly/aKy5a*) (up to Java 8), and its spiritual successor SpotBugs (*https://oreil.ly/W5qww*). JetBrains, the creator of the IntelliJ IDEA and the JVM language *Kotlin*, also provides a package containing the annotations (*https://oreil.ly/My1Zs*).

6 The Checker Framework (*https://oreil.ly/AS8RG*) has an example (*https://oreil.ly/kYY2f*) of such "nonstandard" behavior between different tools.

7 The documentation of Guava's Optional<T> (*https://oreil.ly/8l6mT*) explicitly mentions that the JDK variant should be preferred.

Optionals to the Rescue

Java 8's new `Optional` isn't just a specialized type to deal with `null` consistently; it's also a functional-akin pipeline benefiting from all the functional additions available in the JDK.

What's an Optional?

The simplest way to think of the `Optional` type is to see it as a box containing an actual value that might be `null`. Instead of passing around a possible `null` reference, you use the box, as seen in Figure 9-1.

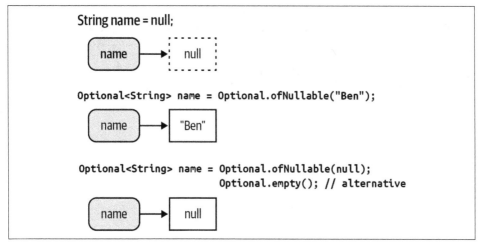

Figure 9-1. Variable versus `Optional<String>`

The box provides a safe wrapper around its inner value. Optionals do not only wrap a value, though. Starting from this box, you can build intricate call chains that depend on a value's existence or absence. They can manage the whole lifecycle of a possible value until the box is unwrapped, including a fallback if no value is present, in such a call chain.

The Purpose and Design Goal of Optional<T>

Looking more closely at Optional's origins and original design goal, they are not the general purpose tool you might think they are.

The original design goal was to create a new type to support the *optional return idiom*, meaning that it represents the result of a query or Collection access. That behavior is clearly visible in the Optional-based terminal Stream operations.

Taking Optionals beyond that initial scope offers many advantages compared to manual null handling. However, remember that any feature, like Optionals, Streams, or a functional approach in general, should always be a deliberate decision because it benefits your code and mental model of what it's supposed to achieve.

The downside of using a wrapper, though, is having to actually look and reach into the box if you want to use its inner value. Like Streams, the additional wrapper also creates an unavoidable overhead regarding method calls and their additional stack frames. On the other hand, the box provides additional functionality for more concise and straightforward code for common workflows with possible null values.

As an example, let's look at the workflow of loading content by an identifier. The numbers in Figure 9-2 correspond to the upcoming code in Example 9-5.

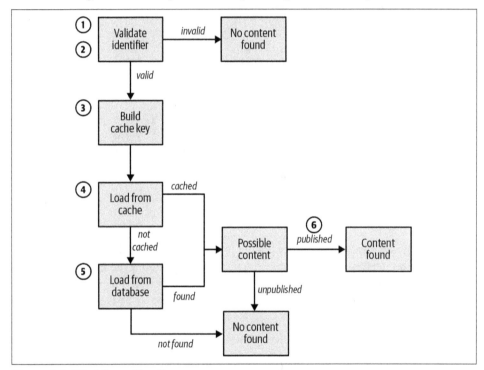

Figure 9-2. Workflow of loading content

The workflow is simplified and doesn't handle all edge cases, but it's a straightforward example of converting a multistep workflow into an Optional call chain. In Example 9-4, you see the workflow implemented without the help of Optionals first.

Example 9-4. Loading content without Optionals

```java
public Content loadFromDB(String contentId) {
  // ...
}

public Content get(String contentId) {
  if (contentId == null) {
    return null;
  }

  if (contentId.isBlank()) {
    return null;
  }

  var cacheKey = contentId.toLowerCase();

  var content = this.cache.get(cacheKey);
  if (content == null) {
    content = loadFromDB(contentId);
  }

  if (content == null) {
    return null;
  }

  if (!content.isPublished()) {
    return null;
  }

  return content;
}
```

The example is exaggerated to make a point but still mostly reflects a typical approach to defensive null handling.

There are three explicit null checks, plus two decisions to be made about a current value and two temporary variables. Even though it's not much code, the overall flow isn't easily graspable with its many if blocks and early returns.

Let's convert the code to a single Optional call chain, as shown in Example 9-5. Don't worry! The upcoming sections will explain the different kinds of operations in detail.

Example 9-5. Loading content with an Optional call chain

```java
public Optional<Content> loadFromDB(String contentId) {
  // ...
}

public Optional<Content> get(String contentId) {
```

```
return Optional.ofNullable(contentId)  ❶
        .filter(Predicate.not(String::isBlank))  ❷
        .map(String::toLowerCase)  ❸
        .map(this.cache::get);  ❹
        .or(() -> loadFromDB(contentId))  ❺
        .filter(Content::isPublished);  ❻
}
```

❶ The first possible `null` check is done by using the `ofNullable` creation method.

❷ The next `if`-block is replaced by a `filter` operation.

❸ Instead of using temporary variables, the `map` operation transforms the value to match the next call.

❹ The content is also retrievable by a `map` operation.

❺ Load the content from the database if no value is present in the pipeline. This call will return another Optional so that the call chain can continue.

❻ Ensure only published content is available.

The Optional call chain condenses the overall code to one operation per line, making the overall flow easily graspable. It perfectly highlights the difference between using an Optional call chain and the "traditional" way of `null` checking everything.

Let's take a look at the steps of creating and working with Optional pipelines.

Building Optional Pipelines

As of Java 17, the `Optional` type provides 3 `static` and 15 instance methods belonging to one of four groups representing different parts of an Optional pipeline:

- Creating a new `Optional<T>` instance
- Checking for values or reacting to the presence or absence of a value
- Filtering and transforming a value
- Getting the value or having a backup plan

These operations can build a fluent pipeline, similar to Streams. Contrary to Streams, though, they are *not* lazily connected until a *terminal*-like operation is added to the pipeline, as I discussed in "Streams as Functional Data Pipelines" on page 117. Every operation resolves as soon as it's added to the fluent call. Optionals only appear lazy because they might return an empty Optional or a fallback value and skip transforming or filtering steps altogether. Still, that doesn't make the call chain itself lazy. However, the executed work is as minimal as possible if a null value is encountered, regardless of the operation count.

You can think of an Optional call chain as two train tracks, as shown in Figure 9-3.

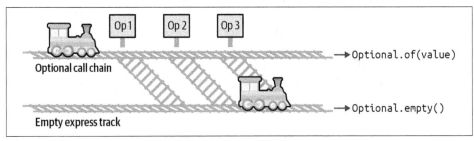

Figure 9-3. Optional "train tracks"

In this analogy, we have two train tracks: the Optional call chain track that leads to returning an Optional<T> with an inner value and the "empty express track" that leads to an empty Optional<T>.

A train always starts on the Optional<T> call train track. When it encounters a track switch (an Optional operation), it looks for a null value, in which case, the train will switch to the empty express track. Once on the express track, there is no chance of returning to the Optional call chain track, at least not until Java 9, as you'll see in "Getting a (fallback) value" on page 230.

Technically, it will still call each method on the Optional call chain after switching to the empty express track, but it'll just validate parameters and move on. If the train didn't encounter a null value by the time it reaches the end of its route, it returns a non-empty Optional<T>. If it encounters a null value at any point along the route, it will return an empty Optional<T>.

To get the train rolling, let's create some Optionals.

Creating an Optional

There are no public constructors available on the Optional type. Instead, it gives you three static factory methods to create new instances. Which one to use depends on your use case and prior knowledge of the inner value:

Optional.ofNullable(T value) *if the value might be* null
> If you know a value might be null or don't care if it might be empty, use the ofNullable method to create a new instance with a possible inner null value. It's the simplest and most bulletproof form of creating an Optional<T>.
>
> ```
> String hasValue = "Optionals are awesome!";
> Optional<String> maybeValue = Optional.ofNullable(hasValue);
> ```

```
String nullRef = null;
Optional<String> emptyOptional = Optional.ofNullable(nullRef);
```

Optional.of(T value) *if the value must be non-*null

Even though Optionals are a great way to deal with null and prevent a NullPointerException, what if you have to make sure you have a value? For example, you already handled any edge cases in your code—which returned empty Optionals—and now you definitely have a value. The of method ensures that the value is non-null and throws an NullPointerException otherwise. This way, the Exception signifies a real problem in your code. Maybe you missed an edge case, or a particular external method call has changed and returns null now. Using the of method in such a context makes your code more future-proof and resilient against unwanted changes in behavior.

```
var value = "Optionals are awesome!";
Optional<String> mustHaveValue = Optional.of(value);

value = null;
Optional<String> emptyOptional = Optional.of(value);
// => throws NullPointerException
```

Optional.empty() *if there's no value*

If you already know there's no value at all, you can use the empty method. The call Optional.ofNullable(null) is unnecessary because there would be just a redundant null check before calling empty itself.

```
Optional<String> noValue = Optional.empty();
```

 The JDK documentation explicitly mentions that the value returned by the static Optional.empty method isn't guaranteed to be a singleton object. So you shouldn't compare empty Optionals with == (double equals), and use equals(Object obj) or compare the result of the isEmpty method instead.

Using Optional.ofNullable(T value) might be the most null-tolerant creation method, but you should strive to use the most fitting one to represent your use case and context knowledge. Code might get refactored or rewritten over time, and it's better to have your code throw a NullPointerException for a suddenly missing value that's actually required as an additional safeguard, even if the API itself is using Optionals.

Checking for and reacting to values

Optionals are meant to wrap a value and represent its existence or absence. They are implemented as a Java type and are, therefore, a runtime-level feature and incur an unavoidable overhead associated with object creation. To compensate for this, checking for values should be as straightforward as possible.

Four methods are available to check for and react to values or their absence. They are prefixed with "`is`" for checks and "`if`" for reactive higher-order functions:

- `boolean isPresent()`
- `boolean isEmpty()` (Java 11+)

Solely checking for a value has its purposes, but checking, retrieving, and using a value requires three separate steps when you use "`is`" methods.

That's why the higher-order "`if`" methods consume a value directly:

- `void ifPresent(Consumer<? super T> action)`
- `void ifPresentOrElse(Consumer<? super T> action, Runnable empty Action)`

Both methods perform the given `action` only if a value is present. The second method runs the `emptyAction` if no value is present. `null` actions aren't allowed and throw a `NullPointerException`. There are no `ifEmpty` equivalents available.

Let's look at how to use these methods in Example 9-6.

Example 9-6. Checking for Optional values

```
Optional<String> maybeValue = ...;

// VERBOSE VERSION
if (maybeValue.isPresent()) {
  var value = maybeValue.orElseThrow();
  System.out.println(value);
} else {
  System.out.println("No value found!");
}

// CONCISE VERSION
maybeValue.ifPresentOrElse(System.out::println,
                           () -> System.out.println("No value found!"));
```

Both `ifPresent` methods perform side-effects-only code due to a lack of a return type. Even though pure functions are generally preferable in a functional approach,

Optionals live somewhere between accepting functional code and fitting right into imperative code.

Filtering and mapping

Safely handling possible null values already removes a considerable burden from any developer, but Optionals allow for more than just checking for the presence or absence of a value.

Similar to Streams, you build a pipeline with intermediate-like operations. There are three operations for filtering and mapping Optionals:

- `Optional<T> filter(Predicate<? super T> predicate)`
- `<U> Optional<U> map(Function<? super T, ? extends U> mapper)`
- `<U> Optional<U> flatMap(Function<? super T, ? extends Optional<? extends U>> mapper)`

The `filter` operation returns `this` if a value is present and matches the given predicate. If no value is present or the predicate doesn't match the value, an empty Optional is returned.

The `map` operation transforms a present value with the provided mapper function, returning a new nullable Optional containing the mapped value. If no value is present, the operation returns an empty `Optional<U>` instead.

The `flatMap` is used if the mapping function returns an `Optional<U>` instead of a concrete value of type `U`. If you would use the `map` in this case, the return value would be an `Optional<Optional<U>>`. That's why the `flatMap` returns the mapped value directly instead of wrapping it into another Optional.

Example 9-7 shows an Optional call chain and the non-Optional equivalent for a hypothetical permissions container and its subtypes. The code callouts are attached to both versions to show the corresponding operations, but their descriptions are for the Optional version.

Example 9-7. Intermediate operations to find an active admin

```
public record Permissions(List<String> permissions, Group group) {

  public boolean isEmpty() {
    return permissions.isEmpty();
  }
}

public record Group(Optional<User> admin) {
  // NO BODY
```

```
}

public record User(boolean isActive) {
    // NO BODY
}

Permissions permissions = ...;

boolean isActiveAdmin =
    Optional.ofNullable(permissions) ❶
            .filter(Predicate.not(Permissions::isEmpty)) ❷
            .map(Permissions::group) ❸
            .flatMap(Group::admin) ❹
            .map(User::isActive) ❺
            .orElse(Boolean.FALSE); ❻
```

❶ The initial null check is covered by creating an Optional<Permissions>.

❷ Filter for non-empty permissions. With the help of the static Predicate.not method, the lambda permissions -> !permissions.isEmpty() is replaced with a more readable wrapped method reference.

❸ Get the group of the permissions object. It doesn't matter if the Permissions::group returns null because the Optional call chain will figuratively skip to its value-retrieving operation if that's the case. In reality, an empty Optional is passing through the fluent calls.

❹ The group might not have an admin. That's why it returns an Optional<User>. If you simply use map(Group::admin), you will have an Optional<Optional<User>> in the next step. Thanks to flat Map(Group::admin), no unnecessarily nested Optional is created.

❺ With the User object, you can filter out nonactive ones.

❻ If any method of the call chain returns an empty Optional, e.g., the group was null, the last operation returns the fallback value Boolean.FALSE. The next section will explain the different types of value-retrieval operations.

Every step of the underlying problem that needs to be solved is laid out in clear, isolated, and directly connected steps. Any validation and decision-making, like null or empty checks, is wrapped up in dedicated operations built on method references. The intent and flow of the problem to be solved are clearly visible and easy to grasp.

Doing the same thing without Optionals results in a nested mess of code, as seen in Example 9-8.

Example 9-8. Finding an active admin without Optionals

```
boolean isActiveAdmin = false;

if (permissions != null && !permissions.isEmpty()) {
  if (permissions.group() != null) {
    var group = permissions.group();
    var maybeAdmin = group.admin();

    if (maybeAdmin.isPresent()) {
      var admin = maybeAdmin.orElseThrow();
      isActiveAdmin = admin.isActive();
    }
  }
}
```

The difference between the two versions is quite noticeable.

The non-Optional version can't delegate any conditions or checks and relies on explicit `if` statements. That creates deeply nested flow structures, increasing the *cyclomatic complexity* of your code. It's harder to understand the overall intent of the code block, and it is not as concise as with an Optional call chain.

 Cyclomatic complexity[8] is a metric used to determine code complexity. It's based on the number of branching paths—or decisions—in your code. The general idea is that straight, non-nested statements and expressions are more accessible to follow and less error-prone than deeply nested decision branches, like nested `if`-statements.

Getting a (fallback) value

Optionals might provide a safe wrapper for possible `null` values, but you might need an actual value at some point. There are multiple ways to retrieve an Optional's inner value, ranging from "brute force" to providing fallback values.

The first method doesn't concern itself with any safety checks:

- `T get()`

The Optional is unwrapped forcefully, and if no value is present, a `NoSuchElement Exception` is thrown, so make sure to check that a value exists beforehand.

The next two methods provide a fallback value if no value is present:

---

8 T.J. McCabe, "A Complexity Measure," IEEE Transactions on Software Engineering (*https://oreil.ly/PwEqN*), Vol. SE-2, No. 4 (Dec. 1976): 308–320. McCabe, TJ. 1976.

- `T orElse(T other)`

- `T orElseGet(Supplier<? extends T> supplier)`

The `Supplier`-based variant allows for lazily getting a fallback, which is immensely useful if creating it is resource intensive.

Two methods are available to throw Exceptions:

- `<X extends Throwable> T orElseThrow(Supplier<? extends X> exception Supplier)`

- `T orElseThrow()` (Java 10+)

Even though one of the main advantages of Optionals is preventing a `NullPointer Exception`, sometimes you still need a domain-specific Exception if there's no value present. With the `orElseThrow` operation, you have fine-grained control about handling a missing value and what Exception to throw, too. The second method, `orElseThrow`, was added as a semantically correct and preferred alternative to the `get` operation. Even though the call isn't as concise, it better fits into the overall naming scheme and confers that an Exception might be thrown.

Java 9 added two additional methods for providing another `Optional<T>` as a fallback or a `Stream<T>`. These allow more complex call chains than before:

The first one, `Optional<T> or(Supplier<? extends Optional<? extends T>> supplier)`, lazily returns another Optional if no value is present. This way, you can continue an Optional call chain, even if no value was present before calling `or`. To go back to the "train track" analogy, the `or` operation is a way to provide a track switch back from the empty express track by creating a new starting point on the Optional call chain track.

The other one, `Stream<T> stream()`, returns a Stream containing the value as its sole element or an empty Stream if no value is present. It is usually used in the intermediate Stream operation `flatMap` as a method reference. The Optional `stream` operation plays a broader role in the interoperability with the Stream API I discussed in Chapter 7.

Optionals and Streams

As discussed in previous chapters, Streams are pipelines that filter and transform elements into the desired outcome. Optionals fit right in as a functional wrapper for possible `null` references, but they must play by the rules of Stream pipelines when used as elements and confer their state to the pipeline.

Optionals as Stream Elements

With Streams, elements are excluded from further processing by using a filtering operation to discard them. In essence, Optionals themselves represent a kind of filtering operation, although not directly compatible with how Streams expect elements to behave.

If a Stream element is excluded by a `filter` operation, it won't traverse the Stream further. This could be achieved by using `Optional::isPresent` as the `filter` operation's argument. However, the resulting Stream in the case of an inner value, `Stream<Optional<User>>`, isn't what you want.

To restore "normal" Stream semantics, you need to map the Stream from `Stream<Optional<User>>` to `Stream<User>`, as seen in Example 9-9.

Example 9-9. Optionals as Stream elements

```
List<Permissions> permissions = ...;

List<User> activeUsers =
  permissions.stream()
              .filter(Predicate.not(Permissions::isEmpty))
              .map(Permissions::group)
              .map(Group::admin) ❶
              .filter(Optional::isPresent) ❷
              .map(Optional::orElseThrow) ❷
              .filter(User::isActive)
              .toList();
```

❶ The `Group::admin` method reference returns an `Optional<User>`. At this point, the Stream becomes a `Stream<Optional<User>>`.

❷ The Stream pipeline requires multiple operations to check for a value and safely unwrap it from its `Optional`.

Filtering and mapping an `Optional<T>` is such a standard use case for Optionals in Streams that Java 9 added the `stream` method to the `Optional<T>` type. It returns a `Stream<T>` containing the inner value if present as its sole element, or otherwise, an empty `Stream<T>`. This makes it the most concise way to combine the power of Optionals and Streams by using the Stream's `flatMap` operation instead of a dedicated `filter` and `map` operation, as seen in Example 9-10.

Example 9-10. Optionals as Stream elements with `flatMap`

```
List<Permissions> permissions = ...;

List<User> activeUsers =
  permissions.stream()
             .filter(Predicate.not(Permissions::isEmpty))
             .map(Permissions::group)
             .map(Group::admin)
             .flatMap(Optional::stream)
             .filter(User::isActive)
             .toList();
```

A singular `flatMap` call replaces the previous `filter` and `map` operations. Even if you save only a single method call—one `flatMap` instead of `filter` plus `map` operation—the resulting code is easier to reason with and better illustrates the desired workflow. The `flatMap` operation conveys all the necessary information for understanding the Stream pipeline without adding any complexity by requiring additional steps. Handling Optionals is a necessity, and it should be done as concisely as possible so that the overall Stream pipeline is understandable and straightforward.

There's no reason to design your APIs without Optionals just to avoid `flatMap` operations in Streams. If `Group::getAdmin` would return `null`, you would still have to add a `null-check` in another `filter` operation. Replacing a `flatMap` operation with a `filter` operation gains you nothing, except the `admin` call now requires explicit `null` handling afterward, even if it's no longer obvious from its signature.

Terminal Stream Operations

Using Optionals in Streams isn't restricted to intermediate operations. Five of the Stream API's terminal operations return an `Optional` to provide an improved representation of their return value. All of them try either to find an element or reduce the Stream. In the case of an empty Stream, these operations need a sensible representation of an absentee value. Optionals exemplify this concept, so it was the logical choice to use them instead of returning `null`.

Finding an element

In the Stream API, the prefix "`find`" represents, as you might have guessed by its name, finding an element based on its existence. There are two `find` operations available with distinct semantics depending on the Stream being parallel or serial:

```
Optional<T> findFirst()
```
Returns an Optional of the first element of a Stream or an empty Optional if the Stream is empty. There's no difference between parallel and serial Streams. Any element might be returned if the Stream lacks an encounter order.

```
Optional<T> findAny()
```
Returns an Optional of any element of a Stream or an empty Optional if the Stream is empty. The returned element is non-deterministic to maximize performance in parallel streams. The first element is returned in most cases, but there's no guarantee for this behavior! So use `findFirst` instead for a consistent return element.

The `find` operations work solely on the concept of existence, so you need to filter the Stream elements accordingly beforehand. If you only want to know if a particular element exists and don't need the element itself, you can use one of the corresponding "`match`" methods:

- `boolean anyMatch(Predicate<? super T> predicate)`
- `boolean noneMatch(Predicate<? super T> predicate)`

These terminal operations include the filtering operation and avoid creating an unnecessary Optional instance.

Reducing to a single value

Reducing a Stream by combining or accumulating its elements into a new data structure is one of a Stream's primary purposes. And just like the `find` operations, reducing operators have to deal with empty Streams.

That's why there are three terminal `reduce` operations available for Streams, with one returning an Optional: `Optional<T> reduce(BinaryOperator<T> accumulator)`.

It reduces the elements of the Stream using the provided `accumulator` operator. The returned value is the result of the reduction, or an empty Optional if the Stream is empty.

See Example 9-11 for an equivalent pseudo-code example from the official documentation.[9]

Example 9-11. Pseudo-code equivalent to the `reduce` operation

```
Optional<T> pseudoReduce(BinaryOperator<T> accumulator) {
  boolean foundAny = false;
```

---

[9] Documentation for `Optional<T> reduce(BinaryOperator<T> accumulator)` (*https://oreil.ly/Iap5u*).

```
    T result = null;

    for (T element : elements]) {
      if (!foundAny) {
        foundAny = true;
        result = element;
      } else {
        result = accumulator.apply(result, element);
      }
    }

    return foundAny ? Optional.of(result)
                    : Optional.empty();
}
```

The two other reduce methods require an initial value to combine the Stream elements with, so a concrete value can be returned instead of an Optional. See "Reducing elements" on page 137 for a more detailed explanation and examples of how to use them in Streams.

Besides the generic reduce methods, two common use cases of reduction are available as methods:

- Optional<T> min(Comparator<? super T> comparator)
- Optional<T> max(Comparator<? super T> comparator)

These methods return the "minimal" or "maximal" element based on the provided comparator or an empty Optional if the Stream is empty.

An Optional<T> is the only suitable type to be returned by min/max. You have to check anyway if there's a result of the operation. Adding additional min/max methods with a fallback value as an argument would clutter up the Stream interface. Thanks to the returned Optional, you can easily check if a result exists or resort to a fallback value or Exception instead.

Optional Primitives

You might ask why you even need an Optional of a primitive because a primitive variable can never be null. If not initialized, any primitive has a value equivalent to zero for their respective type.

Even though that's technically correct, Optionals aren't simply about preventing values from being null. They also represent an actual state of "nothingness"—an absence of a value—that primitives lack.

In many cases, the default values of primitive types are adequate, like representing a networking port: zero is an invalid port number, so you have to deal with it anyway. If zero is a valid value, though, expressing its actual absence becomes more difficult.

Using primitives directly with the Optional<T> type is a no-go because primitives can't be generic types. However, just like with Streams, there are two ways to use primitive values for Optionals: autoboxing or specialized types.

"Primitive Types" on page 44 highlighted the problems of using object-wrapper classes and the overhead they introduce. On the other hand, autoboxing isn't free either.

The usual primitive types are available as dedicated Optional variants in the java.util package:

- OptionalInt
- OptionalLong
- OptionalDouble

Their semantics are almost identical to their generic counterparts, but they do *not* inherit from Optional or share a common interface. The features aren't identical either, as multiple operations, like filter, map, or flatMap, are missing.

The primitive Optional types may remove unnecessary autoboxing, which can improve performance but lacks the full functionality that Optional offers. Also, unlike the primitive Stream variants discussed in "Primitive Streams" on page 159, there's no way to easily convert between a primitive Optional variant and its corresponding Optional<T> equivalent.

Even though it would be easy to create your own wrapper type to improve the handling of Optional values, especially for primitives, I wouldn't recommend doing it under most circumstances. For internal or private implementations, you can use any wrapper you want or need. But the public seams of your code should always strive to stick to the most anticipated and available types. Usually, that means what's already included in the JDK.

Caveats

Optionals can enormously improve null handling for the JDK by providing a versatile "box" to hold possible null values and a (partially) functional API to build pipelines dealing with the presence or absence of that value. Although the upsides are certainly useful, they also come with some noteworthy downsides you need to be aware of to use them correctly and without any unexpected surprises.

Optionals Are Ordinary Types

The most obvious downside of using `Optional<T>` and its primitive variants is that they're ordinary types. Without deeper integration into Java's syntax, such as the new syntax for lambda expressions, they suffer from the same `null` reference problems as any other type in the JDK.

That's why you must still adhere to best practices and informal rules to not counteract the benefits of using Optionals in the first place. If you design an API and decide to use Optionals as a return type, you *must not* return `null` for it under any circumstances! Returning an Optional is a clear signal that anyone using the API will receive at least a "box" that *might* contain a value instead of a possible `null` value. If no value is possible, always use an empty Optional or the primitive equivalent instead.

This essential design requirement has to be enforced by convention, though. The compiler won't help you there without additional tools, like Sonar (*https://oreil.ly/ldteU*).[10]

Identity-Sensitive Methods

Even though Optionals *are* ordinary types, the identity-sensitive methods might work differently from what you expect. This includes the reference equality operator == (double equals), using the `hashCode` method, or using an instance for thread synchronization.

Object identity tells you whether two different objects share the same memory address and are, therefore, the same object. This is tested by the reference equality operator == (double equals). Equality of two objects, which is tested with their `equals` method, means they contain the same state.

Two identical objects are also equal, but the reverse isn't necessarily true. Just because two objects contain the same state doesn't automatically mean they also share the same memory address.

The difference in behavior lies in the Optional's nature of being *value-based* type, meaning its inner value is its primary concern. Methods like `equals`, `hashCode`, and `toString` are based solely on the inner value and ignore the actual object identity. That's why you should treat Optional instances as interchangeable and unsuited

---

10 The Sonar (*https://oreil.ly/ldteU*) rule RSPEC-2789 (*https://oreil.ly/2ZvsP*) checks for Optionals being `null`.

for identity-related operations like synchronizing concurrent code, as stated in the official documentation.[11]

Performance Overhead

Another point to consider when using Optionals is the performance implications, especially outside their primary design goal as return types.

Optionals are easy to (mis-)use for simple `null` checks and provide a fallback value if no inner value is present:

```
// DON'T DO THIS
String value = Optional.ofNullable(maybeNull).orElse(fallbackValue);

// DON'T DO THIS
if (Optional.ofNullable(maybeNull).isPresent()) {
  // ...
}
```

Such simple Optional pipelines require a new `Optional` instance, and every method call creates a new stack frame, meaning that the JVM can't optimize your code as easily as a simple `null` check. Creating an Optional doesn't make much sense without additional operations besides checking for existence or providing a fallback.

Using alternatives like the ternary operator or a direct `null` check should be your preferred solution:

```
// DO THIS INSTEAD
String value = maybeNull != null ? maybeNull
                                  : fallbackValue;

// DO THIS INSTEAD
if (maybeNull != null) {
  // ...
}
```

Using an Optional instead of a ternary operator might look nicer and saves you from repeating `maybeNull`. However, reducing the number of instance creations and method invocations is usually preferable.

If you still want a more visually pleasing alternative to the ternary operator, Java 9 introduced two `static` helper methods on `java.util.Objects`, wrapping the task of checking for `null` and providing an alternative value:

---

11 The official documentation (*https://oreil.ly/KDjQy*) explicitly mentions unpredictable identity method behavior as an "API Note."

- `T requireNonNullElse(T obj, T defaultObj)`
- `T requireNonNullElseGet(T obj, Supplier<? extends T> supplier)`

The fallback value, or in the case of the second method, the result of the `Supplier`, must be non-`null`, too.

Saving a few CPU cycles means nothing compared to a crash due to an unexpected `NullPointerException`. Just like with Streams, there's a trade-off to be made between performance and safer and more straightforward code. You need to find the balance between those based on your requirements.

Special Considerations for Collections

`null` is the technical representation of the absence of a value. Optionals give you a tool to represent this absence safely with an actual object that allows further transformation, filtering, and more. Collection-based types, though, can already represent an absence of their inner values.

A Collection type is already a box that handles values, so wrapping it in an `Optional<T>` creates yet another layer you must deal with. An empty Collection already indicates the absence of inner values, so using an empty Collection as the alternative to `null` eliminates a possible `NullPointerException` *and* the need for an additional layer by using an Optional.

Of course, you still have to deal with the absence of the Collection itself, meaning a `null` reference. If possible, you shouldn't use `null` for Collections at all, neither as arguments nor return values. Designing your code to always use an empty Collection instead of `null` will have the same effect as an Optional. If you still need to discern between `null` and an empty Collection, or the related code isn't under your control or can't be changed, a `null` check might still be preferable to introducing another layer to deal with.

Optionals and Serialization

The `Optional<T>` type and the primitive variants don't implement `java.io.Serializ able`, making them unsuited for `private` fields in serializable types. This decision was made deliberately by its design group because Optionals are supposed to provide the possibility of an optional return value, not be a general-purpose solution for nullability. Making `Optional<T>` serializable would encourage use cases far beyond its intended design goal.

To still reap the benefits of Optionals in your object and maintain serializability, you can use them for your `public` API but use non-Optional fields as an implementation detail, as shown in Example 9-12.

Example 9-12. Using Optionals in `Serializable` types

```java
public class User implements Serializable {

  private UUID id;
  private String username;
  private LocalDateTime lastLogin;

  // ... usual getter/setter for id and username

  public Optional<LocalDateTime> getLastLogin() {
    return Optional.ofNullable(this.lastLogin);
  }

  public void setLastLogin(LocalDateTime lastLogin) {
    this.lastLogin = lastLogin;
  }
}
```

By relying only on an Optional in the getter for `lastLogin`, the type remains serializable but still provides an Optional API.

Final Thoughts on null References

Although it's called a billion-dollar mistake, `null` isn't inherently evil. Sir Charles Antony Richard Hoare, the inventor of `null`, believes that programming language designers should be responsible for errors in programs written in their language.[12]

A language should provide a solid foundation with a good deal of ingenuity and control. Allowing `null` references is one of many design choices for Java, nothing more. Java's catch or specify requirement, as explained in Chapter 10, and `try-catch` blocks provide you with tools against apparent errors. But with `null` being a valid value for any type, every reference is a possible crash waiting to happen. Even if you think something can never be `null`, experience tells us that it may be possible at some point in time.

The existence of `null` references doesn't qualify a language as poorly designed. `null` has its place, but it requires you to be more attentive to your code. This doesn't mean you should replace every single variable and argument in your code with Optionals, either.

Optionals were intended to provide a limited mechanism for optional return values, so don't overuse or misuse them just because it seems convenient. In code under

---

12 Sir Charles Antony Richard Hoare expressed this view in his talk "Null References: The Billion Dollar Mistake" (*https://oreil.ly/ja8Dn*) at QCon London (*https://oreil.ly/6qW4J*) in 2009.

your control, you can make more assumptions and guarantees about the possible nullability of references and deal with it accordingly, even without Optionals. If you follow the other principles highlighted in this book—like small, self-contained, pure functions without side effects—it's way easier to make sure your code won't return a null reference unexpectedly.

Takeaways

- There's no language-level or special syntax available for null handling in Java.
- null is a special case that can represent both the states of "doesn't exist" and "undefined" without you being able to distinguish them.
- The Optional<T> type allows for dedicated null handling of these states with operation chains and fallbacks.
- Specialized types for primitives are also available, although they don't provide feature parity.
- Other approaches for null handling exist, like annotations or best practices.
- Not everything is a good fit for Optionals. If a data structure already has a concept of emptiness, like Collections, adding another layer is counterproductive. You shouldn't wrap it into an Optional unless you are required to represent an "undefined" state, too.
- Optionals and Streams are interoperable without much friction.
- Optionals aren't serializable, so don't use them as private fields if you need to serialize your type. Instead, use Optionals as return values for getters.
- Alternative implementations exist, like in the Google Guava framework (*https://oreil.ly/L8mnq*), even though Google itself recommends using Java's Optional instead.
- null isn't evil per se. Don't replace every variable with Optionals without a good reason.

CHAPTER 10

Functional Exception Handling

As much as we would like to write perfect and error-free code, it's an almost impossible endeavor. That's why we need a way to deal with inevitable problems in our code. Java's mechanism of choice to deal with such disruptive and abnormal control flow conditions is Exceptions.

Exception handling can be tricky, even in imperative and OO code. Combining Exceptions with a functional approach, however, can be a real challenge because the techniques are fraught with considerations and requirements. Although there are third-party libraries that can assist with this, you may not want to rely solely on them in the long term, incurring technical debt due to a new dependency, instead of adapting to a more functional approach overall.

This chapter will show you the different kinds of Exceptions and their impact on functional programming with lambdas. You will learn how to handle Exceptions in lambdas as well as alternative ways to approach control flow disruptions in a functional context.

Java Exception Handling in a Nutshell

In general, an Exception is a special event that happens during the execution of a program that disrupts the normal flow of instructions. This concept is present in many different programming languages, not only in Java, and traces back to the origins of Lisp.[1]

The actual form of how Exceptions are handled depends on the language.

---

[1] Guy L. Steele and Richard P. Gabriel, "The evolution of Lisp," in *History of Programming Languages—II*, (Association for Computing Machinery, 1996), 233-330 (*https://oreil.ly/QFRQP*).

The try-catch block

Java's mechanism of choice is the `try-catch` block, which is an integral element of the language:

```
try {
  return doCalculation(input);
} catch (ArithmeticException e) {
  this.log.error("Calculation failed", e);
  return null;
}
```

The overall concept of it has slightly evolved since its inception. Instead of requiring multiple `catch` blocks, you can catch more than one Exception with a `multi-catch` block (*https://oreil.ly/HdAps*) by using | (pipe) between their types:

```
try {
  return doCalculation(input);
} catch (ArithmeticException | IllegalArgumentException e) {
  this.log.error("Calculation failed", e);
  return null;
}
```

If you need to handle resources, using a `try-with-resources` construct (*https://oreil.ly/1meJf*) will automatically close any resource that implements `AutoCloseable`:

```
try (var fileReader = new FileReader(file);
     var bufferedReader = new BufferedReader(fileReader)) {

  var firstLine = bufferedReader.readLine();
  System.out.println(firstLine);
} catch (IOException e) {
  System.err.println("Couldn't read first line of " + file);
}
```

Regardless of which variant you use, you will end up with an Exception that disrupts the flow of execution of your code by jumping from the origin of the thrown Exception to the nearest `catch` point up the call stack or crashing the current thread if none is available.

The Different Types of Exceptions and Errors

There are three types of control flow disruptions in Java, with disparate requirements regarding their handling in your code: *checked* and *unchecked* Exceptions, and *Errors*.

Checked exceptions

Checked Exceptions are *anticipated* and potentially *recoverable* events outside the normal control flow. For example, you should always expect the possibility of a missing file (`FileNotFoundException`) or an invalid URL (`MalformedURLException`). Because they're anticipated, they must adhere to Java's *catch-or-specify* requirement.

Catch-or-Specify

The *catch-or-specify* requirement declares that your code must honor one of the following conditions while dealing with checked Exceptions:

Catch the Exception in its current context
An appropriate handler—a `catch` block—is provided to catch the specific Exception or one of its base types.

Specify thrown Exceptions in the method's signature
The surrounding method signifies its thrown Exception types by using the `throws` keyword, followed by a comma-separated list of possible checked Exceptions.

This requirement *must* be obliged, and the compiler forces you to adhere to at least one of the two conditions. The reliability and resilience of your code will improve by allowing you to recover gracefully or hand over the liability down the line instead of completely ignoring the Exception. Either flag possible exceptional states or handle them directly.

There's no need to specify an Exception type if you catch and handle it. An unnecessary `throws` declaration forces the caller of such a method to comply with the catch-or-specify requirement, too.

Unchecked exceptions

Unchecked Exceptions, on the other hand, are *not anticipated*, and are often *unrecoverable*, such as:

- `UnsupportedOperationException` in the case of an unsupported operation
- `ArithmeticException` for invalid mathematical calculations
- `NullPointerException` if an empty reference is encountered

They aren't considered part of the methods' public contract but rather represent what happens if any assumed contract preconditions are broken. Therefore, such Exceptions aren't subject to the catch-or-specify requirement, and methods usually don't signify them with the `throws` keyword, even if it's known that a method will throw them under certain conditions.

However, unchecked Exceptions still have to be handled in some form if you don't want your program to crash. If not handled locally, an Exception automatically goes up the call stack of the current thread until it finds an appropriate handler. Or, if none is available, the thread dies. For single-threaded applications, the runtime will terminate, and your program will crash.

Errors

The third kind of control flow disruption, *Errors*, indicates a severe problem you shouldn't catch or can't handle under normal circumstances.

For example, if the runtime runs out of available memory, the runtime throws an `OutOfMemoryError`. Or an endless recursive call will eventually lead to a `Stack OverflowError`. There's nothing you can do without any memory left, regardless of whether it's the heap or the stack. Faulty hardware is another source for Java errors, like `java.io.IOError` in the case of a disk error. These are all grave and not anticipated problems with almost no possibility of recovering gracefully. That's why errors mustn't adhere to the catch-or-specify requirement.

Exception hierarchy in Java

Which category an Exception falls into depends on its base class. All Exceptions are checked, except types subclassing `java.lang.RuntimeException` or `java.lang.Error`. But they share a common base type: `java.lang.Throwable`. Types inheriting from the latter two are either unchecked or an error. The type hierarchy is illustrated in Figure 10-1.

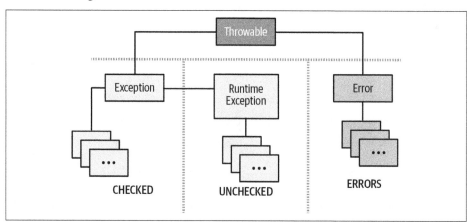

Figure 10-1. Exceptions hierarchy in Java

The concept of having different kinds of Exceptions is rather uncommon among programming languages, and it's a controversial topic of discussion due to their different requirements for how to handle them. Kotlin,[2] for example, inherits the general mechanisms of handling Exceptions but doesn't have any checked Exceptions.

Checked Exceptions in Lambdas

Java's Exception-handling mechanisms were designed to fulfill specific requirements at the time of its inception, 18 years before the introduction of lambdas. That's why throwing and handling Exceptions don't fit nicely into the new functional Java coding style without any special considerations or completely disregarding the catch-or-specify requirement.

Let's take a look at loading the content of a file with a `static` method available on `java.util.Files` with the following method signature:

```
public static String readString(Path path) throws IOException {
  // ...
}
```

The method signature is quite simple and indicates that a checked `IOException` might get thrown, so a `try-catch` block is required. That's why the method can't be used as a method reference, or in a simple lambda:

```
Stream.of(path1, path2, path3)
      .map(Files::readString)
      .forEach(System.out::println);
// Compiler Error:
// incompatible thrown types java.io.IOException in functional expression
```

The problem stems from the functional interface required to satisfy the `map` operation. None of the functional interfaces of the JDK throw checked Exceptions and are, therefore, not compatible with any method that does.

> There are interfaces marked with @FunctionalInterface that throw Exceptions, like `java.util.concurrent.Callable<V>`. They *are* functional interfaces by definition, but it's for compatibility reasons, not because they represent functional types to be used indiscriminately.

The most obvious solution is using `try-catch` block by converting the lambda to a block-based one:

---

2 The official Kotlin documentation (*https://oreil.ly/AosQh*) highlights the differences between Java and Kotlin Exception handling.

```
Stream.of(path1, path2, path3)
    .map(path -> {
      try {
        return Files.readString(path);
      } catch (IOException e) {
        return null;
      }
    })
    .forEach(System.out::println);
```

The code required to satisfy the compiler defeats the purpose of Stream pipeline lambdas in general. The conciseness and straightforward representation of an operation is diluted by the required boilerplate for Exception handling.

Using Exceptions in lambdas feels almost like an antipattern. A `throws` declaration indicates that the caller has to decide how to handle that Exception, and lambdas don't have a dedicated way of dealing with Exceptions except for the preexisting `try-catch`, which can't be used for method references.

Still, there are certain ways of dealing with Exceptions without losing (most of) the simplicity and clarity that lambdas, methods references, and pipelines like Streams or Optionals give you:

- Safe method extraction
- Un-Checking Exceptions
- Sneaky throws

All these options are imperfect workarounds to mitigate Exception handling in functional code. Still, we will have a look at them because they can be useful in certain scenarios if you do not have a built-in way to deal with Exceptions properly.

The last two can even be treacherous or at least become a code smell if used unwisely. Nevertheless, knowing such "last resort" tools can help you navigate more difficult amalgamations of preexisting, non-functional code, and give you a more functional approach.

Safe Method Extraction

Efficiently handling Exceptions in your functional code depends on who effectively controls or owns the code. If the throwing code is entirely under your control, you should *always* adequately handle them. But often, the offending code is *not* yours, or you can't change or refactor it as needed. That's when you can still extract it into a "safer" method with appropriate local Exception handling.

Creating a "safe" method decouples the actual work from handling any Exception, restoring the principle of the caller being responsible for any checked Exceptions. Any functional code can use the safe method instead, as shown in Example 10-1.

Example 10-1. Extract throwing code into a safe method

```
String safeReadString(Path path) { ❶
  try { ❷
    return Files.readString(path);
  } catch (IOException e) {
    return null;
  }
}

Stream.of(path1, path2, path3)
      .map(this::safeReadString) ❸
      .filter(Objects::nonNull) ❹
      .forEach(System.out::println);
```

❶ The "safe" method has the same method signature as the method its wrapping, except for the `throws IOException`.

❷ The Exception is dealt with locally and returns an appropriate fallback.

❸ The wrapper method can be used as a method reference, making the code concise and readable again.

❹ The possibility of a `null` element must be handled accordingly.

The pipeline is concise and straightforward again. The `IOException` is handled in the sense that it doesn't affect the pipeline, but this approach isn't "one-size-fits-all."

Safe method extraction is akin to a more localized version of the *facade pattern*.[3] Instead of wrapping a whole class to provide a safer, context-specific interface, only specific methods get a new facade to improve their handling for particular use cases. That reduces the affected code and still gives you the advantages of a facade, such as reduced complexity and improved readability. It's also a good starting point for future refactoring efforts.

Extracted safe methods might be an improvement over using `try-catch` blocks in a lambda because you keep the expressiveness of inline lambdas and method references and have a chance to handle any Exceptions. But the handling is confined in another abstraction over existing code to regain control of disruptive control flow conditions. The actual caller of the method—the Stream operation—gets no chance to deal with the Exception, making the handling opaque and inflexible.

---

3 Gamma, Helm, Johnson, and Vlissides, *Design Patterns: Elements of Reusable Object-Oriented Software* (Addison-Wesley Professional).

Un-Checking Exceptions

The next way to deal with checked Exceptions goes against the fundamental purpose of using checked Exceptions in the first place. Instead of dealing with a checked Exception directly, you hide it in an unchecked Exception to circumvent the catch-or-specify requirement. It's a nonsensical but effective way to make the compiler happy.

This approach uses specialized functional interfaces that use the `throws` keyword to wrap the offending lambda or method reference. It catches the original Exception and rethrows it as an unchecked `RuntimeException`, or one of its siblings. These functional interfaces extend the original one to ensure compatibility. The original single abstract method uses a `default` implementation to connect it to the throwing one, as shown in Example 10-2.

Example 10-2. Unchecking `java.util.Function`

```
@FunctionalInterface
public interface ThrowingFunction<T, R> extends Function<T, R> { ❶

    R applyThrows(T elem) throws Exception; ❷

    @Override
    default U apply(T t) { ❸
        try {
            return applyThrows(t);
        } catch (Exception e) {
            throw new RuntimeException(e);
        }
    }

    public static <T, R> Function<T, R> uncheck(ThrowingFunction<T, R> fn) { ❹
        return fn::apply;
    }
}
```

❶ The wrapper extends the original type to act as a drop-in replacement.

❷ The single abstract method (SAM) mimics the original but throws an `Exception`.

❸ The original SAM is implemented as a `default` method to wrap any `Exception` as an unchecked `RuntimeException`.

❹ A `static` helper to uncheck any throwing `Function<T, R>` to circumvent the catch-or-specify requirement.

The `ThrowingFunction` type can be used explicitly by calling the uncheck method or implicitly as seen in Example 10-3.

Example 10-3. Using ThrowingFunction<T, R>

```
ThrowingFunction<Path, String> throwingFn = Files::readString; ❶

Stream.of(path1, path2, path3)
     .map(ThrowingFunction.uncheck(Files::readString)) ❷
     .filter(Objects::nonNull)
     .forEach(System.out::println);
```

❶ Any throwing method is assignable as a ThrowingFunction via a method reference and used in a context requiring a Function.

❷ Alternatively, a throwing lambda or method reference can be unchecked on the
   fly by using the static helper uncheck.

Congratulations, the compiler is happy again and won't force you to handle the
Exception anymore. The wrapper type doesn't fix the original problem of possible
control flow disruption but hides it from plain sight. The Stream pipeline will still
blow up if any Exception occurs without any possibility for localized Exception
handling.

> Exception-throwing functional interfaces only disguise their excep-
> tional states. They have their place and can be quite useful, but it
> should be considered a last resort and not a go-to solution.

Sneaky Throws

The *sneaky throws* idiom is a hack to throw a checked Exception without declaring it
with the throws keyword in a method's signature.

Instead of throwing a checked Exception using the throw keyword in a method's
body, which requires a throws declaration in the method signature, the actual Exception is thrown by another method, as follows:

```
String sneakyRead(File input) {

    // ...

    if (fileNotFound) {
        sneakyThrow(new IOException("File '" + file + "' not found."));
    }

    // ...
}
```

The actual throwing of the Exception is delegated to the sneakyThrow method.

Wait a minute, doesn't anyone using a method throwing a checked Exception, like sneakyThrow, have to adhere to the catch-or-specify requirement?

Well, there's one exception to the rule (pun intended). You can take advantage of a change[4] in Java's type inference regarding Generics and Exceptions in Java 8. In simple terms, if there are no upper or lower bounds on a generic method signature with throws E, the compiler assumes the type E to be a RuntimeException. This allows you to create the following sneakyThrow:

```
<E extends Throwable> void sneakyThrow(Throwable e) throws E {
    throw (E) e;
}
```

Regardless of the actual type for the argument e, the compiler assumes throws E to be a RuntimeException and thereby exempts the method from the catch-or-specify requirement. The compiler might not complain, but this approach is highly problematic.

The method signature of sneakyRead no longer signifies its checked Exception. Checked Exceptions are supposed to be anticipated and recoverable, and therefore belong to the method's public contract. By removing the throws keyword and circumventing the catch-or-specify requirement, you reduce the amount of information conferred to the caller by making the method's public contract more opaque for convenience reasons. You still could—and should—list all Exceptions and their reasoning in the method's documentation.

The method no longer follows "normal reasoning" by bypassing the throws keyword and the enforcement of the catch-or-specify requirement. Anyone reading the code has to know what sneakyThrow does. You could add an appropriate return statement after the call to at least convey that it's an exit point. But the significance that a throws keyword emits is lost.

 Sneaky throws circumvent an integral part of the Java language about how to deal with control flow disruptions. There is a place for it in a few edge cases for internal implementations. In external code, however, like public methods, throwing Exceptions sneakily breaks the reasonably expected contract between the method and the caller any Java developer would anticipate.

---

4 The rules for type resolution are listed in §18.4 of the Java SE 8 Language Specification (*https://oreil.ly/o6QD6*).

Sneakily throwing Exceptions might be an acceptable last resort hack for internal code, but you still have to communicate the implications with the help of the context, method names, and documentation. In the next section, I show you an acceptable use case for sneakily throwing an Exception in a specialized implementation for internal code.

A Functional Approach to Exceptions

So far, I've only discussed how to "brute force" Java's Exception handling mechanics to play nice with lambdas by ignoring and circumventing the intended purpose of Exceptions. What's really needed is finding a reasonable compromise and balance between a functional approach and the more traditional constructs.

Your options include designing your code to not throw Exceptions at all or mimicking the Exception-handling approaches of other more functional languages.

Not Throwing Exceptions

Checked Exceptions are an integral part of a method's contract and are designed as control flow disruptions. That's what makes it so difficult to deal with them in the first place! So, instead of finding a better way of handling checked Exceptions and all of their complications, we can instead find an alternative way of dealing with control flow disruption in a functional context.

"Safe Method Extraction" on page 248 discussed a variant of not throwing Exceptions by wrapping an Exception-throwing method with a non-throwing "safer" method. This approach helps if you don't have control over the code and can't design it to not throw any Exceptions in the first place. It replaces disruptive control flow events in the form of Exceptions with another value to represent an exceptional state: Optionals. If you have control over the API, you could design its contracts not to use Exceptions or make them at least more manageable. Exceptions are a reaction to some form of illegal state. The best way to avoid Exception handling is to make the representation of such an illegal state impossible in the first place.

I discussed in Chapter 9 that Optionals are a box to wrap an actual value. It's a specialized type representing the presence or absence of values without risking encountering a null reference and the eventually dreaded NullPointerException.

Let's look at the previous example again. This time, however, let's use an Optional instead of throwing an Exception, as seen in Example 10-4.

Example 10-4. Using `Optional<String>` instead of throwing an `IOException`

```
Optional<String> safeReadString(Path path) { ❶
  try {
    var content = Files.readString(path);
    return Optional.of(content);
  } catch (IOException e) {
    return Optional.empty(); ❷
  }
}
```

❶ An `Optional<String>` is used instead of a plain `String`.

❷ By returning an `Optional<String>`, either with the file content or an empty one in the case of an `IOException`, a valid non-`null` object is returned.

Returning an `Optional<String>` has two advantages over simply returning a `String`. First, a valid object is returned, so no additional `null` checks are required to use it safely. Second, the Optional type is a starting point for a fluent functional pipeline to deal with the inner value, or its absence.

If your API doesn't expose any illegal states requiring control flow disruptions, you, or anyone else calling such methods, don't have to handle them. Optionals are a simple and readily available choice, although they lack some desirable features. The new `safeReadString` conveys that it wasn't able to read the file but doesn't tell you *why* it wasn't able to do so.

Errors as Values

Where Optionals only provide the difference between the presence and absence of a value, a dedicated *result object* conveys more information about *why* an operation might have failed. The concept of dedicated type representing the overall result of an operation isn't a new one. They are wrapper objects indicating whether or not an operation was a success and include a value or, if unsuccessful, a reason why not. Many languages support dynamic tuples as return types, so you don't need an explicit type representing your operation, like in Go:

```
func safeReadString(path string) (string, error) {
  // ...
}

content, err := safeReadString("location/content.md")
if err != nil {
  // error handling code
}
```

Even though Java lacks such dynamic tuples, thanks to Generics, a versatile and functionally inclined result type can be created that leverages tools and concepts discussed in this book.

Let's create a rudimentary Result<V, E extends Throwable> type together.

Creating the scaffold

The main goal of the Result type is to hold a possible value or, if not successful, an Exception representing the reason for failure.

A traditional result object could be implemented as a Record as shown in Example 10-5.

Example 10-5. Traditional result object

```
public record Result<V, E extends Throwable>(V value,    ❶
                                              E throwable,
                                              boolean isSuccess) {

  public static <V, E extends Throwable> Result<V, E> success(V value) {    ❷
    return new Result<>(value, null, true);
  }

  public static <V, E extends Throwable> Result<V, E> failure(E throwable) {    ❷
    return new Result<>(null, throwable, false);
  }
}
```

❶ The Record components reflect the different states. The explicit isSuccess field helps to better determine a successful operation and to support null as a valid value.

❷ Convenience factory methods provide a more expressive API.

Even this simple scaffold provides a certain improvement over using Optionals already, with the convenience factory methods being an expressive way to create appropriate results.

The previous examples of safeReadString can be easily converted to use the Result<V, E> type, as shown in Example 10-6.

Example 10-6. Using Result<V, E> as a return type

```
Result<String, IOException> safeReadString(Path path) {
  try {
    return Result.success(Files.readString(path));
  } catch (IOException e) {
```

```
        return Result.failure(e);
    }
}

Stream.of(path1, path2, path3)
    .map(this::safeReadString)
    .filter(Result::isSuccess)
    .forEach(System.out::println);
```

The new type is just as easy to use in a Stream pipeline as an Optional. But the real
power comes from giving it more functional properties by introducing higher-order
functions that depend on the success state.

Making Result<V, E> functional

The general features of the `Optional` type are the inspiration on how to improve the
`Result` type further, including:

- Transforming its value or Exception
- Reacting to an Exception
- Providing a fallback value

Transforming the `value` or `throwable` field requires dedicated `map` methods or a
combined one to handle both use cases at once, as shown in Example 10-7.

Example 10-7. Adding transformers to Result<V, E>

```
public record Result<V, E extends Throwable> (V value,
                                               E throwable,
                                               boolean isSuccess) {
    // ...

    public <R> Optional<R> mapSuccess(Function<V, R> fn) { ❶
        return this.isSuccess ? Optional.ofNullable(this.value).map(fn)
                              : Optional.empty();
    }

    public <R> Optional<R> mapFailure(Function<E, R> fn) { ❶
        return this.isSuccess ? Optional.empty()
                              : Optional.ofNullable(this.throwable).map(fn);
    }

    public <R> R map(Function<V, R> successFn, ❷
                     Function<E, R> failureFn) {
        return this.isSuccess ? successFn.apply(this.value)
                              : failureFn.apply(this.throwable);
    }
}
```

❶ The singular mapping methods are quite similar and transform the respective result, success or failure. That's why both must return an `Optional` instead of a concrete value.

❷ A combined `map` method allows you to handle both cases, success or failure, in a single call. Because both states are handled, a concrete value instead of an `Optional` is returned.

With the help of the mapper methods, you can now handle either one or both cases directly:

```
// HANDLE ONLY SUCCESS CASE
Stream.of(path1, path2, path3)
      .map(this::safeReadString)
      .map(result -> result.mapSuccess(String::toUpperCase))
      .flatMap(Optional::stream)
      .forEach(System.out::println);


// HANDLE BOTH CASES
var result = safeReadString(path).map(
  success -> success.toUpperCase(),
  failure -> "IO-Error: " + failure.getMessage()
);
```

There also needs to be a way to work with a `Result` without requiring it to transform its value or Exception first.

To react to a certain state, let's add `ifSuccess`, `ifFailure`, and `handle`:

```
public record Result<V, E extends Throwable> (V value,
                                               E throwable,
                                               boolean isSuccess) {

  // ...

  public void ifSuccess(Consumer<? super V> action) {
    if (this.isSuccess) {
      action.accept(this.value);
    }
  }

  public void ifFailure(Consumer<? super E> action) {
    if (!this.isSuccess) {
      action.accept(this.throwable);
    }
  }

  public void handle(Consumer<? super V> successAction,
                     Consumer<? super E> failureAction) {
    if (this.isSuccess) {
      successAction.accept(this.value);
```

```
      } else {
        failureAction.accept(this.throwable);
      }
    }
  }
```

The implementation is almost equivalent to the mapper methods, except they use a Consumer instead of a Function.

 These two additions are side-effect-only and, therefore, not very functional in the purest sense. Nevertheless, such additions provide an excellent stopgap between imperative and functional approaches.

Next, let's add convenience methods for providing fallback values. The most obvious ones are orElse and orElseGet:

```
public record Result<V, E extends Throwable>(V value,
                                              E throwable,
                                              boolean isSuccess) {

  // ...

  public V orElse(V other) {
    return this.isSuccess ? this.value
                          : other;
  }

  public V orElseGet(Supplier<? extends V> otherSupplier) {
    return this.isSuccess ? this.value
                          : otherSupplier.get();
  }
}
```

No surprises here.

However, adding an orElseThrow as a shortcut to rethrow the inner Throwable isn't as straightforward because it still has to adhere to the catch-or-specify requirement. This is actually the one acceptable use case discussed earlier about using a sneaky throw discussed in "Sneaky Throws" on page 251, to circumvent the requirement:

```
public record Result<V, E extends Throwable>(V value,
                                              E throwable,
                                              boolean isSuccess) {

  // ...

  private <E extends Throwable> void sneakyThrow(Throwable e) throws E {
    throw (E) e;
  }

  public V orElseThrow() {
```

```
    if (!this.isSuccess) {
      sneakyThrow(this.throwable);
      return null;
    }

    return this.value;
  }
}
```

In this particular case, a sneaky throw is justified, in my opinion, due to the general context and public contract of orElseThrow. Like with the Optional<T> type, the method force-unwraps the box holding a possible result and warns you about a possible Exception with its name.

There's a lot left to be desired, like adding a Stream<V> stream() method for even better integration into Stream pipelines. Still, the general approach was a great exercise on how to combine functional concepts to provide an alternative to handling disruptive control flow events. The implementation shown in this book is quite simplistic and reduced to a minimal amount of code.

If you intend to use a type like Result<V, E>, you should check out one of the functional libraries of the Java ecosystem. Projects like vavr (*https://oreil.ly/fzFhV*), jOOλ (*https://oreil.ly/qN316*) (pronounced "JOOL"), and Functional Java (*https://oreil.ly/WGpKg*) provide quite comprehensive and battle-tested implementations that are ready to use.

The Try/Success/Failure Pattern

Scala is arguably the closest functional relative to Java available on the JVM, not considering Clojure due to its more foreign syntax and dynamic type system. It addresses many of Java's perceived shortcomings over younger languages and is functional at its core, including an excellent way of dealing with exceptional conditions.

The *try/success/failure* pattern and its related types Try[+T][5], Success[+T], and Failure[+T], are Scala's way of dealing with Exceptions in a more functional fashion.

Where an Optional<T> indicates that a value might be missing, Try[+T] can tell you *why* and gives you the ability to handle any occurred Exception, similar to the Result type discussed earlier in this chapter. If the code succeeds, a Success[+T] object is returned, and if it fails, the error will be contained in a Failure[+T] object. Scala also supports *pattern-matching*, a switch-like concept of handling different outcomes.

---

5 Scala's generic types are declared with [ ] (square brackets) instead of <> (angle brackets). The + (plus) signifies the type's variance. See "Tour of Scala" (*https://oreil.ly/II6Z2G*) for more information about type variance.

That allows for concise and straightforward Exception handling without the usual boilerplate a Java developer is used to.

 Scala-like pattern matching for Java's `switch` construct is available as a preview feature[6] since Java 17.

A `Try[+T]` can either be in a `Success[+T]` or `Failure[+T]` state, with the latter containing a `Throwable`. Even without full knowledge of Scala's syntax, the code in Example 10-8 shouldn't be too foreign to a Java developer.

Example 10-8. Scala's try/success/failure pattern

```
def readString(path: Path): Try[String] = Try { ❶
  // code that will throw an Exception
}

val path = Path.of(...);

readString(path) match { ❷
  case Success(value) => println(value.toUpperCase) ❸
  case Failure(e) => println("Couldn't read file: " + e.getMessage) ❹
}
```

❶ The return type is `Try[String]`, so the method must either return a `Success[String]` containing the content of the `Path`, or a `Failure[Throwable]`. Scala doesn't need an explicit `return` and returns the last value implicitly. Any Exception is caught by the `Try { … }` construct.

❷ Scala's pattern matching simplifies the result handling. The cases are lambdas, and the whole block is similar to an Optional call chain with a `map` and an `orElse` operation.

❸ The `Success` case provides access to the return value.

❹ If an Exception occurs, it's handled by the `Failure` case.

---

6 The first preview of pattern matching for `switch` is described in JEP 406 (*https://oreil.ly/w9oJ7*). A second preview is described in JEP 420 (*https://oreil.ly/XJ7m9*), which was delivered in Java 18. The next release, Java 19, included the third preview described in JEP 427 (*https://oreil.ly/7uxGf*). The feature is still evolving with another preview planned for Java 20, described in JEP 433 (*https://oreil.ly/hd8HL*).

`Try[+A]` is an excellent Scala feature, combining concepts similar to Optionals and Exception handling into a single, easy-to-use type and idiom. But what does that mean for you as a Java developer?

Java doesn't provide anything out-of-the-box that comes even close to the simplicity or language integration of Scala's try/success/failure pattern.

Functional Exception Handling with CompletableFutures

Java actually has a type capable of handling lambdas in the vein of the try/success/failure pattern: `CompletableFuture<T>`. It provides a fluent functional API including error handling, which I will discuss in more detail in Chapter 13.

On the surface, it's quite similar to the custom `Try` implementation. However, its optimal problem context isn't handling throwing lambdas. Instead, `Completable` `Futures` are designed for asynchronous tasks and running lambdas in multi-threaded environments.

Even without language support, you can still implement an approximation of the try/success/failure pattern with the new functional tools since Java 8. So let's do that now.

Creating a pipeline

Similar to how Streams provide a launch pad for a functional pipeline, the `Try` type we're going to create will have a creation step, intermediate but independent operations, and finally, a terminal operation to kickstart the pipeline.

To replicate Scala's functionality, a construct accepting a lambda is needed as a starting point.

 As with other functional constructs, many variants would be needed to support the various available functional interfaces. To simplify the required code, the `Try` type only supports `Function<T, R>` as the initial lambda.

The main requirements of the `Try` type are:

- Accepting a possibly throwing lambda
- Providing a `success` operation
- Providing a `failure` operation
- Starting the pipeline with a value

The Try type could be simplified by only supporting RuntimeException, but then it wouldn't be a flexible alternative to regular try-catch block. To circumvent the catch-or-specify requirement, the ThrowingFunction interface discussed in "Un-Checking Exceptions" on page 250 is used.

The minimum scaffold required to accept a ThrowingFunction and a possible Function to handle a RuntimeException is shown in Example 10-9.

Example 10-9. Minimal Try<T, R> accepting a lambda and Exception handler

```
public class Try<T, R> { ❶

  private final Function<T, R>                fn; ❷
  private final Function<RuntimeException, R> failureFn; ❷

  public static <T, R> Try<T, R> of(ThrowingFunction<T, R> fn) { ❸
    Objects.requireNonNull(fn);
    return new Try<>(fn, null);
  }

  private Try(Function<T, R> fn, ❹
             Function<RuntimeException, R> failureFn) {
    this.fn = fn;
    this.failureFn = failureFn;
  }
}
```

❶ The generic types T and R correspond to Function<T, R>. Using a class instead of a record makes it possible to hide the sole constructor by making it private.

❷ The construct needs to hold the initial Function<T, R> and a possible error-handling Function<RuntimeException, R>. Both fields are final, making the Try type immutable.

❸ The static factory method of provides a similar interface as other functional pipelines. It accepts a ThrowingFunction<T, R> to circumvent the catch-or-specify requirement but assigns it immediately to a Function<T, R>.

❹ The private constructor enforces the use of the factory method.

Even though the type doesn't do anything, creating a new pipeline from an existing lambda or method reference is pretty straightforward:

```
var trySuccessFailure = Try.<Path, String> of(Files::readString);
```

The type hints in front of the of call are required because the compiler can't necessarily infer the type from the surrounding context.

Next, the type needs to handle success and failure.

Handling success and failure

Two new methods are needed to handle the outcome of the Try pipeline, success and failure, as seen in Example 10-10.

Example 10-10. Handling success and failure in Try<T, R>

```java
public class Try<T, R> {

  // ...

  public Try<T, R> success(Function<R, R> successFn) {
    Objects.requireNonNull(successFn);

    var composedFn = this.fn.andThen(successFn); ❶
    return new Try<>(composedFn, this.failureFn);
  }

  public Try<T, R> failure(Function<RuntimeException, R> failureFn) {
    Objects.requireNonNull(failureFn);
    return new Try<>(this.fn, ❷
                     failureFn);
  }
}
```

❶ The successFn is composed to the original lambda to provide the base for the new Try instance. The failureFn is used as is.

❷ Handling an error requires only passing through the original fn and the provided failureFn.

Because the Try type is designed to be immutable, both handling methods return a new instance of Try. The success method uses functional composition to create the fully required task, whereas the failure method creates a new Try instance with the preexisting lambda and the provided error handling Function.

By using functional composition for the success operation instead of an extra control path, like storing successFn in another field, the handler isn't even required in case of no modifications to the result of the initial lambda.

Using the handler methods is as you would expect and feels similar to working with a Stream's intermediate operations:

```java
var trySuccessFailure = Try.<Path, String> of(Files::readString)
                           .success(String::toUpperCase)
                           .failure(str -> null);
```

Unlike a Stream, though, the operations are independent of one another and not in a sequential pipeline. It's more akin to how an Optionals pipeline seems to be sequential but actually has tracks to follow. Which handling operation, success or failure, is supposed to be evaluated depends on the state of the Try evaluation.

It's time to kickstart the pipeline.

Running the pipeline

The last operation needed to complete the pipeline is the ability to push a value down the pipeline and let the handlers do their work, in the form of an apply method, as shown in Example 10-11.

Example 10-11. Applying a value to Try<T, R>

```java
public class Try<T, R> {

  // ...

  public Optional<R> apply(T value) {
    try {
      var result = this.fn.apply(value);
      return Optional.ofNullable(result); ❶
    }
    catch (RuntimeException e) {
      if (this.failureFn != null) { ❷
        var result = this.failureFn.apply(e);
        return Optional.ofNullable(result);
      }
    }

    return Optional.empty(); ❸
  }
}
```

❶ The "happy path" is applying fn to the value. Thanks to designing the success method as a functional composition, no special handling is needed to run the initial lambda and optional success transformation. The code has to be run in a try-catch block to handle the failure case.

❷ Failure handling isn't mandatory, so a null check is necessary.

❸ This point is the ultimate fallback if no error handler was added to the pipeline.

The return type Optional<R> provides another lift-off point for a functional pipeline.

Now our minimalistic Try pipeline has all the operations needed to call a throwing method and handle both the success and failure cases:

```
var path = Path.of("location", "content.md");

Optional<String> content = Try.<Path, String> of(Files::readString)
                                    .success(String::toUpperCase)
                                    .failure(str -> null)
                                    .apply(path);
```

Even though the `Try` pipeline gives you higher-order function operations to deal with a throwing lambda, the pipeline itself isn't functional on the outside. Or is it?

The name `apply`, which I've chosen for the terminal operation, reveals the possible functional interface that `Try` could implement to be more easily usable in other functional pipelines like Streams or Optionals: `Function<T, Optional<R>>`.

By implementing the functional interface the `Try` type becomes a drop-in replacement for any `Function` without requiring actual logic changes, as shown in Example 10-12.

Example 10-12. Implementing Function<T, Optional<R>>

```
public class Try<T, R> implements Function<T, Optional<R>> {

  // ...

  @Override
  public Optional<R> apply(T value) {
    // ...
  }
}
```

Now, any `Try` pipeline is easily usable in any higher-order function that accepts a `Function`, like in a Stream `map` operation:

```
Function<Path, Optional<String>> fileLoader =
  Try.<Path, String> of(Files::readString)
                    .success(String::toUpperCase)
                    .failure(str -> null);

List<String> fileContents = Stream.of(path1, path2, path3)
                                  .map(fileLoader)
                                  .flatMap(Optional::stream)
                                  .toList();
```

As with the `Result` before, the `Try` type is quite minimalistic and should be regarded as an exercise in how to combine functional concepts to create new constructs, like a lazy fluent pipeline consisting of higher-order functions. If you want to use a type like `Try`, you should consider using an established functional third-party library like vavr (*https://oreil.ly/OAr28*), which provides a versatile `Try` type and much more.

Final Thoughts on Functional Exception Handling

Disruptive and abnormal control flow conditions in our code are inevitable, which is why we need a way to deal with them. Exception handling helps to improve program safety. For example, the catch-or-specify requirement is designed to make you think about the anticipated exceptional states and deal with them accordingly to increase code quality. Although it's certainly useful, it's also tricky to carry out.

Handling Exceptions can be quite a pain point in Java, regardless of using a functional approach. There is always a trade-off, no matter which Exception-handling approach you choose, especially if checked Exceptions are involved:

- Extracting unsafe methods to gain localized Exception handling is a good compromise but not an easy-to-use general solution.
- Designing your APIs to not have any exceptional states is not as easy as it sounds.
- Unchecking your Exceptions is a "last-resort" tool that hides them away without a chance to handle them and contradicts their purpose.

So what should you do? Well, it depends.

None of the presented solutions is perfect. You have to find a balance between "convenience" and "usability." Exceptions are sometimes an overused feature, but they are still essential signals to the control flow of your programs. Hiding them away might not be in your best interest in the long run, even if the resulting code is more concise and reasonable, as long as no Exception occurs.

Not every imperative or OOP feature/technique is replaceable with a functional equivalent in Java. Many of Java's (functional) shortcomings are circumventable to gain their general advantages, even if the resulting code is not as concise as in fully-functional programming languages. Exceptions, however, are one of those features that aren't easily replaceable in most circumstances. They're often an indicator that you either should try to refactor your code to make it "more functional" or that a functional approach might not be the best solution for the problem.

Alternatively, several third-party libraries are available, like the Vavr project (*https://oreil.ly/OAr28*) or jOOλ (*https://oreil.ly/x8I3e*), that allow you to circumvent or at least mitigate problems when using (checked) Exceptions in functional Java code. They did all the work implementing all relevant wrapper interfaces and replicating control structures and types from other languages, like pattern matching. But in the end, you end up with highly specialized code that tries to bend Java to its will, without much regard for traditional or common code constructs. Such dependence on a third-party library is a long-term commitment and shouldn't be added lightly.

Takeaways

- There are no specialized constructs for handling Exceptions in functional code like lambda expressions, only the `try-catch` block as usual, which leads to verbose and unwieldy code.

- You can fulfill or circumvent the catch-or-specify requirement in multiple ways, but that merely hides the original problem.

- Custom wrappers can provide a more functional approach.

- Third-party libraries can help reduce the additional boilerplate required for handling Exceptions more functionally. But the newly introduced types and constructs are no lightweight addition to your code and might create a lot of technical debt.

- Choosing the right way to deal with Exceptions in functional code depends highly on the surrounding context.

CHAPTER 11

Lazy Evaluation

Although laziness is often seen as a character flaw in people, it can be considered a favorable feature in programming languages. In computer science terms, *laziness* is the antagonist to *strictness*—or *eagerness*—of code evaluation.

This chapter will show you how being lazy can improve performance. You will learn about the difference between strict and lazy evaluation and its impact on your code's design.

Laziness Versus Strictness

The strictness of a language describes the semantics of how your code is evaluated.

Strict evaluation happens as soon as possible, such as declaring or setting a variable or passing an expression as an argument. *Non-strict* evaluation, however, happens when the result of an expression is actually needed. This way, expressions can have a value even if one or more subexpressions fail to evaluate.

The functional programming language Haskell has non-strict semantics by default, evaluating expressions from the outermost to the inner ones. This allows you to create control structures or infinite data sequences due to the separation of the *creation* and *consumption* of expressions.

Let's take a look at the following strict Java code of a simple method accepting two arguments but using only one for its logic:

```
int add(int x, int y) {
  return x + x;
}
```

The non-strict Haskell equivalent function declaration looks more like a variable assignment:

```
add x y = x + x
```

This function also uses only its first argument and doesn't evaluate the second argument, y, at all. That's why the following Haskell code still yields a result:

```
add 5 (1/0)
=> 10
```

If you call the Java equivalent of this function with the same arguments, the value 1 and the expression (1/0), it will throw an Exception:

```
var result = add(5, (1/0));
// => java.lang.ArithmeticException: Division by zero
```

Even though the second parameter of the add call isn't used in any capacity, Java, as a strict language, evaluates the expression immediately. Method arguments are *passed-by-value*, which means they're evaluated before being passed to the method, which in this case throws an ArithmeticException.

 Java's method arguments are always pass-by-value. In the case of non-primitive types, arguments are passed as *object handles* by the JVM with a special type called references. These are technically still passed-by-value, making the general terminology and semantics quite confusing.

Conversely, lazy evaluation is defined as evaluating expressions only when their result is needed. That means the declaration of an expression doesn't trigger its immediate evaluation, which makes Java lambda expressions the perfect match for lazy evaluation, as seen in Example 11-1.

Example 11-1. Lazy evaluation in Java using Suppliers

```
int add (IntSupplier x, IntSupplier y) {
  var actualX = x.getAsInt();
  return actualX + actualX;
}

var result = add(() -> 5, () -> 1 / 0);
// => 10
```

The declaration of the IntSupplier instances, or their inline equivalents, is a strict statement and is evaluated immediately. The actual lambda body, however, doesn't evaluate until it's explicitly called with getAsInt, preventing the ArithmeticException in this case.

In essence, *strictness* is about "doing things," but *laziness* is about "considering things to do."

How Strict Is Java?

Most programming languages are neither fully lazy nor fully strict. Java is considered a strict language, but with some noteworthy lazy exceptions on a language level and in the available types of the JDK.

Let's go through them.

Short-Circuit Evaluation

Language-integrated laziness is available in Java in the form of the logical *short-circuit evaluation* with the logical operators && (double ampersand) and || (double pipe) for AND and OR. These operators evaluate their operands left to right and only as required. If the logical expression is satisfied by the expression left of the operator, the right operand isn't evaluated at all, as seen in Table 11-1.

Table 11-1. Evaluation of logical short-circuit operators

Operations	Value of `leftExpr`	Is `rightExpr` evaluated?
`leftExpr && rightExpr`	true	yes
	false	no
`leftExpr || rightExpr`	true	no
	false	yes

Bitwise Logical Operators

The similar bitwise operators & (single ampersand) and | (single pipe) evaluate eagerly and serve a different purpose than their logical brethren. Bitwise operators compare individual bits of integer types, resulting in an integer result.

Despite functioning similarly to a control structure, these logical operands can't exist in a vacuum. They must always be part of another statement, like a condition for an `if`-block or a variable assignment, as seen in Example 11-2. Another advantage of short-circuit evaluation for assignments is that they create (effectively) `final` references, as discussed in "Effectively final" on page 21, making them a perfect fit to use with Java's functional approach.

Example 11-2. Usage of logical short-circuit operators

```
// COMPILES: used as if condition
if (left() || right()) {
    // ...
}

// COMPILES: used as variable assignment
var result = left() || right();

// WON'T COMPILE: unused result
left() || right();**
```

Omitting the right-side operand evaluation is extremely helpful if the expression is costly or has any side effects, or doesn't need to be evaluated if the left side was. However, it also might be the source of not evaluating a required expression if the statement is short-circuited and the expression necessary is on the right side. If you make them a part of decision-making, make sure to design them carefully.

Any decision-making code benefits immensely from pure functions. The intended behavior is straightforward and easily understandable, without any lurking side effects that might go unnoticed during redesigning or refactoring your code, introducing subtle bugs that are often hard to pin down. You should make sure that there are either no side effects at all, which, in my opinion, is too absolute and generally an unrealistic goal, or name your methods to reflect their repercussions.

Control Structures

Control structures are responsible for changing the path taken through the instructions of your code. An `if-else` construct, for example, is a conditional branch with one (`if`) or more (`if-else`) blocks of code. These blocks are only evaluated depending on their corresponding condition, which is a lazy trait. Strictly evaluating any part of an `if-else` construct on declaration would defeat its purpose of using it as a conditional branch. This "lazy exception to the eager rules" applies to all branching and loop structures, as listed in Table 11-2.

Table 11-2. Lazy structures in Java

Branching control structures	Looping structures
if-else	for
? : (ternary) operator	while
switch	do-while
catch	

An absolutely strict language with non-lazy control structures is hard to imagine, if not impossible.

Lazy Types in the JDK

So far, I've talked about how Java's laziness was built directly into the language in the form of operators and control structures. The JDK, however, also provides multiple built-in types and data structures with a certain degree of laziness at runtime as well.

Lazy Maps

A common task for Maps is checking if a key already has a mapped value, and providing one if it's missing. The related code requires multiple checks and non (effectively) `final` variables, as follows:

```
Map<String, User> users = ...;

var email = "john@doe.com";

var user = users.get(email);
if (user == null) {
  user = loadUser(email);
  users.put(email, user);
}
```

The code might vary depending on the actual `Map` implementation, but the gist should be clear.

In general, this is already a lazy approach, delaying loading a user until necessary. In the course of retrofitting functional additions to many types in JDK 8, the `Map` type received a more concise and functional alternative with its `computeIf-` methods.

Two methods are available based on the existence of a mapped value for a key:

- `V computeIfAbsent(K key, Function<? super K, ? extends V> mapping Function)`

- `V computeIfPresent(K key, BiFunction<? super K, ? super V, ? extends V> remappingFunction)`

The first one is an ideal replacement for the code of the previous example, as such:

```
Map<String, User> users = ...;

var user = users.computeIfAbsent("john@doe.com", this::loadUser);
```

It requires the desired key as its first argument and a mapper `Function<K, V>` as its second argument that provides the new mapped value for the key if absent. The `computeIfPresent` is the antagonist for remapping values only if one is present.

A combination of both methods is also available in the form of the `V compute(K key, BiFunction<? super K, ? super V, ? extends V> remappingFunction)` method. It's able to update and even delete mapped values depending on the result of the `remapping` function, as illustrated in Figure 11-1.

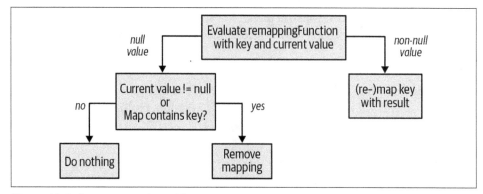

Figure 11-1. Lazy remapping with Map#compute

The general theme of a functional approach is clearly visible in `Map` type's lazy additions. Instead of requiring you to write the verbose and repetitive code of *how* to work with the Map and its mapped values, now you can concentrate on *what* is happening and how to deal with keys and values.

Streams

Java Streams are the perfect example of lazy functional pipelines. You can define an intricate Stream scaffold filled with expensive functional operations that will only start evaluation after calling a terminal operation. The number of processed elements solely depends on the design of the pipeline, allowing you to minimize the required work as much as possible by separating the definition of an expression and its actual evaluation in a data processing pipeline.

Chapter 6 explains Streams and their lazy approach to data processing in detail.

Optionals

Optionals are a non-lazy way of handling `null` values. Their general approach is similar to Streams, but they evaluate strictly compared to Streams. There are lazy operations available such as the `T orElseGet(Supplier<? extends T> supplier)` method that utilizes a `Supplier` to delay the execution to when it's absolutely necessary.

Chapter 9 gives a detailed introduction to Optionals and more information on how to use them.

Lambdas and Higher-Order Functions

Lambdas are a great way to introduce laziness on a code level. Their declaration is a statement and, therefore, strictly evaluated. However, their body—the *single abstract method*—encapsulates the actual logic and evaluates at your discretion. That makes them a simple way to store and transfer expressions for later evaluation.

Let's look at some eager code for providing an argument to a method and how it can be made lazy with the help of lambdas.

An Eager Approach

In Example 11-3, a hypothetical User is updated with a list of roles. The update isn't always done and depends on the inner logic of the update method. The arguments are provided eagerly, requiring a pretty expensive lookup call through the *DAO.*[1]

Example 11-3. Updating a User with eager method arguments

```
User updateUser(User user, List<Role> availableRoles) { ❶
  // ...
}

// HOW TO USE

var user = loadUserById(23L);
var availableRoles = this.dao.loadAllAvailableRoles(); ❷
var updatedUser = updateUser(user, availableRoles); ❸
```

❶ The updateUser method requires the user and a list of all available roles. The update itself depends on the inner logic and might not need the roles after all.

❷ The loadAllAvailableRoles method is called regardless of the updateUser method requiring the roles. This results in a costly trip to the database that might be unnecessary.

❸ All arguments are already evaluated at the time of the method call.

Providing updateUser with all available roles, even if they aren't necessary for every use case, creates unnecessary database calls and wastes performance.

---

1 A *DAO* (data access object) is a pattern to provide an abstract interface to a persistence layer like a database. It translates application calls to specific operations on the underlying persistence layer without exposing details of it.

So how can you make the call nonmandatory if it's not always required? By introducing laziness.

A Lazier Approach

In a strict language like Java, all method arguments are provided up front and as is. The method has no choice but to accept them, even if an argument isn't actually needed. This is especially a problem when it comes to executing expensive operations to create such arguments beforehand, such as database calls, which can be a drain on your available resources and performance.

The naïve approach to remedy unnecessary database calls is to change `updateUser` to accept the DAO directly, to use only if necessary:

```
User updateUser(User user, DAO roleDAO) {
  // ...
}
```

The `updateUser` method now has all the tools necessary to load the available roles by itself. On a superficial level, the initial problem of non-lazy data access is solved, but this "solution" creates a new problem: cohesion.

The `updateUser` method now uses the DAO directly and is no longer isolated from *how* the roles are acquired. This approach will make the method impure, as accessing the database is considered a side effect and makes it harder to verify and test. Thanks to possible API boundaries, it gets even more complicated if the `updateUser` method doesn't know the DAO type at all. So you need to create another abstraction to retrieve the roles. Instead of creating an additional abstract layer to bridge the gap between the DAO and the `updateUser` method, you can make `updateUser` a higher-order function and accept a lambda expression.

A Functional Approach

To create a functional abstraction for retrieving the required user roles in Example 11-3, you must first dissect the problem into a more abstract representation, finding out *what* is actually needed as an argument and not *how* the argument's value came to be.

The `updateUser` method needs access to the available roles, as it is reflected in the original method signature. And that's exactly the point in your code where introducing laziness will give you the most flexible solution.

The `Supplier` type is the most low-level possibility to encapsulate certain logic to retrieve a value at your discretion. Instead of providing `updateUser` directly with the DAO, a lambda expression is the lazy intermediate construct for loading the roles, as seen in Example 11-4.

Example 11-4. Updating a User with a lambda

```
void updateUser(User user, Supplier<List<Role>> availableRolesFn) { ❶
  // ...

  var availableRoles = availableRolesFn.get();

  // ...
}


// HOW TO USE

var user = loadUserById(23L);

updateUser(user, this.dao::loadAllAvailableRoles); ❷
```

❶ The updateUser method signature has to be changed to accept a Supplier<List<Role>> instead of the already loaded List<Role> or the DAO itself.

❷ The logic of how to acquire the roles is now encapsulated in a method reference.

Making updateUser a higher-order function by accepting a Supplier creates a superficial new layer without requiring an additional custom type wrapping the role-loading process.

Using the DAO directly as an argument eliminates the downsides:

- There's no longer a connection between the DAO and the updateUser method, creating the possibility of a pure, side-effect-free method.
- You don't need an additional type to represent the abstraction. The already available Supplier functional interface is the simplest and most compatible form of abstraction possible.
- Testability is restored without requiring the possibly complicated mocking of a DAO.

Costly operations, like database queries, can benefit immensely from a lazy approach if the call is avoidable. That doesn't mean, though, that making all method arguments lazy without a real need is the right approach, either. There are other solutions, too, like caching the result of costly calls, that might be simpler to use than designing your method calls to accept lazy arguments.

Delayed Executions with Thunks

Lambda expressions are a simple and low-level way to encapsulate an expression for later evaluation. One missing thing, though, is storing the result after evaluation—memoization, discussed in Chapter 2—so you don't re-evaluate an expression if called twice. There's an easy way to remedy this omission: *Thunks*.

A Thunk is a wrapper around a computation that is delayed until the result is needed. Unlike a `Supplier`, which also delays a computation, a Thunk evaluates only once and directly returns the result on subsequent calls.

Thunks fall into the general category of *lazy loading/initialization*, a design pattern often found in object-oriented code. Both techniques—lazy loading and lazy initialization—are similar mechanisms for achieving the same goal: non-strict evaluation and caching the result. Where a `Supplier` just defers the evaluation, a Thunk also caches its result.

Let's create a simple Thunk that follows the *virtual proxy* design pattern[2] to be a drop-in replacement for `Supplier`.

Creating a Simple Thunk

The most straightforward approach is wrapping a `Supplier` instance and storing its result after its first evaluation. By also implementing the `Supplier` interface, the Thunk becomes a drop-in replacement, as shown in Example 11-5.

Example 11-5. A simple Thunk<T> implementation

```
public class Thunk<T> implements Supplier<T> { ❶

  private final Supplier<T> expression; ❷

  private T result; ❸

  private Thunk(Supplier<T> expression) {
    this.expression = expression;
  }

  @Override
  public T get() {
    if (this.result == null) { ❹
      this.result = this.expression.get();
```

---

2 The Wikipedia entry on proxies (*https://oreil.ly/XAGo6*) provides an overview of the different kinds of proxies and their use.

```
      }
    return this.result;
  }

  public static <T> Thunk<T> of(Supplier<T> expression) { ❺
    if (expression instanceof Thunk<T>) { ❻
      return (Thunk<T>) expression;
    }
    return new Thunk<T>(expression);
  }
}
```

❶ Thunk<T> implements Supplier<T> to serve as a drop-in replacement.

❷ The actual Supplier<T> needs to be stored to delay evaluation.

❸ The result must be stored after evaluation.

❹ If not evaluated yet, the expression gets resolved, and its result is stored.

❺ A convenience factory method to create a Thunk without needing new or generic type information, so the only constructor can be private.

❻ No need to create a new Thunk<T> for a Thunk<T>.

This Thunk implementation is simple yet powerful. It adds memoization by calling a factory method with any Supplier<T> to create a drop-in replacement. Updating a User, like in the previous section, requires wrapping the method reference in the Thunk.of method:

```
updateUser(user, Thunk.of(this.dao::loadAllAvailableRoles));
```

The functional additions to Thunk<T> don't have to stop here. You can easily add "glue methods," as discussed in Chapter 2, to support functional composition, as shown in Example 11-6.

Example 11-6. Functional additions to Thunk<T>

```
public class Thunk<T> implements Supplier<T> {

  // ...

  public static <T> Thunk<T> of(T value) { ❶
    return new Thunk<T>(() -> value);
  }

  public <R> Thunk<R> map(Function<T, R> mapper) { ❷
    return Thunk.of(() -> mapper.apply(get()));
```

```
    }

    public void accept(Consumer<T> consumer) { ❸
      consumer.accept(get());
    }
}
```

❶   Factory method for creating a Thunk<T> of a single value instead of a
     Supplier<T>.

❷   Creates a new Thunk<R> including the mapper function.

❸   Consumes the result of a Thunk<T> by calling get to force evaluation if necessary.

With the addition of "glue" methods, the Thunk<T> type becomes a more versatile
utility type for creating lazy pipelines for single expressions.

One general problem remains, though: *thread safety*.

A Thread-Safe Thunk

For single-threaded environments, the Thunk implementation I discussed in the previous section works as intended. However, if it's accessed from another thread while
the expression evaluates, a race condition might lead to re-evaluation. The only way
to prevent this is to synchronize it across all accessing threads.

The most straightforward approach would be to add the keyword synchronized to its
get method. However, it has the obvious downside of *always* requiring synchronized
access and the associated overhead, even if the evaluation is already finished. Synchronization might not be as slow as it used to be, but it's still an overhead for every
call to the get method and definitely will slow down your code unnecessarily.

So how do you change the implementation to eliminate the race condition without
affecting the overall performance more than necessary? You do a risk analysis of
where and when a race condition can occur.

The risk of the evaluation-related race condition exists only until the expression is
evaluated. After that, no double evaluation can happen, as the result is returned
instead. That allows you to synchronize only the evaluation itself, not each call to the
get method.

Example 11-7 shows the introduction of a dedicated and synchronized evaluate
method. The actual implementation of it and how to access its result will be explained
shortly.

Example 11-7. Thunk<T> with synchronized evaluation

```
public class Thunk<T> implements Supplier<T> {

  private Thunk(Supplier<T> expression) {
    this.expression = () -> evaluate(expression);
  }

  private synchronized T evaluate(Supplier<T> expression) {
    // ...
  }

  // ...
}
```

The previous version of the Thunk used an additional field, value, to determine if expression was already evaluated. The new, thread-safe variant, however, replaces the stored value and its checks with a dedicated abstraction that holds the value:

```
private static class Holder<T> implements Supplier<T> {

  private final T value;

  Holder(T value) {
    this.value = value;
  }

  @Override
  public T get() {
    return this.value;
  }
}
```

The Holder<T> does two things:

- Holds the evaluated value
- Implements Supplier<T>

As Holder<T> implements Supplier<T>, it becomes a drop-in replacement for the field expressions. Therefore, you can use a technique called *compare & swap* (CAS). It's used for designing concurrent algorithms, by comparing the value of a variable with an expected value, and if they are equal, swapping out the value for the new value. The operation has to be *atomic*, meaning it's all-or-nothing for accessing the underlying data. That's why the evaluate method has to be synchronized. Any thread can see the data before or after, but never during evaluation, therefore eliminating the race condition.

Now, the `private` field `expression` can be replaced by the new type, as shown in Example 11-8.

Example 11-8. Using Holder<T> instead of Supplier<T>

```java
public class Thunk<T> implements Supplier<T> {

  private static class Holder<T> implements Supplier<T> {
    // ...
  }

  private Supplier<T> holder;  ❶

  private Thunk(Supplier<T> expression) {
    this.holder = () -> evaluate(expression);
  }

  private synchronized T evaluate(Supplier<T> expression) {
    if (Holder.class.isInstance(this.holder) == false) {  ❷
      var evaluated = expression.get();
      this.holder = new Holder<>(evaluated);  ❸
    }
    return this.holder.get();
  }

  @Override
  public T get() {
    return this.holder.get();  ❹
  }
}
```

❶ The field gets renamed to better reflect its usage and is also made non-`final`, as it is swapped out after the expression is evaluated.

❷ The expression gets evaluated only if the `holder` field currently isn't a `Holder` instance, but the expression created in the constructor.

❸ The `holder` field, at this point holding the original lambda to evaluate the initial expression, gets swapped out for a `Holder` instance with the evaluated result.

❹ The un-synchronized `get` method uses the `holder` field directly to access the value, as it always references a `Supplier`.

The improved `Thunk` implementation isn't as simple as before, but it eliminates the race condition by decoupling the evaluation of the expression from accessing it.

On first access, the `holder` field will call `evaluate`, which is synchronized, and therefore thread-safe. Any additional calls while the expression is evaluated will call to `evaluate`, too. Instead of a re-evaluation, the type check of the `holder` field skips directly to returning the result of the `this.holder.get()` call. Any access after the `holder` is reassigned will skip any `synchronized` entirely.

That's it; you now have a thread-safe, lazily evaluated `Supplier` drop-in that evaluates only once.

Our `Thunk` implementation uses `synchronized`, but there are multiple approaches to implementing a CAS algorithm. The same general behavior can be accomplished using one of `Atomic-` types available in the JDK's `java.util.concurrent.atomic` package, or even using a `ConcurrentHashMap#computeIfAbsent` to prevent the race condition. The book *Java Concurrency* by Brian Goetz and others[3] provides a good starting point for better understanding atomic variables, non-blocking synchronization, and Java's concurrency model in general.

Final Thoughts on Laziness

At its core, the idea of laziness boils down to deferring required work until a point in time when it's indispensable. The separation of *creating* and *consuming* expressions gives you a new axis of modularity in your code. This approach can improve performance immensely if an operation is optional and not required for each use case. Lazy evaluation also means, though, that you have to give up a certain degree of control over the exact time of evaluation.

The perceived and actual *loss of control* makes it much harder to reason about the required performance and memory characteristics of your code. The total performance requirement is the sum of all evaluated parts. Eager evaluation allows for quite linear and compositional performance assessment. Laziness shifts the actual computational cost from where expressions are defined to when they are used, with the possibility of code not being run at all. That's why idiomatic lazy performance is harder to assess; the perceived performance would most likely improve immediately compared to eager evaluation, especially if your code has many costly but maybe optional code paths. The total performance requirements may vary depending on the general context and what code is actually evaluated. You'd have to analyze your lazy code's average usage patterns and estimate the performance characteristics required under different scenarios, making straightforward benchmarking quite challenging.

Software development is a constant battle of *effectively utilizing scarce resources* to reach the desired, or required, performance. Lazy techniques, like delayed evaluation, or Streams for data processing, are low-hanging fruits[4] to improve your code's performance that are easy to integrate into an existing codebase. These techniques

---

3 Brian Goetz et al., *Java Concurrency in Practice* (Addison-Wesley Professional, 2006).

definitely will reduce the required work to a minimum, maybe even zero, freeing up precious performance for other tasks. If some expression or costly computation can be avoided, making it lazy will most definitely be a worthwhile endeavor in the long run.

Takeaways

- Strict evaluation means expressions and method arguments evaluate immediately on declaration.
- Lazy evaluation separates creating and consuming expressions by deferring their evaluation until their result is necessary, maybe not even evaluating them at all.
- *Strictness* is about "doing things"; laziness is about "considering things to do."
- Java is a "strict" language regarding expressions and method arguments, although certain lazy operators and control structures exist.
- Lambdas encapsulate expressions, making them lazy wrappers to be evaluated at your discretion.
- The JDK has several lazy runtime constructs and helper methods. For example, Streams are lazy functional pipelines, and `Optional` and `Map` provide *lazy* additions to their general interfaces.
- The `Supplier` interface is the simplest way to create a lazy calculation.
- Memoization, in the form of a `Thunk`, helps to avoid re-evaluation and can be used as a drop-in replacement for any `Supplier`.
- Laziness is a performance optimization powerhouse. The best code is the one that's not run at all. The next best alternative is to run it lazily only "on demand."
- The assessment of performance requirements for lazy code is difficult and might conceal performance problems if tested in environments not matching a "real-world" use case.

---

4 The concept of a *low-hanging fruit* describes a goal that is easy to achieve or take advantage of, compared to the alternatives, like redesigning or refactoring your whole codebase.

CHAPTER 12

Recursion

Recursion is an approach to solving a problem that can be broken down into smaller versions of itself. Many developers see *recursion* as another—often complicated—approach to iteration-based problem-solving. Still, it's good to know different techniques for particular groups of problems in a functional way.

This chapter shows the general idea behind recursion, how you implement recursive methods, and their place in your Java code compared to other forms of iteration.

What Is Recursion?

In "Recursion" on page 8, you've seen an illustration of calculating factorials—the product of all positive integers less than or equal to the input parameter. Many books, guides, and tutorials use factorials to demonstrate recursion because it's a perfect problem to solve partially, and it'll be the first example of this chapter, too.

Every step of calculating factorials breaks down into the product of the input parameter and the result of the next factorial operation. When the calculation reaches $fac(1)$ —defined as "1"—the chain terminates and provides the value to the previous step. The complete steps can be seen in Equation 12-1.

Equation 12-1. Formal representation of a factorial calculation

$$fac(n)$$
$$\rightarrow n * fac(n-1)$$
$$\rightarrow n * (n-1) * fac(n-2)$$
$$\rightarrow 4 * (n-1) * (n-2) * \cdots * fac(1)$$
$$\rightarrow 4 * (n-1) * (n-2) * \cdots * 1$$

This generalization of the calculation steps visualizes the underlying concept of recursion: solving a problem by combining smaller instances of the same problem. This is done using methods that call themselves with modified arguments until a base condition is reached.

Recursion consists of two distinct operation types:

Base conditions

A *base condition* is a predefined case—a *solution* to the problem—which will return an actual value and unwind the recursive call chain. It provides its value to the previous step, which can now calculate a result and return it to its predecessor, and so forth.

Recursive call

Until the call chain reaches its base condition, every step will create another one by calling itself with modified input parameters.

Figure 12-1 shows the general flow of a recursive call chain.

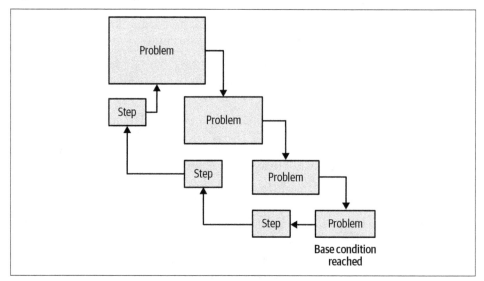

Figure 12-1. Solving problems with smaller problems

The problem becomes smaller until a solution is found for the smallest part. This solution will then become an input for the next bigger problem, and so on until the sum of all parts builds the solution to the original problem.

Head Versus Tail Recursion

Recursive calls fall into two categories, *head* and *tail* recursion, depending on the location of the recursive call in the method body:

Head recursion

> Other statements/expressions are executed/evaluated after the recursive method call, making it not the last statement.

Tail recursion

> The recursive call is the last statement of the method without any further calculations linking its result to the current call.

Let's look at calculating a factorial with both types to illustrate their differences better. Example 12-1 shows how to use head recursion.

Example 12-1. Calculating factorials with head recursion

```
long factorialHead(long n) { ❶
  if (n == 1L) { ❷
    return 1L;
  }

  var nextN = n - 1L;

  return n * factorialHead(nextN); ❸
}

var result = factorialHead(4L);
// => 24
```

❶ The method signature contains only the input parameter of the current recursive step. No intermediate state moves between the recursive calls.

❷ The base condition must come before the recursive call.

❸ The return value is an expression depending on the result of the recursive call, making it not the sole last statement in the method.

Now it's time to look at tail recursion, as shown in Example 12-2.

Example 12-2. Calculating factorials with tail recursion

```
long factorialTail(long n, long accumulator) { ❶
  if (n == 1L) { ❷
    return accumulator;
  }
```

```
    var nextN = n - 1L;
    var nextAccumulator = n * accumulator;

    return factorialTail(nextN, nextAccumulator); ❸
}

var result = factorialTail(4L, 1L); ❹
// => 24
```

❶   The method signature contains an accumulator.

❷   The base condition hasn't changed compared to head recursion.

❸   Instead of returning an expression dependent on the next recursive call, both factorialTail parameters are evaluated beforehand. The method only returns the recursive call itself.

❹   The accumulator requires an initial value. It reflects the base condition.

The main difference between head and tail recursion is how the call stack is constructed.

With *head recursion*, the recursive call is performed before returning a value. Therefore, the final result won't be available until the runtime has returned from each recursive call.

With *tail recursion*, the broken-down problem is solved first before the result is passed on to the next recursive call. Essentially, the return value of any given recursive step is the same as the result of the next recursive call. This allows for optimizing the call stack if the runtime supports it, as you will see in the next section.

Recursion and the Call Stack

If you look at Figure 12-1 again, you can think of every box as a separate method call and, therefore, a new stack frame on the call stack. That is a necessity because every box must be isolated from previous calculations so that their arguments won't affect each other. The total recursive call count is only constrained by how long it takes to reach a base condition. The problem is, though, that the available stack size is finite. Too many calls will fill up the available stack space and eventually throw a StackOverflowError.

A stack frame contains the state of a single method invocation. Each time your code calls a method, the JVM creates and pushes a new frame on the thread's stack. After returning from a method, its stack frame gets popped and discarded.

The actual maximum stack depth depends on the available stack size,[1] and what's stored in the individual frames.

To prevent the stack from overflowing, many modern compilers use *tail-call optimization/elimination* to remove no-longer-required frames in recursive call chains. If no additional calculations take place after a recursive call, the stack frame is no longer needed and can be removed. That reduces the stack frame space complexity of the recursive call from O(N) to O(1), resulting in faster and more memory-friendly machine code without an overflowing stack.

Sadly, the Java compiler and runtime lack that particular ability, as of early 2023.

Nevertheless, recursion is still a valuable tool for a subset of particular problems, even without optimization of the call stack.

Project Loom

Project Loom (*https://oreil.ly/bgKWy*), an effort to support easy-to-use, high-throughput lightweight concurrency and new programming models, will add support for stack frame manipulation. The JVM gains support for unwinding the stack to some point and invoking a method with given arguments, a feature called *unwind-and-inkove*.

That allows for efficient tail calls, even though automatic tail-call optimization is not an explicitly stated project goal. Nevertheless, these pleasant changes to the runtime might lower the barriers to using recursion more often and more efficiently.

A More Complex Example

As good as calculating a factorial is for explaining recursion, it isn't a typical real-world problem. That's why it's time to look at a more realistic example: traversing a tree-like data structure, as seen in Figure 12-2.

The data structure has a single root node, and every node has an optional left and right child node. Their numbers are for identification, not the order of any traversal.

---

1 The default stack size of most JVM implementations is one megabyte. You can set a bigger stack size with the flag -Xss. See the Oracle Java Tools documentation (*https://oreil.ly/jRsor*) for more information.

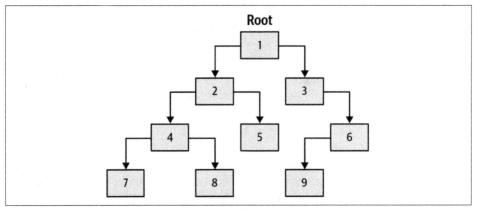

Figure 12-2. Tree-like data structure traversal

The nodes are represented by a generic Record Node<T>, as shown in Example 12-3.

Example 12-3. Tree node structure

```java
public record Node<T>(T value, Node<T> left, Node<T> right) {

  public static <T> Node<T> of(T value, Node<T> left, Node<T> right) {
    return new Node<>(value, left, right);
  }

  public static <T> Node<T> of(T value) {
    return new Node<>(value, null, null);
  }

  public static <T> Node<T> left(T value, Node<T> left) {
    return new Node<>(value, left, null);
  }

  public static <T> Node<T> right(T value, Node<T> right) {
    return new Node<>(value, null, right);
  }
}

var root = Node.of("1",
                Node.of("2",
                        Node.of("4",
                                Node.of("7"),
                                Node.of("8")),
                        Node.of("5")),
                Node.right("3",
                        Node.left("6",
                                Node.of("9"))));
```

The goal is to traverse the tree "in order." That means every node's left child node is traversed first until no other left node is found. Then it will continue traversing down its right child's left nodes before going up again.

First, we will implement the tree traversal with an iterative approach and then compare it to a recursive one.

Iterative Tree Traversal

With the help of a `while` loop, traversing the tree is as you would expect. It requires temporary variables and coordination boilerplate for traversal, as seen in Example 12-4.

Example 12-4. Iterative tree traversal

```
void traverseIterative(Node<String> root) {
  var tmpNodes = new Stack<Node<String>>(); ❶
  var current = root;

  while(!tmpNodes.isEmpty() || current != null) { ❷
    if (current != null) { ❸
      tmpNodes.push(current);
      current = current.left();
      continue;
    }

    current = tmpNodes.pop(); ❹

    System.out.print(current.value()); ❺

    current = current.right(); ❻
  }
}
```

❶ Auxiliary variables are required to save the current state of the iteration.

❷ Iterate until no node is present, or `nodeStack` isn't empty.

❸ A `java.util.Stack` saves all nodes until the bottom is reached.

❹ At this point, the loop can't go deeper because it encountered `current == null`, so it sets `current` to the last node saved in `tmpNodes`.

❺ Output the node value.

❻ Rinse and repeat with the right child node.

The output is as expected: *748251396*.

Although it works as intended, the code isn't very concise and requires mutable auxiliary variables to work properly.

Let's take a look at the recursive approach to see if it's an improvement over iteration.

Recursive Tree Traversal

To create a recursive solution to traverse the tree, you must first clearly define the different steps needed, including the base condition.

Traversing the tree requires two recursive calls, an action, and a base condition:

- Traverse the left node
- Traverse the right node
- Print a node's value
- Stop if no further nodes are found

The Java implementation of these different steps in their correct order is shown in Example 12-5.

Example 12-5. Recursive tree traversal

```
void traverseRecursion(Node<String> node) {
  if (node == null) { ❶
    return;
  }

  traverseRecursion(node.left()); ❷

  System.out.print(node.value()); ❸

  traverseRecursion(node.right()); ❹
}
```

❶ The base condition to stop the traversal if no nodes remain.

❷ First, recursively traverse the left child node. This will call `traverse` again as long as a left node exists.

❸ Second, because no more left child nodes exist, the current value needs to be printed.

❹ Third, traverse the possible right child node with the same logic as before.

The output is the same as before: *748251396*.

The code no longer requires an external iterator or auxiliary variables to hold the state, and the actual processing logic is reduced to a minimum. The traversal is no longer in the imperative mindset of *what to do*. Instead, it reflects the functional approach of *how to achieve* a goal in a more declarative way.

Let's make the tree traversal even more functional by moving the traversal process into the type itself and accepting a `Consumer<Node<T>>` for its action, as shown in Example 12-6.

Example 12-6. Extend Node<T> with a traversal method

```
public record Node<T>(T value, Node<T> left, Node<T> right) {

  // ...

  private static <T> void traverse(Node<T> node, ❶
                                   Consumer<T> fn) { ❷
    if (node == null) {
      return;
    }

    traverse(node.left(), fn);

    fn.accept(node.value());

    traverse(node.right(), fn);
  }

  public void traverse(Consumer<T> fn) { ❸
    Node.traverse(this, fn);
  }
}

root.traverse(System.out::print);
```

❶ The previous `traverse` method can easily be refactored into a `private static` method on the original type.

❷ The new `traverse` method accepts a `Consumer<Node<T>>` to support any kind of action.

❸ A `public` method for traversal simplifies the call by omitting `this` as its first argument.

Traversing the type became even easier. The type itself is now responsible for the best way to traverse itself and provides a flexible solution for anyone using it.

It's concise, functional, and easier to understand compared to the iterative approach. Still, there are advantages to using a loop. The biggest one is the performance discrepancy, trading the needed stack space for available heap space. Instead of creating a new stack frame for every recursive traversal operation, the nodes accumulate on the heap in tmpNodes. That makes the code more robust for larger graphs that might otherwise lead to a stack overflow.

As you can see, there's no easy answer to which approach is best. It always depends highly on the kind of data structure you have and how much data you need to process. Even then, your personal preference and familiarity with a particular approach might be more important than using the "best" solution to a problem and to write straightforward and bug-free processing code.

Recursion-Like Streams

Java's runtime might not support tail-call optimization; however, you can still implement a recursive-like experience with lambda expressions and Streams that doesn't suffer from overflowing stack issues.

Thanks to the lazy nature of Streams, you can build a pipeline that runs infinitely until the recursive problem is solved. But instead of calling a lambda expression recursively, it returns a new expression instead. This way, the stack depth will remain constant, regardless of the number of performed recursive steps.

This approach is quite convoluted compared to recursion or even using loops. It's not commonly used, but it illustrates how to combine various new functional components of Java to solve recursive problems. Take a look at the book's code repository (*https://github.com/benweidig/a-functional-approach-to-java*) if you'd like to learn more.

Final Thoughts on Recursion

Recursion is an often overlooked technique because it's so easy to get it wrong. For example, a faulty base condition may be impossible to fulfill, which inevitably leads to a stack overflow. The recursive flow, in general, is harder to follow and more difficult to understand if you're not used to it. Because Java does not have tail-call optimization, you will have to factor in the unavoidable overhead, which results in slower execution times compared to iterative structures, in addition to the possibility of a StackOverflowError if your call stack is too deep.

You should always consider the additional overhead and stack overflow problems when choosing between recursion and its alternatives. If you're running in a JVM with ample available memory and a big enough stack size, even bigger recursive call chains won't be an issue. But if your problem size is unknown or not fixed, an alternative approach might be more sensible to prevent a StackOverflowError in the long run.

Some scenarios are better suited for a recursive approach, even in Java with its lack of tail-call optimization. Recursion will feel like a more natural way to solve particular problems with self-referencing data structures like linked lists or trees. Traversing tree-like structures can also be done iteratively but will most likely result in more complex code that's harder to reason with.

But remember, choosing the best solution for a problem solely from a technical viewpoint might undermine the readability and reasonability of your code, which will affect long-time maintainability.

Table 12-1 gives you an overview of the differences between recursion and iteration, so you can use them to choose more effectively.

Table 12-1. Recursion versus iteration

	Recursion	Iteration
Approach	Self-calling function	Loop construct
State	Stored on Stack	Stored in control variables (e.g., a loop index)
Progression	Toward base condition	Toward control value condition
Termination	Base condition reached	Control variable condition reached
Verbosity	Lower verbosity Minimal boilerplate and coordination code required	Higher verbosity Explicit coordination of control variables and state
If not terminated	StackOverflowError	Endless loop
Overhead	Higher overhead of repeated method calls	Lower overhead with constant stack depth
Performance	Lower performance due to overhead and missing tail-call optimization	Better performance thanks to constant call stack depth
Memory Usage	Each call requires stack space	No additional memory besides control variables
Execution speed	Slower	Faster

Which to choose—recursion or iteration—depends highly on the problem you want to solve and in which environment your code runs. Recursion is often the preferred tool for solving more abstract problems, and iteration is a better match for more low-level code. Iteration might provide better runtime performance, but recursion can improve your productivity as a programmer.

Don't forget that you can always start with a familiar iterative approach and convert it to use recursion later.

Takeaways

- Recursion is the functional alternative to traditional iteration.
- Recursion is best used for partially solvable problems.
- Java lacks tail-call optimization, which can lead to `StackOverflowExceptions`.
- Don't force recursion just to make it more functional. You can always start with an iterative approach and convert it to a recursive approach later.

CHAPTER 13

Asynchronous Tasks

Modern workloads require more thought about how to use available system resources efficiently. Asynchronous tasks are an excellent tool for improving the responsiveness of your application by avoiding performance bottlenecks.

Java 8 introduced the new generic type, `CompletableFuture<T>`, which improved upon the previously available `Future<T>` type to create async tasks by utilizing a declarative and functional approach.

This chapter explains why and how to utilize asynchronous programming and how `CompletableFuture<T>` is a more flexible and functional approach to asynchronous tasks than what was included in the JDK before.

Synchronous versus Asynchronous

The concept of synchronous and asynchronous tasks is not restricted to software development.

For example, an in-person meeting or conference call is a synchronous activity, at least if you pay attention. You can't do anything else except participate and maybe take notes. Every other task is blocked until the meeting/call is over. If the meeting/call would have been an e-mail instead—as most of my meetings could and should be—your current task isn't interrupted by requiring immediate attention before you could resume your previous task. Therefore, an e-mail is *non-blocking* communication.

The same principles are true for software development. Synchronously executed tasks run in sequence, blocking further work until they're finished. From a single-threaded point of view, a blocking task means waiting for the result, possibly wasting resources by not doing anything else until the task is finished.

Asynchronous tasks are about starting a task that is processed "somewhere else" and you get notified when it's done. Such tasks are non-blocking by using concurrency techniques to spin off their work—usually to another thread—so they don't have to wait for them to finish. Therefore, the current thread isn't blocked and can continue with other tasks, as illustrated in Figure 13-1.

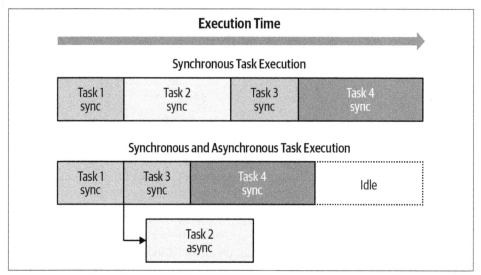

Figure 13-1. Comparison of synchronous and asynchronous execution

Parallel execution, as discussed in Chapter 8, strives for maximum throughput as its primary objective; the completion time of a single task is generally of lesser concern in the greater scheme of things. An asynchronous execution model, like CompletableFuture use, on the other hand, is focused on the overall latency and responsiveness of the system. Spinning off tasks ensures a responsive system even in single-threaded or resource-constrained environments.

Java Futures

Java 5 introduced the interface `java.util.concurrent.Future` as a container type for an eventual result of an asynchronous computation. To create a `Future`, a task in the form of a `Runnable` or a `Callable<T>` gets submitted to an `ExecutorService` which starts the task in a separate thread but immediately returns a Future instance. This way, the current thread can continue to do more work without waiting for the eventual result of the `Future` computation.

The result is retrievable by calling the `get` method on a `Future` instance, which might block the current thread, though, if the computation hasn't finished yet. A simple example of the general flow is visualized in Example 13-1.

Example 13-1. Future<T> flow of execution

```java
var executor = Executors.newFixedThreadPool(10); ❶

Callable<Integer> expensiveTask = () -> { ❷
    System.out.println("(task) start");

    TimeUnit.SECONDS.sleep(2);

    System.out.println("(task) done");

    return 42;
};

System.out.println("(main) before submitting the task");

var future = executor.submit(expensiveTask); ❸

System.out.println("(main) after submitting the task");

var theAnswer = future.get(); ❹

System.out.println("(main) after the blocking call future.get()");
// OUTPUT:
// (main) before submitting the task
// (task) start
// (main) after submitting the task
// ~~ 2 sec delay ~~
// (task) done
// (main) after the blocking call future.get()
```

❶ An explicit ExecutorService is needed to spin off a Callable<T> or Runnable.

❷ The Callable<T> interface has been available since before the introduction of lambdas of functional interfaces. Its intended use case is equivalent to Supplier<T> but it throws an Exception in its single abstract method.

❸ The computation of expensiveTask starts immediately, reflected in the output.

❹ At this point, the calculation isn't finished yet, so calling the get method on future blocks the current thread until it is finished.

Although the Future type achieves the essential requirement of being a non-blocking container for asynchronous computation, its feature set is limited to only a few methods: checking if the computation is done, canceling it, and retrieving its result.

To have a versatile tool for asynchronous programming, there are a lot of features left to be desired:

- An easier way of retrieving a result, like callbacks on completion or failure.
- Chaining and combining multiple tasks in the spirit of functional composition.
- Integrated error handling and recovery possibilities.
- Manual creation or completion of tasks without requiring an `ExecutorService`.

Java 8 improved upon Futures to remedy the lacking features by introducing the interface `CompletionStage<T>`, and its sole implementation, `CompletableFuture<T>`, in the same package `java.util.concurrent`. They're versatile tools to build asynchronous task pipelines with a richer feature set than Futures before them. Where `Future<T>` is a container type for an asynchronous computation of an eventual value, `CompletionStage<T>` represents a single stage of an asynchronous pipeline with a massive API of over 70 methods!

Designing Asynchronous Pipelines with CompletableFutures

The general design philosophy of CompletableFutures is similar to Streams: both are task-based pipelines offering parameterized methods accepting common functional interfaces. The new API adds a myriad of coordination tools that return new instances of `CompletionStage` or `CompletableFuture`. This amalgamation of a container for asynchronous computation and coordination tools provides all the previously missing features in a fluently composable and declarative API.

Due to the massive `CompletableFuture` API and the complex mental model of asynchronous programming in general, let's start with a simple metaphor: making breakfast.

The imaginary breakfast consists of coffee, toast, and eggs. Preparing the breakfast in synchronous—or blocking—order doesn't make much sense. Waiting for the coffee maker to finish or for the toast to be done before starting with the eggs is a poor use of available resources that will add unnecessarily to the total prep time, leaving you hungry by the time you sit down to eat. Instead, you can start frying the eggs while the coffee maker and toaster do their thing and react to them only when the toaster pops or the coffeemaker is done.

The same logic applies to programming. The available resources should be allocated as needed and not wasted by waiting for computationally expensive or long-running tasks. The underlying concept of such asynchronous pipelines is available in many languages under a different, maybe more common name: Promises.

Promising a Value

Promises are the building blocks for asynchronous pipelines with built-in coordination tools that allow chaining and combining multiple tasks, including error handling. Such a building block is either *pending* (not settled), *resolved* (settled and computation completed), or *rejected* (settled, but in the error state). Moving between states in the compositional pipeline is done by switching between two channels: *data* and *error*, as shown in Figure 13-2.

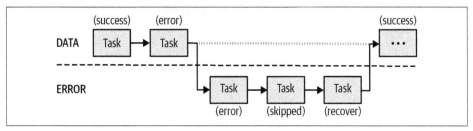

Figure 13-2. Promise data and error channels

The data channel is the happy path if everything goes right. However, if a Promise fails, the pipeline switches to the error channel. This way, a failure doesn't crash the whole pipeline, like with Streams, and can be handled gracefully or even recover and switch the pipeline back to the data channel.

As you will see, the CompletableFuture API is a Promise by another name.

Creating a CompletableFuture

Like its predecessor, `Future`, the new `CompletableFuture` type doesn't provide any constructors to create an instance. New `Future` instances are created by submitting tasks to an `ExecutorService` which returns an instance with its task already started.

`CompletableFuture` follows the same principle. However, it doesn't necessarily require an explicit `ExecutorService` to schedule tasks, thanks to its **static** factory methods:

- `CompletableFuture<Void> runAsync(Runnable runnable)`

- `CompletableFuture<U> supplyAsync(Supplier<U> supplier)`

Both methods are also available with a second argument, accepting a `java.util.concurrent.Executor`, which is the base interface of the `ExecutorService` type. If you choose the `Executor`-less variants, the common `ForkJoinPool` is used, just like for parallel Stream pipelines as explained in "Streams as Parallel Functional Pipelines" on page 195.

The most apparent difference in submitting tasks to an Executor Service for creating a Future is the use of Supplier instead of Callable. The latter explicitly throws an Exception in its method signature. Therefore, supplyAsync isn't a drop-in replacement for submitting a Callable to an Executor.

Creating a CompletableFuture instance is almost equivalent to creating a Future one, as shown in Example 13-2. The example doesn't use type inference, so the returning types are visible. Usually, you would prefer the var keyword instead of using the explicit type.

Example 13-2. CompletableFuture creation with convenience methods

```
// Future<T>

var executorService = ForkJoinPool.commonPool();

Future<?> futureRunnable =
  executorService.submit(() -> System.out.println("not returning a value"));

Future<String> futureCallable =
  executorService.submit(() -> "Hello, Async World!");

// CompleteableFuture<T>

CompletableFuture<Void> completableFutureRunnable =
  CompletableFuture.runAsync(() -> System.out.println("not returning a value"));

CompletableFuture<String> completableFutureSupplier =
  CompletableFuture.supplyAsync(() -> "Hello, Async World!");
```

Though the creation of instances is similar between Future and CompletableFuture, the latter is more concise by not necessarily requiring an ExecutorService. The bigger difference, though, is that a CompletableFuture instance provides a starting point for a declarative and functional pipeline of CompletionStage instances instead of a singular isolated async task as in the case of a Future.

Compositing and Combining Tasks

After starting with a CompletableFuture instance, it's time to combine and compose them further to create a more complex pipeline.

The broad range of operations available to build your asynchronous pipelines is separable into three groups, depending on their accepted arguments and intended use cases:

Transforming a result

Like the `map` operation of Streams and Optionals, the CompletableFuture API gives you the similar `thenApply` method, which uses a `Function<T, U>` to transform the previous result of type T, and returns another `CompletionStage<U>`. If the transformation function returns another `CompletionStage`, using the `then Compose` method prevents additional nesting, similar to Stream's and Optional's `flatMap` operation.

Consuming a result

As its name suggests, the `thenAccept` method requires a `Consumer<T>` to work with the previous result of type T and returns a new `CompletionStage<Void>`.

Executing after finishing

If you don't require access to the previous result, the `thenRun` method executes a `Runnable` and returns a new `CompletionStage<Void>`.

There are too many methods to discuss each one in detail, especially with the additional -`Async` methods. Most of these methods have two additional -`Async` variants: one matching the non-`Async` and another one with an additional Executor argument.

The non-`Async` methods execute their task in the same thread as the previous task, even though that's not guaranteed, as explained later in "About Thread Pools and Timeouts" on page 320. The -`Async` variants will use a new thread, created by the common `ForkJoinPool` or by the provided `Executor`.

I will discuss the non-`Async` variants to keep things simple.

Compositing tasks

Compositing tasks creates a serial pipeline of connected `CompletionStage` instances.

All compositing operations follow a general naming scheme:

```
<operation>[Async](argument [, Executor])
```

The `<operation>` name derives from the type of operation and its arguments, mainly using the prefix `then` plus the name of the SAM of the functional interface they accept:

- `CompletableFuture<Void> thenAccept(Consumer<? super T> action)`
- `CompletableFuture<Void> thenRun(Runnable action)`
- `CompletableFuture<U> thenApply(Function<? super T,? extends U> fn)`

Thanks to the API's proper naming scheme, using any of the operations results in a fluent and straightforward call chain. For example, imagine a bookmark manager that scrapes its websites for storing a permanent copy. The overall task could be run async so it won't stop the UI thread. The task itself consists of three steps: downloading the website, preparing the content for offline consumption, and finally, storing it, as shown in Example 13-3.

Example 13-3. Async bookmark manager workflow

```
var task = CompletableFuture.supplyAsync(() -> this.downloadService.get(url))
                    .thenApply(this.contentCleaner::clean)
                    .thenRun(this.storage::save);
```

Compositing operations are 1:1 only, meaning they take the result of the previous stage and do their intended job. If your task pipeline requires multiple flows to converge, you need to combine tasks.

Combining tasks

Compositing interconnected futures to create a more complex task can be immensely helpful. Sometimes, however, the different tasks don't need combination or can run in serial. In this case, you can combine `CompletionStage` instances by using operations that accept another stage in addition to their usual arguments.

Their naming scheme is similar to the previous 1:1 compositing operations:

```
<operation><restriction>[Async](other, argument [, Executor])
```

The additional `restriction` indicates if the operation works on both stages, or either, using the aptly named suffixes `-Both` and `-Either`.

Table 13-1 lists the available 2:1 operations.

Table 13-1. Combinational Operations

Method	Argument	Notes
thenCombine	BiFunction<T, U, V>	Applies the BiFunction after *both* stages have been completed normally.
thenAcceptBoth	BiConsumer<T, U>	Like thenCombine, but doesn't produce any value.
runAfterBoth	Runnable	Evaluates the Runnable after both given stages have been completed normally.
applyToEither	Function<T, U>	Applies the Function to the first completed stage.
acceptEither	Consumer<T, U>	Like applyToEither, but doesn't produce any value.
runAfterEither	Runnable	Evaluates the Runnable after either of the given stages has been completed normally.

Like with other functional Java features, the many different operations are owed to Java's static type system and how generic types are resolved. Unlike other languages, like JavaScript, methods can't accept multiple types in a single argument or as a return type.

The composing operations can easily be mixed with the compositing ones, as illustrated in Figure 13-3.

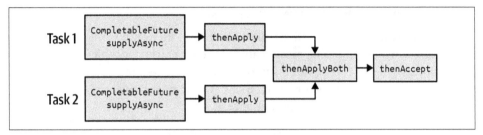

Figure 13-3. Compositing and combining tasks

The available operations provide a variety of functionality for almost any use case. Still, there are certain blindspots in Java's asynchronous API; especially, a particular variant is missing: combining the result of two stages with a `BiFunction` returning another stage without creating a nested `CompletionStage`.

The `thenCombine` behavior is similar to other `map` operations in Java. In the case of a nested return value, a `flatMap`-like operation is required, which is missing for the `CompletableFuture` type. Instead, you need an additional `thenCompose` operation to flatten the nested values, as shown in Example 13-4.

Example 13-4. Unwrapping nested stages

```
CompletableFuture<Integer> future1 = CompletableFuture.supplyAsync(() -> 42); ❶
CompletableFuture<Integer> future2 = CompletableFuture.supplyAsync(() -> 23); ❶

BiFunction<Integer, Integer, CompletableFuture<Integer>> task = ❷
  (lhs, rhs) -> CompletableFuture.supplyAsync(() -> lhs + rhs);

CompletableFuture<Integer> combined = future1.thenCombine(future2, task) ❸
                                        .thenCompose(Function.identity()); ❹
```

❶ The two stages that should combine their results.

❷ The task consuming the combined results of the previous stage.

❸ The return value of `task` is wrapped into another stage by `thenCombine`, resulting in an unwanted `CompletionStage<CompletionStage<Integer>>`.

❹ The thenCompose call with `Function.identity()` unwraps the nested stage and the pipeline is a `CompletionStage<Integer>` again.

This approach is helpful if the task returns a `CompletableFuture` instead of relying on the caller to handle it asynchronously by wrapping it into a `CompletableFuture` if needed.

Running more two CompletableFuture instances at once

The previously discussed operations allow you to run up to two CompletableFutures to create a new one. Handling more than two, however, isn't possible with combinational operations like `thenCombine` without creating a nested method-call nightmare. That's why the `CompletableFuture` type has two `static` convenience methods for dealing with more than two instances at once:

- `CompletableFuture<Void> allOf(CompletableFuture<?>… cfs)`
- `CompletableFuture<Object> anyOf(CompletableFuture<?>… cfs)`

The `allOf` and `anyOf` methods coordinate preexisting instances. Therefore, both of them don't provide matching `-Async` variants because each given `CompletableFuture` instance already has its designated `Executor`. Another aspect of the coordination-only nature is their restrictive return types. Because both accept any kind of `CompletableFuture` instances, signified by the generic bound `<?>`, no definitive `T` for the overall result is determinable, as the types can be mixed freely. The return type of the `allOf` is a `CompletableFuture<Void>`, so you don't have access to any result of the given instances in later stages. However, it's possible to create helper methods that support returning a result as an alternative. I'll show you how to do that in "Creating a CompletableFuture Helper" on page 309, but for now, let's go through the other operations of `CompletableFuture` first.

Exception Handling

So far, I've shown you pipelines that have only trotted along the "happy path" without any hiccups. However, a Promise can be rejected, or as it is called in Java, *complete exceptionality*, if an Exception occurs in the pipeline.

Instead of blowing up the whole pipeline in the case of an Exception, as Streams or Optionals do, the CompletableFuture API sees Exceptions as first-class citizens and an essential part of its workflow. That's why Exception handling isn't imposed on the tasks themselves, and there are multiple operations available to handle possibly rejected Promises:

- `CompletionStage<T> exceptionally(Function<Throwable, T> fn)`
- `CompletionStage<U> handle(BiFunction<T, Throwable, U> fn)`
- `CompletionStage<T> whenComplete(BiConsumer<T, Throwable> action)`

Using the `exceptionally` operation adds an Exception hook into the pipeline, which will complete normally with the previous stage's result if no Exception has occurred in any previous stage. In the case of a rejected stage, its Exception is applied to the hook's `fn` for a recovery effort. To recover, `fn` needs to return any value of type `T`, which will switch the pipeline back to the data channel. If no recovery is possible, throwing a new Exception, or rethrowing the applied one, will keep the pipeline in the exceptionally completed state and on the error channel.

The more flexible `handle` operation combines the logic of `exceptionally` and `thenApply` into a single operation. The `BiFunction` arguments depend on the result of the previous stage. If it was rejected, the second argument of type `Throwable` is non-`null`. Otherwise, the first argument of type `T` has value. Be aware that it still might be a `null` value.

The last operation, `whenComplete`, is similar to `handle` but doesn't offer a way to recover a rejected Promise.

Data and error channel revisited

Even though I explained that Promises have technically two channels, data and error, a CompletableFuture pipeline is actually a straight line of operations, like Streams. Each pipeline stage looks for the next compatible operation, depending on which state the current stage has completed. In case of completing normally, the next `then`/`run`/`apply`/etc. executes. These operations are "pass-through" for exceptionally completed stages, and the pipeline looks further for the next `exceptionally`/`handle`/`whenComplete`/etc. operation.

A CompletableFuture pipeline might be a straight line created by a fluent call. Visualizing it as two channels, though, as done previously in Figure 13-2, gives you a better overview of what's happening. Each operation exists in either the data or error channel, except the `handle` and `whenComplete` operations, which exist in between, as they're executed regardless of the pipeline's state.

Rejected either tasks

A straight pipeline might get another CompletableFuture injected by using a combinatorial operation. You might think the suffix `-Either` might imply that *either* pipelines might complete normally to create a new, non-rejected stage. Well, you're in for a surprise!

If the previous stage is rejected, the `acceptEither` operation remains rejected regardless of whether the other stage is completed normally, as shown in Example 13-5.

Example 13-5. Either operations and rejected stages

```
CompletableFuture<String> notFailed =
  CompletableFuture.supplyAsync(() -> "Success!");

CompletableFuture<String> failed =
  CompletableFuture.supplyAsync(() -> { throw new RuntimeException(); });

// NO OUTPUT BECAUSE THE PREVIOUS STAGE FAILED
var rejected = failed.acceptEither(notFailed, System.out::println);

// OUTPUT BECAUSE THE PREVIOUS STAGE COMPLETED NORMALLY
var resolved = notFailed.acceptEither(failed, System.out::println);
// => Success!
```

The gist to remember is that all operations, except the error-handling ones, require a non-rejected previous stage to work properly, even for `-Either` operations. If in doubt, use an error-handling operation to ensure a pipeline is still on the data channel.

Terminal Operations

Up to this point, any operation returns another `CompletionStage` to extend the pipeline further. The `Consumer`-based operations might fulfill many use cases, but at some point, you need the actual value even if it might block the current thread.

The `CompletionStage` type itself doesn't provide any additional retrieval methods compared to the `Future` type. Its implementation `CompletableFuture`, though, gives you two options: the `getNow` and `join` methods. This ups the number of terminal operations to four, as listed in Table 13-2.

Table 13-2. Getting a value from a CompletableFuture<T> pipeline

Method signature	Use case	Exceptions
`T get()`	Blocks the current thread until the pipeline is completed.	`InterruptedException` (checked) `ExecutionException` (checked) `CancellationException` (unchecked)
`T get(long timeout, TimeUnit unit)`	Blocks the current thread until the pipeline is completed but throws an Exception after the timeout is reached.	`TimeoutException` (checked) `InterruptedException` (checked) `ExecutionException` (checked) `CancellationException` (unchecked)

Method signature	Use case	Exceptions
`T getNow` `(T valueIfAbsent)`	Returns the pipeline's result if completed normally or throws an `CompletionException`. If the result is still pending, the provided fallback value `T` is returned immediately without canceling the pipeline.	`CompletionException` (unchecked) `CancellationException` (unchecked)
`join()`	Blocks the current thread until the pipeline is done.	If it completes exceptionally, the Exception is wrapped into a `CompletionException`.

The `CompletableFuture` type also adds another pipeline coordination method, `isCompletedExceptionally`, giving you a total of four methods for affecting or retrieving the pipeline's state, as listed in Table 13-3.

Table 13-3. CompletableFuture<T> coordination methods

Method Signature	Returns
`boolean cancel(boolean mayInterruptIfRunning)`	Completes a not already completed stage exceptionally with a `CancellationException`. The argument `mayInterruptIfRunning` is ignored because interrupts aren't used for control, unlike for the `Future` type.
`boolean isCancelled()`	Returns `true` if the stage was canceled before it has been completed.
`boolean isDone()`	Returns `true` if the stage has been completed in any state.
`boolean isCompletedExceptionally()`	Returns `true` if the stage has been completed exceptionally or is already in the rejected state.

That's quite a humongous API, covering a lot of use cases. Still, depending on your requirements, some edge cases might be missing. But adding your helper to fill any gaps is easy, so let's do it.

Creating a CompletableFuture Helper

Although the CompletableFuture API is massive, it's still missing certain use cases. For example, as mentioned earlier in "Combining tasks" on page 304, the return type of the `static` helper `allOf` is `CompletableFuture<Void>`, so you don't have access to any result of the given instances in later stages. It's a flexible coordination-only method that accepts any kind of `CompletableFuture<?>` as its arguments but with the trade-off of not having access to any of the results. To make up for this, you can create a helper to complement the existing API as needed.

Let's create a helper in the vein of `allOf`, running more than two `CompletableFuture` instances at once, but still giving access to their results:

```
static CompletableFuture<List<T>> eachOf(CompletableFuture<T> cfs...)
```

The proposed helper `eachOf` runs all of the given `CompletableFuture` instances, like `allOf`. However, unlike `allOf`, the new helper uses the generic type T instead of ? (question mark). This restriction to a singular type makes it possible that the `eachOf` method can actually return a `CompletableFuture<List<T>>` instead of a resultless `CompletableFuture<Void>`.

The helper scaffold

A convenience `class` is needed to hold any helper methods. Such helper methods are useful for particular edge cases that aren't possible to solve otherwise in a concise way, or even at all, with the provided API. The most idiomatic and safe way is to use a `class` with a `private` constructor as shown as follows to prevent anyone from accidentally extending or instantiating the type.

```
public final class CompletableFutures {

  private CompletableFutures() {
    // suppress default constructor
  }
}
```

 Helper classes with a `private` default constructor don't have to be `final` per se to prevent extendability. The extending class won't compile without a visible implicit `super` constructor. Nevertheless, making the helper class `final` signifies the desired intent without relying on implicit behavior.

Designing eachOf

The goal of `eachOf` is almost identical to the `allOf` method. Both methods coordinate one or more `CompletableFuture` instances. However, `eachOf` is going further by managing the results, too. This leads to the following requirements:

- Returning a `CompletableFuture` containing all the given instances, like `allOf`.
- Giving access to the results of successfully completed instances.

The first requirement is fulfilled by the `allOf` method. The second one, however, requires additional logic. It requires you to inspect the given instances individually and aggregate their results.

The simplest way of running any logic after a previous stage completes in any way is using the `thenApply` operation:

```
public static
<T> CompletableFuture<List<T>> eachOf(CompletableFuture<T>... cfs) {
  return CompletableFuture.allOf(cfs)
                    .thenApply(???);
}
```

Using what you've learned so far in the book, the aggregation of the results of success-fully completed CompletableFuture instances can be done by creating a Stream data processing pipeline.

Let's go through the steps needed to create such a pipeline.

First, the Stream must be created from the given CompletableFuture<T> instan-ces. It's an vararg method argument so it corresponds to an array. The helper Arrays#stream(T[] arrays) is the obvious choice when dealing with a vararg:

```
Arrays.stream(cfs)
```

Next, the successfully completed instances are filtered. There is no explicit method to ask an instance if it is completed normally, but you can ask the inverse, thanks to Predicate.not:

```
Arrays.stream(cfs)
      .filter(Predicate.not(CompletableFuture::isCompletedExceptionally))
```

There are two methods for getting a result immediately from a CompletableFuture: get() and join(). In this case, the latter is preferable, because it doesn't throw a checked Exception, simplifying the Stream pipeline as discussed in Chapter 10:

```
Arrays.stream(cfs)
      .filter(Predicate.not(CompletableFuture::isCompletedExceptionally))
      .map(CompletableFuture::join)
```

Using the join method blocks the current thread to get the result. However, the Stream pipeline is run after allOf is completed anyway, so all results are already available. And by filtering not-successfully-completed elements beforehand, no Exception is thrown that might implode the pipeline.

Finally, the results are aggregated into a List<T>. This can be either done with a collect operation, or if you're using Java 16+, the Stream<T> type's toList method:

```
Arrays.stream(cfs)
      .filter(Predicate.not(CompletableFuture::isCompletedExceptionally))
      .map(CompletableFuture::join)
      .toList();
```

The Stream pipeline can now be used to gather the results in the thenApply call. The full implementation of CompletableFutures and its eachOf helper method is shown in Example 13-6.

Example 13-6. Complete implementation of eachOf

```
public final class CompletableFutures {

    private final static Predicate<CompletableFuture<?>> EXCEPTIONALLY = ❶
        Predicate.not(CompletableFuture::isCompletedExceptionally);

    public static <T> CompletableFuture<List<T>> eachOf(CompletableFuture<T>... cfs) {
        Function<Void, List<T>> fn = unused -> ❷
            Arrays.stream(cfs)
                  .filter(Predicate.not(EXCEPTIONALLY))
                  .map(CompletableFuture::join)
                  .toList();

        return CompletableFuture.allOf(cfs) ❸
                                .thenApply(fn);
    }

    private CompletableFutures() {
        // suppress default constructor
    }
}
```

❶ The Predicate for testing successful completion isn't bound to a specific CompletableFuture instance and, therefore, is reusable as a final static field.

❷ The result-gathering action is represented by Function<Void, List<T>>, which matches the inner types of the return type of allOf and the intended return type of eachOf.

❸ The overall task is merely calling the preexisting allOf and combining it with the result-aggregating pipeline.

That's it! We've created an alternative to allOf for certain use cases when the results should be easily accessible.

The final implementation is an example of the functional approach to solving problems. Each task in itself is isolated and could be used on its own. By combining them, though, you create a more complex solution built of smaller parts.

Improving the CompletableFutures helper

The eachOf method works as you would expect it to as a complementary method to allOf. If any of the given CompletableFuture instances fail, the returned CompletableFuture<List<T>> has also completed exceptionally.

Still, there are "fire & forget" use cases, where you are interested only in the successfully completed tasks and don't care about any failures. A failed CompletableFuture, though, will throw an Exception if you try to extract its value with get or similar methods. So let's add a bestEffort helper method based on eachOf that always completes successfully and returns only the successful results.

The main goal is almost identical to eachOf, except if the allOf call returns an exceptionally completed CompletableFuture<Void>, it must recover. Adding an Exception hook by interjecting an exceptionally operation is the obvious choice:

```
public static
<T> CompletableFuture<List<T>> bestEffort(CompletableFuture<T>... cfs) {
  Function<Void, List<T>> fn = ...; // no changes to Stream pipeline

  return CompletableFuture.allOf(cfs)
                      .exceptionally(ex -> null)
                      .thenApply(fn);
}
```

The exceptionally lambda ex -> null might look weird at first. But if you check out the underlying method signature, its intention becomes clearer.

In this case, the exceptionally operation requires a Function<Throwable, Void> to recover the CompletableFuture by returning a value of type Void instead of throwing an Exception. This is achieved by returning null. After that, the aggregation Stream pipeline from eachOf is used to gather the results.

 The same behavior could be achieved with the handle operation, which would handle both states, success or rejection, in a singular BiFunction. Still, handling the states in separate steps makes a more readable pipeline.

Now that we have two helper methods with shared logic, it might make sense to extract common logic into their own methods. This underlies the functional approach of combining isolated logic to create a more complex and complete task. A possible refactored implementation of CompletableFutures is shown in Example 13-7.

Example 13-7. Refactored implementation of CompletableFutures

```
public final class CompletableFutures {

  private final static Predicate<CompletableFuture<?>> EXCEPTIONALLY = ❶
    Predicate.not(CompletableFuture::isCompletedExceptionally);

  private static <T> Function<Void, List<T>>
```

```
                        gatherResultsFn(CompletableFuture<T>... cfs) { ❷
     return unused -> Arrays.stream(cfs)
                            .filter(Predicate.not(EXCEPTIONALLY))
                            .map(CompletableFuture::join)
                            .toList();
   }

   public static
   <T> CompletableFuture<List<T>> eachOf(CompletableFuture<T>... cfs) { ❸
     return CompletableFuture.allOf(cfs)
                            .thenApply(gatherResultsFn(cfs));
   }

   public static
   <T> CompletableFuture<List<T>> bestEffort(CompletableFuture<T>... cfs) { ❸
     return CompletableFuture.allOf(cfs)
                            .exceptionally(ex -> null)
                            .thenApply(gatherResultsFn(cfs));
   }

   private CompletableFutures() {
     // suppress default constructor
   }
}
```

❶ The Predicate is unchanged.

❷ The result-gathering logic is refactored into a private factory method to ensure consistent handling across both the eachOf and bestEffort methods.

❸ Both public helper methods are reduced to the absolute minimum.

The refactored CompletableFutures helper is simpler and more robust than before. Any sharable complex logic is reused so it provides consistent behavior throughout its method and minimizes the required documentation that you should definitely add to communicate the intended functionality to any caller.

Manual Creation and Completion

The only way to create Future instances besides implementing the interface yourself is by submitting a task to an ExecutorService. The static convenience factory methods runAsync or supplyAsync of CompletableFuture are quite similar. Unlike their predecessor, they're not the only way to create instances.

Manual Creation

Thanks to being an actual implementation and not an interface, the Completable Future type has a constructor that you can use to create an unsettled instance, as follows:

```
CompletableFuture<String> unsettled = new CompletableFuture<>();
```

Without an attached task, however, it will never be completed or fail. Instead, you need to complete such a task manually.

Manual Completion

There are a couple of ways to settle an existing CompletableFuture instance and kickstart the attached pipeline:

- boolean complete(T value)
- boolean completeExceptionally(Throwable ex)

Both methods return true if the call transitions the stage to the expected state.

Java 9 introduced additional complete methods for normally completed stages, in the form of -Async variants, and a timeout-based one:

- CompletableFuture<T> completeAsync(Supplier<T> supplier)
- CompletableFuture<T> completeAsync(Supplier<T> supplier, Executor executor)
- CompletableFuture<T> completeOnTimeout(T value, long timeout, TimeUnit unit)

The -Async variants complete the current stage with the result of the supplier in a new asynchronous task.

The other method, completeOnTimeout, settles the current stage with the given value if the stage doesn't complete otherwise before the timeout is reached.

Instead of creating a new instance and then manually completing it, you can also create an already completed instance with one of these static convenience factory methods:

- CompletableFuture<U> completedFuture(U value)
- CompletableFuture<U> failedFuture(Throwable ex) (Java 9+)
- CompletionStage<U> completedStage(U value) (Java 9+)

- `CompletionStage<U> failedStage(Throwable ex)` (Java 9+)

Such already completed futures can then be used in any of the combinatorial operations, or as a starting point for a CompletableFutures pipeline, as I'm going to discuss in the next section.

Use Cases for Manually Created and Completed Instances

In essence, the CompletableFuture API provides an easy way to create an asynchronous task pipeline with multiple steps. By creating and completing a stage manually, you gain fine-grained control over how the pipeline is executed afterward. For example, you can circumvent spinning off a task if the result is already known. Or you can create a partial pipeline factory for common tasks.

Let's look at a few possible use cases.

CompletableFutures as return values

The `CompletableFuture` type makes an excellent return value for possible costly or long-running tasks.

Imagine a weather report service that calls a REST API to return a `WeatherInfo` object. Even though weather changes over time, it makes sense to cache the `WeatherInfo` for a particular place for some time before updating the information with another REST call.

A REST call is naturally costlier and requires more time than a simple cache lookup, and therefore might block the current thread too long to be acceptable. Wrapping it in a `CompletableFuture` provides an easy way to offload the task from the current thread, leading to the following general `WeatherService` with a singular `public` method:

```
public class WeatherService {

  public CompletableFuture<WeatherInfo> check(ZipCode zipCode) {
    return CompletableFuture.supplyAsync(
      () -> this.restAPI.getWeatherInfoFor(zipCode)
    );
  }
}
```

Adding a cache requires two methods, one for storing any result, and one for retrieving existing ones:

```
public class WeatherService {

  private Optional<WeatherInfo> cached(ZipCode zipCode) {
    // ...
  }
```

```
private WeatherInfo storeInCache(WeatherInfo info) {
  // ...
}

// ...
}
```

Using `Optional<WeatherInfo>` provides you with a functional launchpad to connect each part later. The actual implementation of the caching mechanism doesn't matter for the purpose and intent of the example.

The actual API call should be refactored, too, to create smaller logic units, leading to a singular `public` method and three `private` distinct operations. The logic to store a result in the cache can be added as a `CompletableFuture` operation, `CompletableFuture<WeatherInfo>`, by using `thenApply` with the `storeInCache` method:

```
public class WeatherService {

    private Optional<WeatherInfo> cacheLookup(ZipCode zipCode) {
      // ...
    }

    private WeatherInfo storeInCache(WeatherInfo info) {
      // ...
    }

    private CompletableFuture<WeatherInfo> restCall(ZipCode zipCode) {
      Supplier<WeatherInfo> restCall = this.restAPI.getWeatherInfoFor(zipCode);

      return CompletableFuture.supplyAsync(restCall)
                            .thenApply(this::storeInCache);
    }

    public CompletableFuture<WeatherInfo> check(ZipCode zipCode) {
      // ...
    }
}
```

Now all parts can be combined to fulfill the task of providing a cached weather service, as shown in Example 13-8.

Example 13-8. Cached weather service with CompletableFutures

```
public class WeatherService {

  private Optional<WeatherInfo> cacheLookup(ZipCode zipCode) { ❶
    // ...
  }

  private WeatherInfo storeInCache(WeatherInfo info) { ❶
```

```
    // ...
}

private CompletableFuture<WeatherInfo> restCall(ZipCode zipCode) { ❷
  Supplier<WeatherInfo> restCall = () -> this.restAPI.getWeatherInfoFor(zipCode);

  return CompletableFuture.supplyAsync(restCall)
                          .thenApply(this::storeInCache);
}

public CompletableFuture<WeatherInfo> check(ZipCode zipCode) { ❸
  return cacheLookup(zipCode).map(CompletableFuture::completedFuture) ❹
                          .orElseGet(() -> restCall(zipCode)); ❺
}
}
```

❶ The cache lookup returns an Optional<WeatherInfo> to provide a fluent and functional jump-off point. The storeInCache method returns the stored Weather Info object to be usable as a method reference.

❷ The restCall method combines the REST call itself and stores the result, if successfully completed, in the cache.

❸ The check method combines the other methods by looking in the cache first.

❹ If a WeatherInfo is found, it returns an already completed CompletableFuture<WeatherInfo> immediately.

❺ If no object is found, the orElseGet call on the returned empty Optional<WeatherInfo> executes the restCall method lazily.

The advantage of combining CompletableFutures with Optionals this way is that it doesn't matter what happens behind the scenes for the caller, whether the data is loaded via REST or is coming directly from a cache. Each private method does a singular task most efficiently, with the sole public method combining them as an asynchronous task pipeline doing its expensive work only if absolutely required.

Pending CompletableFuture pipelines

A pending CompletableFuture instance never completes by itself with any state. Similar to Streams that won't start their data processing until a terminal operation is connected, a CompletableFuture task pipeline won't do any work until the first stage completes. Therefore, it provides a perfect starting point as the first stage of a more intricate task pipeline or even a scaffold for a predefined task to be executed on demand later.

Imagine you want to process image files. There are multiple independent steps involved that might fail. Instead of processing the files directly, a factory provides unsettled CompletedFuture instances, as shown in Example 13-9.

Example 13-9. Designing an image processor with unsettled CompletableFutures

```
public class ImageProcessor {

  public record Task(CompletableFuture<Path> start, ❶
                     CompletableFuture<InputStream> end) {
    // NO BODY
  }

  public Task createTask(int maxHeight,
                         int maxWidth,
                         boolean keepAspectRatio,
                         boolean trimWhitespace) {
    var start = new CompletableFuture<Path>(); ❷

    var end = unsettled.thenApply(...) ❸
                       .exceptionally(...)
                       .thenApply(...)
                       .handle(...);

    return new Task(start, end); ❹
  }
}
```

❶ The caller needs access to the unsettled first stage to start the pipeline but also requires the stage to access the final result.

❷ The generic type of the returned CompletableFuture instance must match the type you want the caller to provide when they actually execute the pipeline. In this case, the Path to an image file is used.

❸ The task pipeline starts with an unsettled instance so the required processing operations can be added lazily.

❹ The Task Record is returned to provide easy access to the first and last stages.

Running the task pipeline is done by calling any of the complete methods on the first stage, start. Afterward, the last stage is used to retrieve a potential result, as shown below:

```
// CREATING LAZY TASK
var task = this.imageProcessor.createTask(800, 600, false, true);

// RUNNING TASK
```

```
var path = Path.of("a-functional-approach-to-java/cover.png");
task.start().complete(path);

// ACCESSING THE RESULT
var processed = task.end().get();
```

Just like a Stream pipeline without a terminal operation creates a lazy processing pipeline for multiple items, a pending CompletableFuture pipeline is a lazily usable task pipeline for a singular item.

About Thread Pools and Timeouts

Two last aspects of concurrent programming shouldn't be ignored: timeouts and thread pools.

By default, all -Async operations use the JDK's common ForkJoinPool. It's a highly optimized thread pool based on runtime settings with sensible defaults.[1] As its name implies, the "common" pool is a shared one also used by other parts of the JDK, like parallel Streams. Unlike parallel Streams, though, the async operations can use a custom Executor instead. That allows you to use a thread pool fitting your requirements[2] without affecting the common pool.

Daemon Threads

An important difference between using Threads via the ForkJoin Pool and user-created ones via an Executor is their ability to outlive the main thread. By default, user-created Threads are non-daemon, which means they outlive the main thread and prevent the JVM from exiting, even if the main thread has finished all its work. Threads used via the ForkJoinPool, however, might get killed with the main thread. See this blog post (*https://oreil.ly/_0ej3*) by Java Champion A N M Bazlur Rahman for more details on the topic.

Running your tasks on the most efficient thread is only the first half of the equation; thinking about timeouts is the other half. A CompletableFuture that never completes or times out will remain pending for eternity, blocking its thread. If you try to retrieve its value, for example, by calling the get method, the current thread is blocked, too. Choosing appropriate timeouts can prevent eternally blocked threads.

---

1 The default settings of the common ForkJoinPool and how to change them is explained in its documentation (*https://oreil.ly/NhI-b*).

2 The excellent book *Java Concurrency in Practice* by Joshua Bloch et al. (Addison-Wesley Professional) has all the information you might need in Part II: Ch. 8, "Applying Thread Pools" to better understand how thread pools work and are utilized best.

However, using timeouts means that you also have to deal with a possible TimeoutEx
ception now.

There are multiple operations available, both intermediate and terminal, as listed in
Table 13-4.

Table 13-4. Timeout-related operations

Method signature	Use case

CompletableFuture<T>
completeOnTimeout(T value,
        long timeout,
        TimeUnit unit)
	Completes the stage normally with the provided value after the timeout is reached. (Java 9+)

CompletableFuture<T> orTimeout(long timeout, TimeUnit unit)	Completes the stage exceptionally after the timeout is reached. (Java 9+)
T get(long timeout, TimeUnit unit)	Blocks the current thread until the end of the computation. If the timeout is reached, a TimeoutException is thrown.

The intermediate operations completeOnTimeout and orTimeout provide an
interceptor-like operation to handle timeouts at any position on a Completable
Future pipeline.

An alternative to timeouts is canceling a running stage by calling boolean
cancel(boolean mayInterruptIfRunning). It cancels an unsettled stage and its
dependents, so it might require some coordination and keeping track of what's
happening to cancel the right one.

Final Thoughts on Asynchronous Tasks

Asynchronous programming is an important aspect of concurrent programming to
achieve better performance and responsiveness. However, it can be difficult to reason
about asynchronous code execution, because it's no longer obvious when and on
which thread a task is executed.

Coordinating different threads is nothing new to Java. It can be a hassle and is
hard to do right and efficiently, especially if you're not used to multi-threaded programming. That's where the CompletableFuture API really shines. It combines the
creation of intricate asynchronous, possibly multistep, tasks and their coordination
into an extensive, consistent, and easy-to-use API. This allows you to incorporate
asynchronous programming into your code way easier than before. Furthermore,
you don't require the common boilerplate and "handrails" normally associated with
multi-threaded programming.

Still, like with all programming techniques, there's an *optimal problem context*. If used indiscriminately, asynchronous tasks might achieve the opposite of their intended goal.

Running tasks asynchronously is a good fit for any of these criteria:

- Many tasks need to be done simultaneously with at least one being able to make progress.

- Tasks performing heavy I/O, long-running computations, network calls, or any kind of blocking operation.

- Tasks are mostly independent and don't have to wait for another one to complete.

Even with a quite high-level abstraction like the `CompletableFuture` type, multi-threaded code trades simplicity for possible efficiency.

Like other concurrent or parallel high-level APIs, such as the parallel Stream API discussed in Chapter 8, there are nonobvious costs involved in coordinating multiple threads. Such APIs should be chosen deliberately as an optimization technique, not as a one-size-fits-all solution to hopefully use the available resources more efficiently.

If you're interested in the finer details of how to navigate multi-threaded environments safely, I recommend the book *Java Concurrency in Practice* by Brian Goetz,[3] the Java Language Architect at Oracle. Even with all the new concurrent features introduced since its release in 2006, this book is still the de facto reference manual on the topic.

Takeaways

- Java 5 introduced the type `Future` as a container type for asynchronous tasks with an eventual result.

- The CompletableFuture API improves upon the `Future` type by providing many desirable features previously unavailable. It's a declarative, reactive, lambda-based coordination API with 70+ methods.

- Tasks can be easily chained or merged into a more complex pipeline that runs each task in a new thread if required.

- Exceptions are first-class citizens and you can recover within the functional fluent call, unlike with the Streams API.

---

3 Brian Goetz et al., *Java Concurrency in Practice* (Addison-Wesley Professional, 2006).

- `CompletableFuture` instances can be created manually with either a preexisting value without requiring any threads or other coordination, or as a pending instance to provide an on-demand starting point for its attached operations.
- As the CompletableFuture API is a concurrency tool, the usual concurrency-related aspects and issues need to be considered, too, like timeouts and thread pools. Like parallel Streams, running tasks asynchronously should be considered an optimization technique, not necessarily the first option to go to.

CHAPTER 14

Functional Design Patterns

Functional programming's answer to object-oriented design patterns is usually "just use functions instead." Technically, that's correct; it's *turtles all the way down*[1] with functional programming. However, coming from an object-oriented mindset wanting to augment your code with functional principles, more practical advice is required to utilize known patterns in a functional fashion.

This chapter will examine some of the commonly used object-oriented design patterns described by the "Gang of Four,"[2] and how they can benefit from a functional approach.

What Are Design Patterns?

You don't have to reinvent the wheel every time you need to solve a problem. Many of them have already been solved, or at least a general approach to a fitting solution exists in the form of a design pattern. As a Java developer, you most likely used or came across one or more object-oriented design patterns already, even if you didn't know it at the time.

In essence, object-oriented design patterns are tested, proven, formalized, and repeatable solutions to common problems.

---

1 The saying *turtles all the way down* describes the problem of *infinite regress*: an infinite series of entities governed by a recursive principle. Each entity depends on or is produced by its predecessor, which matches a lot of the functional design philosophy.

2 Erich Gamma, Richard Helm, Ralph Johnson, and John Vlissides, who wrote *Design Patterns: Elements of Reusable Object-Oriented Software* (Addison-Wesley Professional).

The "Gang of Four" categorized the patterns they describe into three groups:

Behavioral patterns
How to deal with responsibilities of and communication between objects.

Creational patterns
How to abstract the object creation/instantiation process, to help create, compose, and represent objects.

Structural patterns
How to compose objects to form larger or enhanced objects.

Design patterns are general scaffolds to make knowledge shareable with concepts on applying them to specific problems. That's why not every language or approach fits every pattern. Especially in functional programming, many problems don't require a certain pattern besides "just functions."

(Functional) Design Patterns

Let's take a look at four commonly used object-oriented design patterns and how to approach them functionally:

- Factory pattern (creational)
- Decorator pattern (structural)
- Strategy pattern (behavioral)
- Builder pattern (creational)

Factory Pattern

The *factory pattern* belongs to the group of *creational patterns*. Its purpose is to create an instance of an object without exposing the implementation details of *how to create* such objects by using a *factory* instead.

Object-oriented approach

There are multiple ways of implementing the factory pattern. For my example, all objects have a shared interface, and an enum is responsible for identifying the desired object type:

```
public interface Shape {
  int corners();
  Color color();
  ShapeType type();
}
```

```
public enum ShapeType {
  CIRCLE,
  TRIANGLE,
  SQUARE,
  PENTAGON;
}
```

Shapes are represented by Records, which only need a Color, as they can deduce their other properties directly. A simple Circle Record might look like this:

```
public record Circle(Color color) implements Shape {

  public int corners() {
    return 0;
  }

  public ShapeType type() {
    return ShapeType.CIRCLE;
  }
}
```

A Shape factory needs to accept the type and color to create the corresponding Shape instance, as follows:

```
public class ShapeFactory {

  public static Shape newShape(ShapeType type,
                               Color color) {
    Objects.requireNonNull(color);

    return switch (type) {
      case CIRCLE -> new Circle(color);
      case TRIANGLE -> new Triangle(color);
      case SQUARE -> new Square(color);
      case PENTAGON -> new Pentagon(color);
      default -> throw new IllegalArgumentException("Unknown type: " + type);
    };
  }
}
```

Looking at all the code involved so far, there are four distinct parts to the pattern:

- The shared interface Shape
- The shape-identifying enum ShapeType
- The concrete implementations of shapes (not shown)
- The ShapeFactory to create shapes based on their type and color

These parts depend on each other, which is expected. Still, this interdependence of the factory and the enum makes the whole approach fragile to change. If a new ShapeType is introduced, the factory has to account for it, or an

`IllegalArgumentException` is thrown in the `default` case of the `switch`, even if a concrete implementation type exists.

 The `default` case isn't necessarily needed, as all cases are declared. It's used to illustrate the dependency between `ShapeType` and `ShapeFactory` and how to alleviate it.

To improve the factory, its fragility can be reduced by introducing compile-time validation with a more functional approach.

A more functional approach

This example creates quite simple Records that need only a singular argument: `Color`. These identical constructors give you the possibility to move the "factory" directly into the `enum`, so any new shape automatically requires a corresponding factory function.

Even though Java's `enum` types are based on constant names, you can attach a corresponding value for each constant. In this case, a factory function for creating the discrete object in the form of a `Function<Color, Shape>` value:

```java
public enum ShapeType {
  CIRCLE,
  TRIANGLE,
  SQUARE,
  PENTAGON;

  public final Function<Color, Shape> factory;

  ShapeType(Function<Color, Shape> factory) {
    this.factory = factory;
  }
}
```

The code no longer compiles, because the constant declaration now requires an additional `Function<Color, Shape>`. Luckily, the Shapes' constructors are usable as method references to create quite concise code for the factory methods:

```java
public enum ShapeType {
  CIRCLE(Circle::new),
  TRIANGLE(Triangle::new),
  SQUARE(Square::new),
  PENTAGON(Pentagon::new);

  // ...
}
```

The enum gained the discrete creation methods as an attached value to each of its constants. This way, any future additions, like, for example, HEXAGON, force you to provide an appropriate factory method without the possibility of missing it, as the compiler will enforce it.

Now all that's left is the ability to create new instances. You could simply use the factory field and its SAM accept(Color color) directly, but I prefer an additional method to allow for sanity checks:

```
public enum ShapeType {

  // ...

  public Shape newInstance(Color color) {
    Objects.requireNonNull(color);
    return this.factory.apply(color);
  }
}
```

Creating a new Shape instance is now quite easy:

```
var redCircle = ShapeType.CIRCLE.newInstance(Color.RED);
```

The public field factory might seem redundant now that a dedicated method for instance creation is available. That's kind of true. Still, it provides a functional way to interact with the factory further, like functional composition to log the creation of a shape:

```
Function<Shape, Shape> cornerPrint =
  shape -> {
    System.out.println("Shape created with " + shape.corners() + " corners.");
    return shape;
  };

ShapeType.CIRCLE.factory.andThen(cornerPrint)
                        .apply(Color.RED);
```

By fusing the factory with the enum, the decision-making process—what factory method to call—gets replaced by binding the factory methods directly with ShapeType counterparts. The Java compiler now forces you to implement the factory on any addition to the enum.

This approach reduces the required boilerplate with added compile-time safety for future extensions.

Decorator Pattern

The decorator pattern is a structural pattern that allows for modifying object behavior at runtime. Instead of subclassing, an object is wrapped inside a "decorator" that contains the desired behavior.

Object-oriented approach

The object-oriented implementation of this pattern requires that the decorators share an interface with the type they're supposed to decorate. To simplify writing a new decorator, an `abstract` class implementing the shared interface is used as a starting point for any decorator.

Imagine a coffee maker with a single method to prepare coffee. The shared interface and the concrete implementation are:

```
public interface CoffeeMaker {
  List<String> getIngredients();
  Coffee prepare();
}

public class BlackCoffeeMaker implements CoffeeMaker {

    @Override
    public List<String> getIngredients() {
      return List.of("Robusta Beans", "Water");
    }

    @Override
    public Coffee prepare() {
      return new BlackCoffee();
    }
}
```

The goal is to decorate the coffee maker to add functionality like adding milk or sugar to your coffee. Therefore, a decorator has to accept the coffee maker and decorate the `prepare` method. A simple shared `abstract` decorator appears:

```
public abstract class Decorator implements CoffeeMaker { ❶

    private final CoffeeMaker target;

    public Decorator(CoffeeMaker target) { ❷
      this.target = target;
    }

    @Override
    public List<String> getIngredients() { ❸
      return this.target.getIngredients();
    }

    @Override
    public Coffee prepare() { ❸
      return this.target.prepare();
    }
}
```

❶ The `Decorator` implements `CoffeeMaker` so it's usable as a drop-in replacement.

❷ The constructor accepts the original CoffeeMaker instance that's supposed to be decorated.

❸ The getIngredients and prepare methods simply call the decorated CoffeeMaker, so any actual decorator can use a super call to get the "original" result.

The abstract Decorator type aggregates the minimal required functionality to decorate a CoffeeMaker in a singular type. With its help, adding steamed milk to your coffee is straightforward. All you need now is a milk carton, as seen in Example 14-1.

Example 14-1. Adding milk with a decorator

```java
public class AddMilkDecorator extends Decorator {

  private final MilkCarton milkCarton;

  public AddMilkDecorator(CoffeeMaker target,
                          MilkCarton milkCarton) { ❶
    super(target);
    this.milkCarton = milkCarton;
  }

  @Override
  public List<String> getIngredients() { ❷
    var newIngredients = new ArrayList<>(super.getIngredients());
    newIngredients.add("Milk");
    return newIngredients;
  }

  @Override
  public Coffee prepare() { ❸
    var coffee = super.prepare();
    coffee = this.milkCarton.pourInto(coffee);
    return coffee;
  }
}
```

❶ The constructor needs to accept all the requirements, so a MilkCarton is needed in addition to the CoffeeMaker.

❷ The decorator hooks into the getIngredients call by first calling super, making the result mutable, and adding the milk to the list of previously used ingredients.

❸ The prepare call also tasks super to do its intended purpose and "decorates" the resulting coffee with milk.

Creating a café con leche[3] is quite easy now:

```
CoffeeMaker coffeeMaker = new BlackCoffeeMaker();

CoffeeMaker decoratedCoffeeMaker = new AddMilkDecorator(coffeeMaker,
                                                new MilkCarton());

Coffee cafeConLeche = decoratedCoffeeMaker.prepare();
```

The decorator pattern is pretty straightforward to implement. Still, that's quite a lot
of code to pour some milk into your coffee. If you take sugar in your coffee, too, you
need to create another decorator with redundant boilerplate code and need to wrap
the decorated `CoffeeMaker` again:

```
CoffeeMaker coffeeMaker = new BlackCoffeeMaker();

CoffeeMaker firstDecorated = new AddMilkDecorator(coffeeMaker,
                                                new MilkCarton());

CoffeeMaker lastDecorated = new AddSugarDecorator(firstDecorated);


Coffee sweetCafeConLeche = lastDecorated.prepare();
```

There has to be a simpler way to improve the creation of a decorator and the process
of using multiple decorators.

So let's take a look at how to use functional composition instead.

A more functional approach

The first step to any refactoring effort toward a more functional approach is dissect-
ing what's actually happening. The decorator pattern consists of two parts that are
suitable for improvement:

- Decorating a `CoffeeMaker` with one or more decorators
- Creating a `Decorator` itself

The first part of "how to decorate" boils down to taking an existing `CoffeeMaker` and
"somehow" adding the new behavior and returning a new `CoffeeMaker` to be used
instead. In essence, the process looks like a `Function<CoffeeMaker, CoffeeMaker>`.

As before, the logic is bundled as a `static` higher-order method in a convenience
type. This method accepts a `CoffeeMaker` and a decorator and combines them with
functional composition:

---

3 A café con leche is a coffee variant prevalent in Spain and Latin America. The name means literally "coffee
with milk." I didn't use a "flat white" for my example because then I would have needed to steam the milk first.

```
public final class Barista {

  public static
  CoffeeMaker decorate(CoffeeMaker coffeeMaker,
                       Function<CoffeeMaker, CoffeeMaker> decorator) {
    return decorator.apply(coffeeMaker);
  }

  private Barista() {
    // suppress default constructor
  }
}
```

The `Barista` class has a parameterized `decorate` method that inverts the flow by accepting a `Function<CoffeeMaker, CoffeeMaker>` to actually do the process of decoration. Even though the decoration "feels" more functional now, accepting only a singular `Function` makes the process still tedious for more than one decorator:

```
CoffeeMaker decoratedCoffeeMaker =
  Barista.decorate(new BlackCoffeeMaker(),
                   coffeeMaker -> new AddMilkDecorator(coffeeMaker,
                                                       new MilkCarton())));

CoffeeMaker finalCoffeeMaker =
  Barista.decorate(decoratedCoffeeMaker,
                   AddSugarDecorator::new);
```

Thankfully, there's a functional API to process multiple elements in sequence I discussed in Chapter 6: Streams.

The decoration process is effectively a *reduction*, with the original `CoffeeMaker` as its initial value, and the `Function<CoffeeMaker, CoffeeMaker>` accepting the previous value to create the new `CoffeeMaker`. Therefore, the decoration process would look like Example 14-2.

Example 14-2. Multiple decorations by reduction

```
public final class Barista {

  public static
  CoffeeMaker decorate(CoffeeMaker coffeeMaker, ❶
                       Function<CoffeeMaker, CoffeeMaker>... decorators) {
    Function<CoffeeMaker, CoffeeMaker> reducedDecorations = ❷
      Arrays.stream(decorators)
            .reduce(Function.identity(),
                    Function::andThen);

    return reducedDecorations.apply(coffeeMaker); ❸
  }
}
```

❶ The decorate method still accepts the original CoffeeMaker to decorate. However, an arbitrary number of decorations can be provided thanks to the vararg argument.

❷ The decorations are composed with a Stream<Function<CoffeeMaker, Coffee Maker> by creating a Stream from the array and reducing all the elements to a single Function<CoffeeMaker, CoffeeMaker> by composing each of them.

❸ Finally, the singular reduced decoration is composed with CoffeeMaker.

Making a café con leche is now simpler thanks to combining multiple functional and functional-akin techniques:

```
CoffeeMaker decoratedCoffeeMaker =
  Barista.decorate(new BlackCoffeeMaker(),
                coffeeMaker -> new AddMilkDecorator(coffeeMaker,
                                                    new MilkCarton())),
                AddSugarDecorator::new);
```

The decoration process is an improvement over nesting the decorators one by one, by simplifying it into a single call. Still, the creation of a decorator could be improved with functions, too.

Instead of creating the decorator in the form of a Function<CoffeeMaker, Coffee Maker> yourself by using either a lambda or method reference, you could use another convenience type to group them together. This way, you don't even have to expose the concrete types of the decorators, because only the CoffeeMaker type and additional ingredients like MilkCarton are involved.

The implementation of a Decorations convenience type with static factory methods is quite straightforward, as shown in the following code:

```
public final class Decorations {

  public static
  Function<CoffeeMaker, CoffeeMaker> addMilk(MilkCarton milkCarton) {
    return coffeeMaker -> new AddMilkDecorator(coffeeMaker, milkCarton);
  }

  public static Function<CoffeeMaker, CoffeeMaker> addSugar() {
    return AddSugarCoffeeMaker::new;
  }

  // ...
}
```

All possible ingredients are available through a single type, without any callee needing to know the actual implementation or other requirements besides the arguments of each method. This way, you can use a more concise and fluent call to decorate your coffee:

```
CoffeeMaker maker = Barista.decorate(new BlackCoffeeMaker(),
                                     Decorations.addMilk(milkCarton),
                                     Decorations.addSugar());
var coffee = maker.prepare();
```

The main advantage of a functional approach is the possible elimination of explicit nesting and exposing the concrete implementation types. Instead of littering your packages with additional types and repetitive boilerplate, the already existing functional interfaces of the JDK can lend you a hand with more concise code to achieve the same result. You still should group the related code together, so related functionality is in a single file that can be split up if it would create a better hierarchy, but it doesn't have to.

Strategy Pattern

The *strategy pattern* belongs to the group of behavioral patterns. Due to the *open-closed*[4] principle that dominates most object-oriented designs, different systems are usually coupled by abstractions, like programming against interfaces, instead of concrete implementations.

This *abstract coupling* provides a useful fiction of more theoretical components working together to be realized later on without your code knowing the actual implementation. Strategies are using this decoupled code style to create interchangeable small logic units based on an identical abstraction. Which one is chosen is decided at runtime.

Object-oriented approach

Imagine you work on an e-commerce platform that sells physical goods. Somehow these goods must be shipped to the customer. There are multiple ways to ship an item, like different shipping companies or the type of shipping.

Such various shipping options share a common abstraction that is then used in another part of your system, like a `ShippingService` type, to ship the parcel:

```
public interface ShippingStrategy {
  void ship(Parcel parcel);
}

public interface ShippingService {
```

---

4 The *open-closed* principle is part of the *SOLID principles*. It states that entities, like classes, methods, functions, etc., should be *open* for extension, but *closed* for modification. See the Wikipedia pages for open-closed principle (*https://oreil.ly/PlJJ1*) and SOLID (*https://oreil.ly/dpBcy*) for more details.

```
    void ship(Parcel parcel, ShippingStrategy strategy);
}
```

Each of the options is then implemented as a `ShippingStrategy`. In this case, let's just look at standard and expedited shipping:

```
public class StandardShipping implements ShippingStrategy {
  // ...
}

public class ExpeditedShipping implements ShippingStrategy {

  public ExpeditedShipping(boolean signatureRequired) {
    // ...
  }

  // ...
}
```

Each strategy requires its own type and concrete implementation. This general approach looks quite similar to the decorators I discussed in the previous section. That's why it can be simplified in almost the same functional way.

A more functional approach

The overall concept behind the strategy pattern boils down to *behavioral parameterization*. That means that the `ShippingService` provides a general scaffold to allow a parcel to be shipped. How it's actually shipped, though, needs to be filled with a `ShippingStrategy` that is passed to it from the outside.

Strategies are supposed to be small and context-bound decisions and are often representable by a functional interface. In this case, you have multiple options for how to create and use strategies:

- Lambdas and method references
- Partial-applied functions
- Concrete implementations

Simple strategies without any additional requirements are best grouped in a `class` and used via method references to signature-compatible methods:

```
public final class ShippingStrategies {

  public static ShippingStrategy standardShipping() {
    return parcel -> ...;
  }
}
```

```
// HOW TO USE
shippingService.ship(parcel, ShippingStrategies::standardShipping);
```

More complex strategies might require additional arguments. That's where a partially-applied function will accumulate the code in a singular type to give you a simpler creation method:

```
public final class ShippingStrategies {

  public static ShippingStrategy expedited(boolean requiresSignature) {
    return parcel -> {
      if (requiresSignature) {
        // ...
      }
    };
  }
}
```

```
// HOW TO USE
shippingService.ship(parcel, ShippingStrategies.expedited(true));
```

These two functional options to create and use strategies are already a more concise way to handle strategies. They also eliminate the requirement of additional implementation types to represent a strategy.

However, if both functional options aren't doable due to a more complex strategy or other requirements, you can always use a concrete implementation. If you transition from object-oriented strategies, they will be concrete implementations, to begin with. That's why the strategy pattern is a prime candidate for introducing a functional approach by gradually converting existing strategies to functional code, or at least using them for new strategies.

Builder Pattern

The *builder pattern* is another creational pattern for creating more complex data structures by separating the construction from the representation itself. It solves various object creation problems, like multistep creation and validation, and improves nonmandatory argument handling. Therefore, it's a good companion for Records, which can only be created in a single swoop. In Chapter 5, I've already discussed how to create a builder for a Record. However, this section will look at builders from a functional perspective.

Object-oriented approach

Let's say you have a simple User Record with three properties and a component validation:

```
public record User(String email, String name, List<String> permissions) {
```

```
    public User {
      if (email == null || email.isBlank()) {
        throw new IllegalArgumentException("'email' must be set.");
      }

      if (permissions == null) {
        permissions = Collections.emptyList();
      }
    }
  }
```

If you need to create a User in multiple steps, like adding the permissions later on, you're out of luck without additional code. So let's add an inner builder:

```
public record User(String email, String name, List<String> permissions) {

  // ...

  public static class Builder { ❶

    private String email;
    private String name;
    private final List<String> permissions = new ArrayList<>();

    public Builder email(String email) { ❷
      this.email = email;
      return this;
    }

    public Builder name(String name) { ❷
      this.name = name;
      return this;
    }

    public Builder addPermission(String permission) { ❸
      this.permissions.add(permission);
      return this;
    }

    public User build() { ❹
      return new User(this.email, this.name, this.permissions);
    }
  }

  public static Builder builder() { ❺
    return new Builder();
  }
}
```

❶ The builder is implemented as an inner static class mimicking all the components of its parent Record.

❷ Each component has its dedicated set-only method that returns the `Builder` instance for fluent call chains.

❸ Additional methods for Collection-based fields allow you to add single elements.

❹ The `build` method simply calls the appropriate `User` constructor.

❺ A `static builder` method is added so you don't need to create a `Builder` instance yourself.

That's quite a lot of boilerplate and duplication to allow a more versatile and simpler creation flow like this:

```
var builder = User.builder()
                    .email("ben@example.com")
                    .name("Ben Weidig");

// DO SOMETHING ELSE, PASS BUILDER ALONG

var user = builder.addPermission("create")
                    .addPermission("edit")
                    .build();
```

Usually, a builder is made even more complex by adding better support for optional and non-optional fields with telescoping constructors or additional validation code.

Telescoping Constructors

Telescoping constructors are a way to supply default values via a constructor. This design pattern was actually used in "Component default values and convenience constructors" on page 91 to simplify Record creation.

In the case of the `User` builder, a constructor like `public Builder(String email)` would communicate that `email` is a required field. Still, telescoping constructors are often seen as an antipattern unless they delegate the call directly to another constructor, as I used them in Chapter 5.

To be honest, there aren't many ways to optimize or change the builder pattern in its current design. You might use a tool-assisted approach that generates the builder for you, but that will only reduce the amount of required code you need to write, not the necessity of the builder itself.

However, that doesn't mean the builder could not be improved with a few functional touches.

A more functional approach

Most of the time, a builder is strongly coupled with the type it's building, as an inner class with fluent methods to provide arguments and a build method to create the actual object instance. A functional approach can improve this creation flow in multiple ways.

First, it enables lazy computation of expensive values. Instead of accepting a value directly, a Supplier gives you a lazy wrapper that's only resolved in the build call:

```
public record User(String email, String name, List<String> permissions) {

  // ...

  private Supplier<String> emailSupplier;

  public Builder email(Supplier<String> emailSupplier) {
    this.emailSupplier = emailSupplier;
    return this;
  }

  // ...

  public User build() {
    var email = this.emailSupplier.get();
    // ...
  }
}
```

You can support both lazy and non-lazy variants. For example, you can change the original method to set emailSupplier instead of requiring both the email and emailSupplier fields:

```
public record User(String email, String name, List<String> permissions) {

  // ...

  private Supplier<String> emailSupplier;

  public Builder email(String email) {
    this.emailSupplier = () -> email;
    return this;
  }

  // ...
}
```

Second, the builder could mimic Groovy's with[5] as follows:

---

5 Groovy has a with method that accepts a closure to simplify repeated use of the same variable. See the official Groovy style guide (*https://oreil.ly/fjtBO*) for more information.

```
var user = User.builder()
                .with(builder -> {
                  builder.email = "ben@example.com";
                  builder.name = "Ben Weidig";
                })
                .withPermissions(permissions -> {
                  permissions.add("create");
                  permissions.add("view");
                })
                .build();
```

To achieve this, `Consumer`-based higher-order methods must be added to the builder, as shown in Example 14-3.

Example 14-3. Add with-methods to User builder

```
public record User(String email, String name, List<String> permissions) {

  // ...

  public static class Builder {

    public String email; ❶
    public String name;

    private List<String> permissions = new ArrayList<>(); ❷

    public Builder with(Consumer<Builder> builderFn) { ❸
      builderFn.accept(this);
      return this;
    }

    public Builder withPermissions(Consumer<List<String>> permissionsFn) { ❸
      permissionsFn.accept(this.permissions);
      return this;
    }

    // ...
  }

  // ...
}
```

❶ The builder fields need to be `public` to be mutable in the `Consumer`.

❷ However, not all fields should be `public`. For example, Collection-based types are better served by their own `with` methods.

❸ Adding another `with` method for `permissions` prevents setting it to `null` by accident and reduces the required code in the `Consumer` to the actual desired action.

Of course, the builder could've used `public` fields, to begin with. But then, no fluent call would've been possible. Adding `Consumer`-based `-with` methods to it, the overall call chain is still fluent, plus you can use lambdas or even method references in the creation flow.

Even if a design pattern, like the builder pattern, doesn't have a coequal functional variant, it could still be made more versatile with a few functional concepts sprinkled into the mix.

Final Thoughts on Functional Design Patterns

Calling them functional design patterns often feels like an oxymoron because they are almost the opposite of their object-oriented counterpart. OO design patterns are by definition formalized and easy-to-repeat solutions for common (OO) problems. This formalization usually comes with a lot of strict conceptual metaphors and boilerplate with little room for deviation.

The functional approach to the problems to be solved by OO design patterns uses the first-class citizenship of functions. It replaces the previously explicitly formalized templates and required type structures with functional interfaces. The resulting code is more straightforward and concise, and it can also be structured in new ways, like `static` methods returning concrete implements, or partially-applied functions, instead of intricate custom type-hierarchies.

Still, is it a good thing to remove the boilerplate in the first place? More straightforward and concise code is always an admirable goal to strive for. However, the initial boilerplate also has a use other than *just* being a requirement for an object-oriented approach: creating a more sophisticated domain to operate in.

Replacing all intermediate types with already available functional interfaces removes a certain amount of directly visible information to the reader of your code. So a middle ground must be found between replacing a more expressive domain-based approach with all of its types and structures, and simplification with a more functional approach.

Thankfully, as with most of the techniques I discuss in this book, it's not either-or. Identifying functional possibilities in classical object-oriented patterns requires you to take a more high-level view of how a problem is solved. For example, the *chain of responsibility* design pattern deals with giving more than one object a chance to process an element in a predefined chain of operations. That sounds quite familiar to how Stream or Optional pipelines work, or how functional composition creates a chain of functionality.

Object-oriented design patterns help you identify the general approach to a problem. Still, moving to a more functional solution, either partially or completely, often gives you a simpler and more concise alternative.

Takeaways

- Object-oriented design patterns are a proven and formalized way of knowledge sharing. They usually require multiple types to represent a domain-specific solution to a common problem.

- A functional approach uses first-class citizenship to replace any additional types with already available functional interfaces.

- Functional principles allow the removal of a lot of the boilerplate code usually required by many object-oriented design patterns.

- Pattern implementations become more concise, but the explicit expressiveness of the used types might suffer. Use domain-specific functional interfaces to regain expressiveness if necessary.

- Even for design patterns without a functional equivalent, adding certain functional techniques can improve their versatility and conciseness.

CHAPTER 15

A Functional Approach to Java

Many programming languages support both a functional and imperative code style. However, the syntax and facilities of a language typically incentivize specific approaches to common problems. Even with all the functional additions to the JDK discussed in this book, Java still favors imperative and object-oriented programming, with most of the core libraries' available types and data structures reflecting this preference.

However, as I've discussed throughout this book, that doesn't mean it has to be an either-or kind of situation. You can augment your OO code with functional principals without going fully functional. Why not have the best of both worlds? To do so, you need to adopt a functional mindset.

This chapter pulls together what you've learned in this book so far and highlights the most important aspects that will influence your functional mindset. It also shows a practical application of functional programming techniques on an architectural level that fits right into an object-oriented environment.

OOP Versus FP Principles

To better understand where functional principles can improve your code, it makes sense to revisit the underlying principles of both paradigms—object-oriented and functional—to recognize their dissimilarities and possible interconnection points. This builds the base knowledge to identify opportunities to incorporate a functional approach into your OO code, and where it doesn't make sense to force it.

Object-oriented programming's main concerns are encapsulating data and behavior, polymorphism, and abstraction. It's a *metaphor-based* approach to solving problems where its objects and connecting code mimic a particular problem domain. These objects interact by messaging through public contracts, like interfaces, and each has responsibilities and usually manages its own state. Using such metaphors bridges the gap between the computer, which requires a set of instructions, and the developer, who can express their intent in a straightforward manner. OOP is an excellent approach to structuring and organizing imperative code after the "real world" and its constant and endless changes.

Functional programming, however, uses mathematical principles to solve problems, utilizing a declarative code style. Instead of requiring a metaphor to model your code like the "real world," its foundation—lambda calculus—cares only about data structures and their transformation using high-level abstractions. Functions take an input and create an output; that's about it! Data and behavior aren't encapsulated; functions and data structures just are. FP circumvents many typical OOP and Java problems, like handling mutable state in a concurrent environment or unexpected side effects, by trying not to have any side effects to begin with.

These two short summaries already highlight the dissimilarity of the core principles of object-oriented and functional programming. OOP tries to tame complexity by encapsulating the moving parts of your code in a familiar domain, whereas FP strives to have fewer parts in total by adhering to mathematical principles. The more abstract way of thinking in FP is why OOP is often the preferred first approach to teaching and learning Java.

As I discussed in Chapter 14, both paradigms are just divergent approaches able to solve the same problems coming from different directions. It would be foolish to declare that one principle is, no pun intended, objectively better than the other. Metaphors in OO are a powerful tool to make code feel more natural to non-programmers and programmers alike. Some complex problems benefit from a good metaphorical representation way more than a maybe more concise but highly abstracted functional approach.

A Functional Mindset

> Any fool can write code that a computer can understand. Good programmers write code that humans can understand.
>
> —Martin Fowler, Refactoring: Improving the Design of Existing Code (*https://oreil.ly/dxtOA*)

You can have all the functional tools available at your fingertips, but using them efficiently requires the right mindset. Having a functional mindset involves having the reasoning to identify code that could be improved with a functional approach, be it going fully functional or just injecting a few functional techniques and principles at critical, and appropriate, places. This mindset won't come overnight; you have to hone it with practice to gain experience and intuition.

Developing this functional mindset starts with wanting to eliminate or reduce any accidental complexity in your code. The techniques and principles you use to solve your problems should lead to code that is reasonable and easier to understand.

To reason with a complex system means grasping and figuring out any code with only the information that's *right in front of you* rather than relying on hidden-away implementation details or maybe outdated comments, without any surprises waiting for you. You don't need to look across multiple files or types to understand the problem that is solved, or you don't need to ponder many of the decisions that went into the code itself.

The correctness of your code is informally proven because any claim about its functionality is backed up by its reasonability and accompanying comments. Anyone using such code can make strong assumptions about it and rely on its public contracts. The opaque nature of OOP and its encapsulation of behavior and data often makes it harder to reason with than alternative approaches.

Let's revisit the different aspects of functional programming that will influence your decisions about when to apply a functional approach.

Functions Are First-Class Citizens

Functional programming is all about functions and their first-class citizenship. That means that functions are tantamount to other constructs of the language because you can:

- Assign functions to variables
- Pass functions as arguments to another function/method
- Return a function from a function/method
- Create anonymous functions without a name

These properties are pretty similar to how anonymous classes are usable in Java, even before the introduction of lambda expressions. Unlike anonymous classes, though, functional interfaces—Java's representation of the concept of functions—are conceptionally more generalized and usually detached from an explicit class or domain type. Furthermore, the JVM uses them differently thanks to the invokedynamic opcode, as explained in "The invokedynamic Instruction" on page 25, which allows for a greater variety of optimizations compared to anonymous classes.

Even though Java doesn't have on the fly types and requires any lambda expression to be represented by concrete functional interfaces, it still manages to allow you to use one of the big differentiators between OO and FP because it provides a higher level of abstraction. Functional abstractions are on a higher level than their OO counterparts.

That means that FP focuses on values instead of discrete domain-specific types with rigid data structures.

Think of functions and their higher level of abstraction as small cogs in a machine. Object-oriented cogs are bigger and specifically designed for a narrower scope of tasks; they fit only into specific parts of the machine. The smaller functional cogs, however, are more uniform and generalized, and therefore easier to use throughout the machine. They can then be composed into groups, going from a singular simple task toward a complex and more complete one. The bigger task is the sum of all its smaller parts, with the parts themselves being as small and generic as possible, reusable, and easily testable. This way, you can build a library of reusable functions to be composed as necessary.

Still, Java's dependence on functional interfaces to represent functions and lambdas is both a blessing and a curse.

It's a curse because you can't have a detached lambda that's based only on its arguments and return type without a corresponding functional interface. Type inference eases the pain but, at some point, the actual type must be available for the compiler to infer the type down the line.

It's also a blessing because it's the perfect way of bridging between Java's static type system and predominantly imperative object-oriented code style and a new way of thinking, without breaking backward compatibility.

Avoiding Side Effects

> Asking a question shouldn't change the answer.
> —Bertrand Meyer, French academic

Having a functional mindset also involves avoiding side effects. From a functional point of view, side effects refer to the modification of any kind of state which can have many forms. It doesn't have to be hidden or unexpected; quite the contrary. Many forms of side effects, like accessing a database, or doing any kind of I/O, are intended actions and are a crucial part of almost every system. Nevertheless, fewer side effects usually mean fewer surprises in your code and a smaller bug surface.

There are several functional ways to reduce the number of side effects, or at least make them more manageable.

Pure functions

The most basic approach to avoid side effects is using the functional programming concept of *pure functions* because they rely on two elemental guarantees:

- The same input will *always* create the same output.
- Pure functions are *self-contained* without any side effects.

Seems simple enough.

In reality, however, there are more aspects you have to look out for when improving the purity of your Java code.

Any pure function can only rely on the declared input arguments to produce its result. Any hidden state or invisible dependencies are a big no-no.

Think of a function that creates a greeting for a User instance with a method signature as follows:

```
public String buildGreeting(User user)
```

The method signature, its public contract, discloses a singular dependency: the User argument. If you don't know the actual implementation, it would be safe to assume that this is a pure function that produces the same salutation for repeated calls with the same user.

Let's take a look at its implementation:

```
public String buildGreeting(User user) {
  String greeting;
  if (LocalTime.now().getHour() < 12) {
    greeting = "Good morning";
  } else {
    greeting = "Hello"
  }

  return String.format("%s, %s", greeting, user.name());
}
```

Checking out the implementation, however, a second dependency reveals itself: the time of day. This invisible dependency that relies on an out-of-context state makes the whole method impure.

To regain purity, the second internal dependency must be made part of the public contract instead:

```
public String buildGreeting(User user, LocalTime time)
```

Purity is restored and the public contract no longer hides the internal dependency on the time of day and communicates it clearly, without requiring any documentation.

The method signature could still be simplified further. Why bind the method to the User type if only its `name` is used? Why use `LocalTime` if only its hour is used? Creating a more versatile `buildGreeting` method would accept only the `name` and not a whole User instance.

The lowest common denominator of arguments will give the most versatile and broadly applicable pure function possible. Try to avoid nested calls to broaden the applicability of a method by going closer to the actual required value instead of relying on specific domain types.

The best way to think about pure functions is to see them totally isolated in their own space-time continuum detached from the rest of the system. That's why they need to receive all of their requirements explicitly as values, preferably with as few intermediate objects as possible. However, such a higher abstraction forfeits some of the method signature's expressiveness, so you must find an acceptable balance.

Pure functions are a cornerstone of functional programming. Reducing a task to "same input + processing → same output" makes method signatures more meaningful and easier to comprehend.

Pure object methods

Pure functions exist only within their own context, which is why they can only rely on their input arguments to create their output. Translating this principle into an object-oriented environment is a little bit more difficult.

Looking deeper at the two guarantees of pure functions from the point of view of an object-oriented programmer, they reveal the possibility of applying them in a broader sense to create a more hybrid approach I call *pure object methods*.

If a method on an object type is truly pure in the previously discussed sense (see "Pure Functions and Referential Transparency" on page 6), it could be made `static` and doesn't even need to be in the object type anymore. Still, binding methods to the related type that's a part of their input is an advantage and won't go away anytime soon.

Take the `buildGreeting` method from the previous section as an example. Even though it can be made a pure function in the form of a `static` method, adding it directly to the User type as an instance method makes sense. However, this will harm reusability because it no longer exists in complete isolation and is interconnected with its surrounding type itself. This relationship doesn't mean it can't be "as pure as possible," though.

As good object types do, the `User` type encapsulates its state and creates its own microcosmos mostly disconnected from the outside. A pure object method might access that microcosmos and treat it as additional input arguments. The main caveat, though, is the non-reusable nature of methods bound to specific types.

Other multiparadigm languages supporting an object-oriented programming style, like Python, make this approach more visible, as the following code shows:

```python
class User:

  name = ''

  def __init__(self, name):
    self.name = name

  def buildGreeting(self, time):
    # ...
```

Using `self`—Python's equivalent to Java's `this`—as an explicit input parameter on each method highlights the interdependence between a method and the instance itself. Even if an object's method affects its state, it can still be a pure object method as it doesn't have any side effects besides its internal state. The object and its current state becomes part of the input, as it encapsulates the side effect. The new state after the method call represents the output.

The functional design principles of pure functions are still useful if you have to deal with object types and can't refactor them to a new design. The same rules apply, but the object state counts as an input argument. That's why further dependencies like `time` in `buildGreeting` shouldn't be hidden away from anyone using the method. Calling the same method with the same input on two identical objects should result in an equal output or new object state.

Pure object methods might not bring in all the advantages of a fully functional approach with pure functions and immutable data structures, especially regarding reusability. Still, the functional mindset injected into the object-oriented style gives you more approachable, safe, and predictable, and therefore more reasonable, types.

Isolating side effects

It's impossible to write applications with absolutely zero side effects. OOP, or imperative code in general, is usually intertwined with mutable states and side effects. Still, side effects affecting your state are often invisible at the surface, easily breaking the reasonability of code and introducing subtle bugs if used incorrectly. If you can't completely avoid a side effect with techniques such as pure functions, they should be *isolated*, preferably on the edges of your logical units, instead of littered throughout the code. By splitting bigger units of code into smaller tasks, the possible side effects will be restricted to and affect only some of the tasks and not the overall unit.

This mindset is also present in the *Unix philosophy*, originated by Ken Thompson, the co-creator of the UNIX operating system. Doug McIlroy—head of the Bell Labs Computing Sciences Research Center at the time and inventor of the *Unix pipe*—summarized[1] it as such:

> Write programs that do one thing and do it well. Write programs to work together.
> —Doug McIlroy

Transferring this philosophy to a functional approach means that functions should strive to do one thing only and do it well without affecting their environment. Design your functions to be as small as possible but as large as necessary. A complex task is better served by multiple composed functions that preserve pureness as long as possible than a bigger function that is impure from the start.

I/O is a classic case of side effects. Loading files, talking to a database, etc., are impure operations and should therefore be separated from pure functions. To encapsulate a side effect you must think about the seams between the actual side effect and the processing of its result. Instead of loading a file and processing its content as a singular operation, it's better to separate them into the side effect of loading a file, and processing the actual data, as illustrated in Figure 15-1.

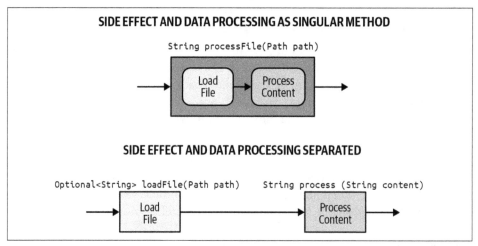

Figure 15-1. Splitting operations into discrete functions

The data processing is no longer bound to the file loading, or files in general, rather than only processing the incoming data. This makes the operation a pure and reusable function, with the side effect restricted to the loadFile method, with the returned Optional<String> giving you a functional bridge to it.

---

1 Quoted by Peter H. Salus in *A Quarter Century of Unix* (Addison-Wesley Professional, 1994).

If side effects can't be avoided, split up the task into smaller and preferably pure functions to isolate and encapsulate any remaining side effects.

Favor expressions over statements

As discussed in Chapter 1, a key differentiator between an object-oriented and a functional approach is the prevalence of either statements or expressions. To recapitulate, statements perform actions, like assigning a variable or control statements, and are therefore literal side effects. Expressions, on the other hand, evaluate their input to *just* yield output.

If you want to reduce side effects, using expressions leads to safer and more reasonable code, based on the following rationale:

- Pure expressions, like pure functions, don't have any side effects.
- Expressions are (mostly) definable in code; the types of available statements are predefined by the language.
- Evaluating pure expressions multiple times will yield the same output, ensuring predictability and enabling certain caching techniques, such as memoization.
- Expressions can be small to remain pure and still be composed with other expressions to solve a bigger task.

The control flow `if-else` statements are often a good candidate for replacing it with a more functional approach, especially to assign variables or create. The previous `buildGreeting` method becomes more concise and straightforward by using the ternary operator for the pretty simplistic decision of which greeting to choose, as seen as follows:

```
public String buildGreeting(User user, LocalTime time) {
    String greeting = time.getHour() < 12 ? "Good Morning"
                                          : "Hello";

    return String.format("%s, %s", greeting, user.name());
}
```

The ternary operator gives you two other advantages.

First, the variable `greeting` is declared and initialized in a single expression instead of it being uninitialized outside of the `if-else`-block.

Second, the variable is effectively `final`. In this particular case, it doesn't matter. Still, having a variable that can be easily used in a lambda expression is better than requiring you to refactor your code when you eventually need a variable to be effectively `final`.

Breaking down complex statement lists and blocks into smaller expressions makes code more concise and easier to reason with, plus it has the added benefit of effectively `final` variables, which is, as you may remember from earlier chapters, a non-negotiable requirement for using variables in lambda expressions.

Expressions are often preferable over statements because they are a combination of values and functions intended to create a new value. They're usually more compact and isolated than statements, making them safer to use. Statements, on the other hand, are more of a standalone unit to execute a side effect.

Moving toward immutability

> If it is not necessary to change, it is necessary not to change.
> —Lucius Cary, 2nd Viscount Falkland

Another way to avoid unintended change, thus side effects and potential bugs, is to embrace immutability whenever possible and sensible. Even without utilizing any other functional principles, your codebase will become more robust thanks to immutability by eliminating the source of way too many bugs: *unintended change*.

To prevent any unforeseen mutations, immutability should be the default approach to any type used in your programs, especially in concurrent environments, as discussed more deeply in Chapter 4. You don't have to reinvent the wheel for many use cases, as the JDK provides you with multiple options for immutable data structures:

Immutable Collections
Even though Java doesn't provide "fully" immutable Collection types, it still has structurally immutable ones where you can't add or remove elements. The concept of *unmodifiable* views of Collections was expanded in Java 9 by `static` factory methods like `List.of` to easily create structurally immutable Collections, as discussed in "Immutable Collection factory methods" on page 67.

Immutable math
The package `java.math` and its two immutable arbitrary-precision types, `Big Integer` and `BigDecimal`, are safe and immutable options for doing high-precision calculations.

Records (JEP 395 (https://oreil.ly/3GmKt))
Introduced as a preview feature in Java 14 and refined in 15, Records provide a completely new data structure as an easy-to-use data aggregation type. They're a great alternative for POJOs and sometimes Java Beans, or you could use them as small, localized immutable data holders, as discussed in Chapter 5.

Java Date and Time API (JSR-310 (https://oreil.ly/X_LZY))

> Java 8 also introduced a new way to store and manipulate dates and times with immutable types from the ground up. The API gives you a fluent, explicit, and straightforward way of dealing with anything related to date and time.

As you can see, more and more Java APIs are built on or at least improve their support for immutability, and so should you. Designing your data structures and code with immutability in mind from the get-go saves you a lot of headaches in the long run. No more worrying about unintended or unexpected changes, and no more worries about thread safety in concurrent environments.

However, one thing to remember is that immutability is suited best for, well, immutable data. Creating a new immutable data structure for any change becomes cumbersome really quickly regarding the required code and memory consumption by all those new objects.

Immutability is one of the most important aspects you can introduce into your codebase, regardless of a functional approach. An "immutable first" mindset gives you safer and more reasonable data structures. Still, your usual modus operandi might not fit into the new challenges that data management with immutability incurs. Remember though, it's easier to (partially) break immutability if there's no other option available than to retroactively tack on immutability in a mature code base.

Functional Data Processing with Map/Filter/Reduce

Most data problems boil down to iterating over a sequence of elements, choosing the correct one, maybe manipulating them, performing an action, or gathering them into a new data structure. The following example—iterating over a list of users, filtering the correct ones, and notifying them—is a typical example of these basic steps:

```
List<User> usersToNotify = new ArrayList<>();

for (var user : availableUsers) {
  if (user.hasValidSubscription()) {
    continue;
  }

  usersToNotify.add(user);
}

notify(usersToNotify);
```

Such problems are a perfect match for a functional approach with Streams and map/filter/reduce, as discussed in "Map/Filter/Reduce" on page 127.

Instead of explicitly iterating over the users with a for-loop and collecting the correct elements in a previously defined List, a Stream pipeline does the whole task in a fluent, declarative call:

```
List<User> usersToNotify = availableUsers.stream()
                                .filter(User::hasValidSubscription)
                                .toList();
notify(usersToNotify);
```

Stream pipelines express *what* to do without the boilerplate of *how* to iterate over the elements. They are a perfect scaffold for converting statement-based data filtering and transformation to a functional pipeline. The fluent call concisely describes the steps necessary to solve the problem, especially if you use method references or method calls returning the required functional interface.

Abstractions Guide Implementations

Every project is built upon abstractions designed after the requirements.

Object-oriented design uses low-level abstractions in the form of powerful metaphors, defining the characteristics and constraints of a system. This domain-based approach is quite expressive and powerful but also restricts the versatility of types and the ease of introducing change. As requirements usually change over time, too-restrictive abstractions lead to misalignment between different parts of your systems. Misaligned abstractions create friction and subtle bugs and might require a lot of work to realign.

Functional programming tries to avoid misaligned abstractions by using higher abstractions not bound to a specific domain. Chapter 14 reflects that by almost unconditionally replacing commonly used object-oriented abstractions with generalized functional interfaces of the JDK instead. This decoupling of abstractions from the original problem context creates simpler and easy-to-reuse components that are combined and mixed as necessary, enabling easier change of any functional system.

Object-oriented and imperative code is a good match for encapsulating functionality, object state, and representing a problem domain. Functional concepts are an excellent choice for implementation logic and higher-level abstractions. Not every data structure must be represented in the problem domain, so using more versatile functional types instead creates reusable and broader types that are driven by their use cases instead of the domain concept.

To resolve this problem, you must find a balance between the two levels of abstraction if you want to use both in the same system. In "Functional Architecture in an Imperative World" on page 364, I discuss how to combine both as an architectural decision that gives the benefits of high-level functional abstractions wrapped in a familiar imperative layer.

Building Functional Bridges

A functional approach means your code most likely lives in an imperative and object-oriented environment that needs to work hand in hand with any functional technique or concept you want to integrate. In "Functional Architecture in an Imperative World" on page 364, I will discuss how to integrate functional code into an imperative environment.

But first, let's look at how to bridge the gap between your existing code and the new functional APIs.

Method references-friendly signatures

Every method, `static` or not, and any constructor is a potential method reference to be used in higher-order functions or represented by a functional interface. That's why it can make sense to design your APIs with other functional APIs in mind.

For example, the commonly used Stream operations `map`, `filter`, and `sort` accept a `Function<T, R>`, a `Predicate<T>`, and a `Comparator<T>`, respectively, that translate well into simple method signatures.

Look at the required functional interface's SAM; it's the blueprint for the required method signature. As long as the input arguments and the return type match, you can name your method any way you want.

 One exception to simply mapping a SAM signature to a method reference is an unbound non-`static` method reference. As the method is referenced via the type itself and isn't bound to a specific instance, the underlying lambda expression accepts the type as its first argument.

For example, `String::toLowerCase` accepts a `String` and returns a `String`, and is, therefore, a `Function<String, String>`, despite `toLowerCase` not having any arguments.

When designing any API, it makes sense to think about how it might be used by higher-order functions and provide method reference-friendly signatures. Your methods still have expressive names depending on their surrounding context, but they also build a bridge to functional APIs with simple method references.

Using retroactive functional interfaces

Functional interfaces are usually marked with the `@FunctionalInterface` annotation. Still, as long as they fulfill the general requirements, as explained in "Functional Interfaces" on page 17, an interface is automatically a functional interface. Therefore, already existing code can benefit from the conciseness of lambdas and method references, and their specialized handling by the JVM.

Many longstanding interfaces of the JDK are now marked with `@FunctionalInterface`, but your code might not have adapted yet and could benefit from these changes. The following "now functional" interfaces were widely used even before Java 8:

- `java.lang.Comparable<T>`
- `java.lang.Runnable`
- `java.util.Comparator<T>`
- `java.util.concurrent.Callable<V>`

For example, before lambdas, sorting a Collection was quite a handful because of all the boilerplate code:

```
users.sort(new Comparator<User>() {
  @Override
  public int compare(User lhs, User rhs) {
    return lhs.email().compareTo(rhs.email());
  }
});
```

The lambda variant tames the boilerplate quite a bit:

```
users.sort((lhs, rhs) -> lhs.email().compareTo(rhs.email()));
```

But why stop here? If you check out the functional interface `Comparator<T>`, you will find `static` and non-`static` helper methods to make the overall call even more concise without losing any expressiveness:

```
users.sort(Comparator.comparing(User::email));
```

Java 8 not only introduced new functional interfaces but also improved existing interfaces so they fit nicely into the new APIs with lots of `default` and `static` methods. Always check out the non-SAM methods available in functional interfaces to find hidden gems to simplify your code with functional composition, or common tasks that can be condensed into a declarative call chain.

Lambda factories for common operations

Designing your APIs to match other functional APIs so you can use method references isn't always a possibility. That doesn't mean that you can provide lambda factories to simplify the use of higher-order functions, though.

For example, if a method doesn't match a particular functional interface, because it requires additional arguments, you can use *partial application* to make it fit the method signature of a higher-order function.

Image a `ProductCategory` type that has a method for a localized description as follows:

```
public class ProductCategory {

  public String localizedDescription(Locale locale) {
    // ...
  }
}
```

The method is representable by a `BiFunction<ProductCategory, Locale, String>`, so you can't use it in a Stream's `map` operation and have to rely on a lambda expression:

```
var locale = Locale.GERMAN;

List<ProductCategory> categories = ...;

categories.stream()
          .map(category -> category.localizedDescription(locale))
          ...;
```

Adding a `static` helper to `ProductCategory` that accepts a `Locale` and returns a `Function<ProductCategory, String>` allows you to use it instead of creating a lambda expression:

```
public class ProductCategory {

  public static Function<ProductCategory, String>
              localizedDescriptionMapper(Locale locale) {
    return category -> category.localizedDescription(locale);
  }

  // ...
}
```

This way, the `ProductCategory` is still responsible for creating a localized mapper function that it expects. However, the call is simpler, and reusable:

```
categories.stream()
          .map(ProductCategory.localizedDescriptionMapper(locale))
          ...;
```

Providing lambda operations for common operations by binding factory methods to their related type gives you a predefined set of intended tasks and saves the caller the repetitive creation of identical lambda expressions.

Implementing functional interfaces explicitly

The most common functional interfaces, discussed in "The Big Four Functional Interface Categories" on page 39, go a long way before you need to create your own specialized types, especially if you include multi-arity variants. Still, creating your own functional interfaces has a big advantage: a more expressive domain.

Looking at an argument or return type alone, a `Function<Path, Path>` could represent anything. A type named `VideoConvertJob`, however, tells you exactly what's going on. To use such a type in a functional approach, though, it has to be a functional interface. Instead of creating a new and isolated functional interface, you should extend an existing one:

```
interface VideoConverterJob extends Function<Path, Path> {
  // ...
}
```

By choosing an existing functional interface as the baseline, your specialized variant is now compatible with `Function<Path, Path>` and inherits the two `default` methods `andThen` and `compose` to support functional composition out of the box. The custom variant narrows the domain and is compatible with its ancestor. Extending an existing interface also inherits the SAM signature.

To improve the domain even further, you could add a `default` method to create an expressive API:

```
interface VideoConverterJob extends Function<Path, Path> {

  Path convert(Path sourceFile);

  default Path apply(Path sourceFile) {
    return convert(sourceFile);
  }

  // ...
}
```

Adding a `default` method to implement a SAM is also the approach to make an existing interface conform to a functional interface without changing the original public contract, except for the additional functionality provided by the functional interface.

Compatibility of Functional Interfaces

Designing APIs using types that extend functional interfaces requires some considerations due to Java's inheritance rules. Even though both interfaces are structurally equal concerning `Function<Path, Path>` compatibility, the types aren't interchangeable.

`VideoConverterJob` is a `Function<Path, Path>` by definition and, therefore, usable wherever an argument requires a `Function<Path, Path>`. The other way around,

---

though, using `Function<Path, Path>` for an argument of type `VideoConverterJob` isn't possible.

Here is a simple rule to follow when using types that extend functional interfaces in method signatures: always return a type as specific as possible, in this case, `Video ConverterJob`, but accept only a type as distinct as necessary, like `Function<Path, Path>`.

Making your interfaces extend a functional interface, or letting your classes explicitly implement a functional interface, bridges between existing types and higher-order functions. There are still considerations to be made to satisfy Java's type hierarchy rules, but accepting the least common denominator as input and returning the most specific type possible is a good rule of thumb.

Functional null handling with Optionals

Optionals are an elegant way to deal with (possible) `null` values. That alone is a big plus in many scenarios. Another one of its advantages is its capability to provide a functional starting point between a possible `null` value and subsequent operations.

Where a `null` reference was previously a dead end requiring additional code to not explode with a `NullPointException`, an Optional gives you a declarative pipeline replacing the usual boilerplate required to handle `null` values:

```
Optional<User> tryLoadUser(long id) {
  // ...
}

boolean isAdminUser =
  tryLoadUser(23L).map(User::getPermissions)
                  .filter(Predicate.not(Permissions::isEmpty))
                  .map(Permissions::getGroup)
                  .flatMap(Group::getAdmin)
                  .map(User::isActive)
                  .orElse(Boolean.FALSE);
```

This pipeline replaces two `null` checks (initial and `Group::getAdmin`) and an if-statement (the `filter` operation), plus accessing the required properties and providing a sensible fallback. The overall task is directly expressed in the fluent declarative call over six lines instead of a more complex and harder-to-follow block of individual statements.

It's hard to argue against the reduction of control statements combined with being a functional jump-off point, and this will likely increase your desire to (over)use Optionals, as it did for me in the beginning. Remember that Optionals were designed as a specialized *return* type, not as a ubiquitous replacement for null-related code. Not every value needs to be wrapped in an Optional, especially simple null checks:

```
// BAD: wrapping a value for a simple lookup
var nicknameOptional = Optional.ofNullable(customer.getNickname())
                               .orElse("Anonymous");

// BETTER: simpler null-check
var nicknameTernary = customer.getNickname() != null ? customer.getNickname()
                                                     : "Anonymous";
```

Using an Optional might *feel* cleaner—easier to follow the flow, no control structure, no explicit null check—but as a normal Java type, creating an Optional isn't free. Each operation requires checking for null to do its intended job and might create a new Optional instance. The ternary operator might not be as appealing as an Optional, but it sure requires fewer resources.

Since Java 9, the utility class `java.util.Objects` got two additions to do simple null checks with a single method call that doesn't create additional instances, which are the preferred alternative to an Optional with only an `orElse` or `orElseGet` operation:

```
var nickname = Objects.requireNonNullElse(customer.getNickname(), "Anonymous");

var nicknameWithSupplier = Objects.requireNonNullElse(customer.getNickname(),
                                                      () -> "Anonymous");
```

Using Optionals should be restricted to their intended use case as improved return containers for possible null values, and, in my opinion, intricate Optional pipelines with multiple operations. You shouldn't use them in your code to perform simple null checks, nor should methods accept them directly as their arguments. Method overloading provides a better alternative if an argument isn't always required.

Parallelism and Concurrency Made Easy

Writing concurrent or parallel programs isn't easy. Creating additional threads is the simple part. However, coordinating more than one thread can become quite complicated. The most common root of all problems related to parallelism and concurrency is sharing data between different threads.

Shared data across multiple threads comes with its own requirements you don't have to consider in sequential programs, like synchronization and locks to ensure data integrity and to prevent data races and deadlocks.

Functional programming creates a lot of opportunities to use concurrency and parallelism safely thanks to the principles that functional principles are built on, most evidently the following:

Immutability
> Without change, there can't be data races or deadlocks. Data structures can safely traverse thread boundaries.

Pure functions
> Without side effects, pure functions are self-contained and can be called from any thread, as they rely only on their input to generate their output.

Essentially, functional techniques don't concern themselves with the distinction of sequential or concurrent execution because FP, at its most strict interpretation, doesn't allow for an environment where a distinction is necessary.

Java's concurrency features like parallel Streams (Chapter 8) and `CompletableFuture` (Chapter 13) still require thread coordination even with fully functional code and data structures. However, the JDK will do it for you in a way that fits most scenarios.

Be Mindful of Potential Overhead

Functional techniques provide a great productivity boost and make your code more expressive and robust. That doesn't automagically mean that it's more performant, though, or even at the same performance level as imperative and object-oriented code.

Java is such a versatile language that is trusted by many companies and individuals because its backward compatibility and general API stability are among the best. However, this comes at the steep price of fewer changes to the language itself, at least compared to others. That's why many features covered in this book, like Streams, CompleteFutures, or Optionals, aren't native language features but are implemented in the JDK with ordinary Java code instead. Even Records, a totally new construct with distinct semantics, boils down to a typical class extending `java.lang.Record`, similar to how Enums work, with the compiler generating the required code behind the scenes. Still, that doesn't mean these features aren't optimized in any way. They still profit from all the optimizations available to all Java code. In addition, lambdas are a language feature utilizing a specialized opcode in the JVM, with multiple optimization techniques.

I know that using functional structures like Streams and Optionals for every single data processing or `null` check is quite tempting because I fell for it after years of Java language stagnation. Even though they are excellent and highly optimized tools, you have to remember they aren't free to use and will incur a certain unavoidable overhead.

Usually, the overhead is negligible compared to the productivity gains and more concise and straightforward code. Always remember the quote by Kent Beck: "First make it work, then make it right, and, finally, make it fast." Don't forgo functional features and APIs in fear of the potential overhead without knowing if it'll affect your code negatively in the first place. If in doubt, measure first, refactor second.

Functional Architecture in an Imperative World

Choosing a particular architecture isn't an easy endeavor and has far-reaching consequences for any project. It's a significant decision that can't be changed without much effort. If you want to apply a more functional approach on an architectural level, it has to fit into an existing imperative and object-oriented code base without disrupting the status quo (too much).

Unsurprisingly, functions are the most basic and essential unit in functional architectures, representing isolated chunks of business logic. These chunks are the building blocks of workflows by being composed as needed. Each workflow represents a bigger logical unit, like a feature, a use case, a business requirement, etc.

A typical architectural approach to utilizing FP in an OO world is to separate the business logic from how it communicates with the outside world with well-defined boundaries. The *functional core, imperative shell* (FC/IS) approach to architecture is one that's flexible in size and can be as low-impact as you want.

Although it's feasible to build a system from scratch with an FC/IS design, it's also possible to integrate the design into an existing code base. An FC/IS is an excellent choice for gradual rewrites and refactoring to introduce functional principles and techniques into your OO project.

If you think about code and its actual purpose detached from any paradigms or concepts, it falls into two distinct groups: *doing* the work, and *coordinating* it. Instead of organizing the code and its responsibilities into a single paradigm, FC/IS draws a distinct line of separation between the two involved paradigms, as shown in Figure 15-2.

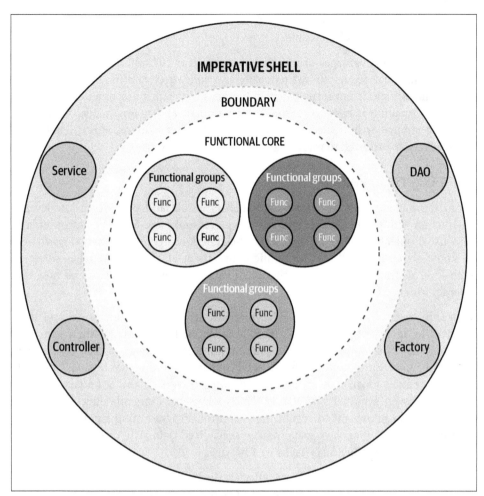

Figure 15-2. Basic layout of functional core, imperative shell

The *functional core* encapsulates the business logic and decisions in isolated and purely functional units. It utilizes all that FP has to offer and does what it does best: working directly with data without worrying about side effects or state-related problems thanks to pure functions and immutability. This core is then wrapped by an *imperative shell*, a thin layer to protect it from the outside world, encapsulating all the side effects and any mutable state.

The *shell* contains the dependencies to other parts of the system and provides the public contract to interact with the FC/IS from the outside. Everything non-functional is kept away from the core and restricted to the shell. To keep the shell as thin as possible, most of the decisions remain in the core, so the shell only needs to delegate the work through its boundary and interpret the core's results. It's a glue layer handling the real world with all its dependencies and mutable state but with as few paths and decisions as possible.

One of the main advantages of this design is the clear-cut split of responsibilities by encapsulation that occurs almost naturally as a side effect of a functional approach. The business logic is encapsulated in the core, built with pure functions, immutability, etc., making it easy to reason with, modular, and maintainable. Conversely, anything impure or mutable, or any contact with other systems, is restricted to the shell, which isn't allowed to make many decisions by itself.

From Objects to Values

From the outside, only the imperative shell is visible and provides a low level of abstraction with problem domain-specific types. It looks and feels like any other layer in a usual object-oriented Java project. The functional core, however, doesn't need to know about the shell and its public contracts at all. Instead, it relies solely on high-level abstractions and the exchange of values rather than objects and how they interact with each other.

This shift from objects to values is required to keep the core functional and independent by leveraging all available functional tools. But it also highlights the split in responsibilities. To keep the core pure, any mutability, state, or side effects must happen beyond the boundary in the shell, outside of the actual business logic. In its most refined form, that means that *anything* traversing the boundary needs to be a value, even eventual side effects! That's why separating side effects from pure functions is so important to regain more control. Programming languages that are "more functional" than Java usually have specialized data structures to handle side effects, like for example Scala's Maybe or Try types.

Java's closest type for handling a side effect is the Optional type, which is capable of representing two states in a single type. In Chapter 10, I also discussed how to recreate Scala's try/success/failure pattern in Java to handle control flow disruptions due to Exceptions in a more functional manner. Still, the additional code and boilerplate required to tame side effects is a clear indicator that they should be handled in the imperative shell where the appropriate tools and constructs are available, unlike in the functional core, where it's at least not desirable to do so.

Separation of Concerns

Functions come to their conclusions solely based on their arguments, without accessing or changing the world around them. Still, at some point, change might be necessary, like with persisting data or mutating state in the shell.

The core is responsible for decision-making but not for acting on such decisions. That's why all changes, even side effects, must be representable as values, too.

Imagine you want to scrape a website for certain information and store it in a database. The overall task consists, broadly speaking, of the following steps:

1. Load the content of a website
2. Extract the necessary information
3. Decide if the information is relevant
4. Persist the data in a database

To fit the task into an FC/IS system, you first need to categorize the steps into shell or core based on their responsibilities.

Loading the content and persisting the data is clearly I/O, which includes side effects, and therefore belongs to the shell. Information extraction and deciding if it's relevant is data processing that fits into the core. This categorization leads to the separation of tasks as illustrated in Figure 15-3.

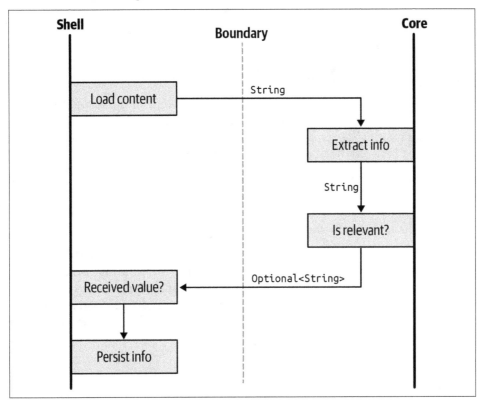

Figure 15-3. Web-scraping responsibilities in FC/IS

As you can see in the figure, the shell interacts with the network and passes the content immediately to the core. The core receives an immutable `String` value and returns an `Optional<String>` to indicate if the information is relevant based on its business logic. If a value is received back in the shell, it persists the value and any other information it still has access to in its context.

The separation of concerns brings another advantage to the code. From a modularity standpoint, the core is capable of using any input source, not just a website. This makes data processing more flexible and reusable. For example, instead of scraping a single site and passing its content directly to the core for processing, multiple pages could be scraped beforehand and persisted in a database for later processing. The core doesn't care and doesn't even need to know where the content comes from; it's entirely focused on its isolated task: extracting and evaluating information. So even if the overall requirements change, the core doesn't necessarily have to change, too. And if it does, you can recombine the existing small logical units as needed.

The Different Sizes of an FC/IS

An FC/IS might seem like a singular organizational layout that your system is built around. That's one way to do it, yet there's a more flexible way to integrate the FC/IS architecture into a system: multiple FC/ISs with different sizes.

Unlike other architectural designs, it doesn't have to define or dominate a project. It doesn't matter if your whole application is built around a singular or multiple FC/ISs. Even creating an FC/IS for a sole task is possible. As long as an imperative shell integrates with the rest of the system, you're good to go!

The dynamic sizing and integration of an FC/IS allows for a gradual transition toward more functional logic in your codebase without breaking preexisting structures. Multiple FC/ISs, as seen in Figure 15-4, can coexist and interact with prior systems without anyone even noticing it from the outside.

A sensible approach for sizing an FC/IS is thinking about its context and capabilities. The boundaries to the outside world—the shell's surface—are the first indicator of the required size. Reducing the coupling between different systems ensures modularity, extensibility, and maintainability over time. The context is defined by the encapsulated specialized domain knowledge represented in the core, and by extension, the public contract of the shell.

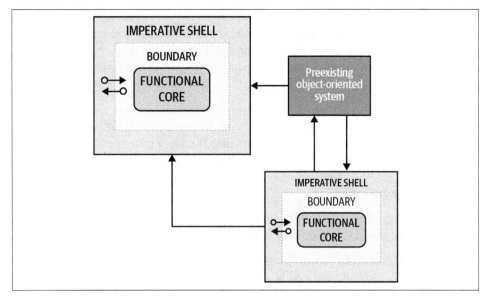

Figure 15-4. Multiple FI/CSs interacting with an existing system

Defining the correct context and appropriate boundaries is crucial and gets easier with experience. An FC/IS should be as small as possible but as big as necessary. Functional units or whole functional groups of a core can be reused in other FC/ISs to facilitate multiple small but specialized FC/ISs instead of a singular "all-inclusive" one. With these smaller and isolated ones it's easier to start replacing and integrating them into even complex preexisting systems step-by-step.

Testing an FC/IS

As with any other refactoring effort, when you adopt an FC/IS design, you should verify your new structures with appropriate testing, such as unit and integration tests. If your code has dependencies, or I/O like a database, testing usually requires mocks or stubs to better isolate the tested components.

While libraries are available to streamline creating such replacements, the whole concept comes with some drawbacks:

Knowledge of implementation details
Mocks often require detailed implementation knowledge to work as intended. Such details might change over time, and every refactor attempt tends to break the mocks and stubs mimicking them, even without changing the public contracts or the test logic.

Incidental testing

Tests should be on point, testing only the absolute minimum to ensure correctness. Dependencies create additional layers to consider, though, even if the intended story of the test hides underneath. Debugging such tests can be a nuisance because you no longer debug the test and functionality itself but also any other layer present.

Fictional testing

Typically, a dependency is correctly initialized and in a guaranteed meaningful state. On the other hand, Mocks and Stubs are essentially fictional implementations to reduce the coupling between components and fulfill the minimal set of requirements for the test.

The FC/IS architecture reduces these usual drawbacks thanks to its clear separation of responsibilities, which is mirrored in its testability.

The functional core—the business logic of the system—consisting of pure functions which are often naturally isolated is a perfect match for unit testing. The same test input needs to fulfill the same assertions. That's why the core is usually easy to verify with small and on-point unit tests without test doubles compared to larger interconnected systems with more complex setup requirements. This general lack of dependencies eliminates the need for mocks and stubs.

The imperative shell still has dependencies and side effects and is obviously not as easily testable as the core; it still needs integration tests. However, having most of the logic in the core, which is easily unit-testable, means fewer tests are required to verify the shell. Any new FC/IS can rely on tested and verified functional code that's easy to reason with, with only a new shell needing to be verified.

Final Thoughts on a Functional Approach to Java

Although I'm obviously a proponent of functional techniques wherever possible and sensible, my day-to-day Java work is still shaped by primarily imperative and object-oriented code. You may also be in a similar situation. In my company, Java 8 and its successors allowed us to introduce functional techniques step-by-step and at our own pace without the need to rewrite the whole architecture or codebase.

For example, slowly establishing immutability throughout the code and as the new baseline for data structures eliminated a whole category of problems that is usually present in an OO approach. Even hybrid approaches, like using partially immutable data structures for critical state management, eliminates certain unfavorable scenarios that could introduce subtle and hard-to-debug problems.

Another significant improvement is designing method signatures with Optionals in mind. It makes the intent of a method more evident, communicating the possibility of missing values clearly with the caller, resulting in fewer `NullPointerExceptions` without requiring an abundance of `null` checks.

Functional idioms, concepts, and techniques aren't as far out from object-oriented ones as is often proclaimed. Sure, they are different approaches to solving similar problems. Most benefits of functional programming can be reaped in object-oriented and imperative environments, too.

Java, as a language, might be lacking support for certain functional constructs. However, Java, the platform with a vast ecosystem, brings in so many benefits regardless of the chosen paradigm.

Fundamentally, functional programming is a thought process, not a specific language per se. You don't have to start a system from scratch to benefit from it. Starting from scratch often brings focus to productivity instead of required breadth. Due to an ever-changing and evolving codebase, it's easy to overlook the necessary edge cases and non-common constructs most systems rely on. Instead of going back to square one, you can reduce the overall complexity by gradually rewriting, refactoring, and injecting a *functional mindset* step-by-step.

Still, not every data structure needs to be redesigned, and not each type to be made fully functional. The way to build a functional mindset is to exercise it. Start small, and don't force it. The more you use functional constructs, the easier you will identify code that can benefit from the functional tools that Java provides.

The overarching goal of a functional approach is reducing the required cognitive capacity to understand and reason with your code. More concise and safer constructs, like pure functions and immutable data structures, improve reliability and long-term maintainability. Software development is about controlling complexity with the right tools, and in my opinion, the functional toolset that Java 8+ provides is quite powerful to tame your imperative and object-oriented Java code.

No matter which functional techniques and concepts you integrate into your projects, the most important lesson that I hope you take away from my book is that it doesn't actually matter if you do OOP or FP. Brian Goetz, the Java Language Architect at Oracle, said it quite well in one of his talks:

> Don't be a functional programmer.
> Don't be an object-oriented programmer.
> Be a better programmer.
>
> —Brian Goetz, FP vs OO: Choose Two[2]

Software development is about choosing the most appropriate tool for a given problem. Incorporating the functional concepts and techniques available to us as Java

---

2 Devoxx, "FP vs OO: Choose Two by Brian Goetz," https://oreil.ly/uLf87.

developers in our day-to-day work adds invaluable new tools to our toolbox, which create more readable, reasonable, maintainable, and testable code.

Takeaways

- OOP and FP are quite dissimilar in their core concepts. However, most of their concepts aren't mutually exclusive or completely orthogonal. Both can solve the same problems but with different approaches.
- Reasonable code is the ultimate goal, and a functional mindset helps achieve it.
- A functional mindset starts with small steps, like avoiding side effects with the help of pure functions or embracing immutability.
- Functional principles can also be part of architectural decisions, like separating concerns by splitting the business logic and the exposed surface to other systems with designs like a functional core, imperative shell.
- The functional core, imperative shell design is an excellent tool for gradually introducing functional principles and concepts into existing code.

Index

null handling and, 217
re-finalizing a reference, 22
Vlissides, John, 93

W

walk methods, 170-171

weakly consistent directory content, 175
work-stealing thread execution, 195
wrappers
    Optionals and, 221, 230, 236
    primitive, 69

About the Author

Using his first computer at the age of four, **Ben Weidig** is a self-taught developer with almost two decades of experience in professional web, mobile, and systems programming in various languages.

After learning the ropes of professional software development and project management at an international clinical research organization, he became a self-employed software developer. He merged with a SaaS company after prolonged and close collaboration on multiple projects. As co-director, he shapes the company's general direction, is involved in all aspects of their Java-based main product, and oversees and implements its mobile strategy.

In his free time, he shares his expertise and experiences by writing articles about Java, functional programming, best practices, and code style in general. He also participates in the open source community, either as a committer to established projects or releasing code of his own.

Colophon

The animal on the cover of *A Functional Approach to Java* is a bare-throated tiger heron (*Tigrisoma mexicanum*), native to Mexico and Central America. This bird frequents open habitat near river and lake banks, where it hunts fish, crustaceans, or frogs by standing still until prey comes within reach of its long, sharp beak.

The tiger heron is a medium-sized bird, about 31 inches in length. As a juvenile, its plumage is cinnamon-brown, with dense, irregular lines (known as vermiculation) across its wings, throat, and belly. Adults develop darker coloration, with gray-and-black mottled feathers and a black crest. These birds also sport bright yellow throats and lores (the area between the eye and beak). The scientific name *Tigresoma* comes from the Greek for "tiger body," referring to its striped appearance.

Normally solitary, the herons build platform nests in trees during breeding season, and lay 2–3 eggs per clutch. These nests are constructed from a jumble of twigs, and occasionally there are gaps large enough to allow eggs to fall through. Nevertheless, the IUCN does not consider the species threatened.

Many of the animals on O'Reilly covers are endangered; all of them are important to the world.

The cover illustration is by Karen Montgomery, based on a black and white engraving from *Zoological Gardens*. The cover fonts are Gilroy Semibold and Guardian Sans. The text font is Adobe Minion Pro; the heading font is Adobe Myriad Condensed; and the code font is Dalton Maag's Ubuntu Mono.

Printed in the USA
CPSIA information can be obtained
at www.ICGtesting.com
JSHW061253140823
46507JS00005B/66